The Sculptural Body in Victorian Literature

Edinburgh Critical Studies in Victorian Culture
Series Editor: Julian Wolfreys

Recent books in the series:

Rudyard Kipling's Fiction: Mapping Psychic Spaces
Lizzy Welby

The Decadent Image: The Poetry of Wilde, Symons and Dowson
Kostas Boyiopoulos

British India and Victorian Literary Culture
Máire ní Fhlathúin

Anthony Trollope's Late Style: Victorian Liberalism and Literary Form
Frederik Van Dam

Dark Paradise: Pacific Islands in the Nineteenth-Century British Imagination
Jenn Fuller

Twentieth-Century Victorian: Arthur Conan Doyle and the Strand Magazine, 1891–1930
Jonathan Cranfield

The Lyric Poem and Aestheticism: Forms of Modernity
Marion Thain

Gender, Technology and the New Woman
Lena Wånggren

Self-Harm in New Woman Writing
Alexandra Gray

Suffragist Artists in Partnership: Gender, Word and Image
Lucy Ella Rose

Victorian Liberalism and Material Culture: Synergies of Thought and Place
Kevin A. Morrison

The Victorian Male Body
Joanne-Ella Parsons and Ruth Heholt

Nineteenth-Century Settler Emigration in British Literature and Art
Fariha Shaikh

The Pre-Raphaelites and Orientalism
Eleonora Sasso

The Late-Victorian Little Magazine
Koenraad Claes

Coastal Cultures of the Long Nineteenth Century
Matthew Ingleby and Matt P. M. Kerr

Dickens and Demolition: Literary Afterlives and Mid-Nineteenth-Century Urban Development
Joanna Hofer-Robinson

Artful Experiments: Ways of Knowing in Victorian Literature and Science
Philipp Erchinger

Victorian Poetry and the Poetics of the Literary Periodical
Caley Ehnes

The Victorian Actress in the Novel and on the Stage
Renata Kobetts Miller

Dickens's Clowns: Charles Dickens, Joseph Grimaldi and the Pantomime of Life
Jonathan Buckmaster

Italian Politics and Nineteenth-Century British Literature and Culture
Patricia Cove

Cultural Encounters with the Arabian Nights in Nineteenth-Century Britain
Melissa Dickson

Novel Institutions: Anachronism, Irish Novels and Nineteenth-Century Realism
Mary L. Mullen

The Fin-de-Siècle Scottish Revival: Romance, Decadence and Celtic Identity
Michael Shaw

Contested Liberalisms: Martineau, Dickens and the Victorian Press
Iain Crawford

Plotting Disability in the Nineteenth-Century Novel
Clare Walker Gore

The Aesthetics of Space in Nineteenth-Century British Literature, 1843–1907
Giles Whiteley

The Persian Presence in Victorian Poetry
Reza Taher-Kermani

Rereading Orphanhood: Texts, Inheritance, Kin
Diane Warren and Laura Peters

Plotting the News in the Victorian Novel
Jessica R. Valdez

Reading Ideas in Victorian Literature: Literary Content as Artistic Experience
Patrick Fessenbecker

Home and Identity in Nineteenth-Century Literary London
Lisa Robertson

Writing the Sphinx: Literature, Culture and Egyptology
Eleanor Dobson

Oscar Wilde and the Radical Politics of the Fin de Siècle
Deaglán Ó Donghaile

The Sculptural Body in Victorian Literature: Encrypted Sexualities
Patricia Pulham

Forthcoming volumes:

Her Father's Name: Gender, Theatricality and Spiritualism in Florence Marryat's Fiction
Tatiana Kontou

Olive Schreiner and the Politics of Print Culture, 1883–1920
Clare Gill

Victorian Auto/Biography: Problems in Genre and Subject
Amber Regis

Gissing, Shakespeare and the Life of Writing
Thomas Ue

Women's Mobility in Henry James
Anna Despotopoulou

Michael Field's Revisionary Poetics
Jill Ehnenn

The Americanisation of W. T. Stead
Helena Goodwyn

Literary Illusions: Performance Magic and Victorian Literature
Christopher Pittard

Pastoral in Early-Victorian Fiction: Environment and Modernity
Mark Frost

Edmund Yates and Victorian Periodicals: Gossip, Celebrity, and Gendered Spaces
Kathryn Ledbetter

Literature, Architecture and Perversion: Building Sexual Culture in Europe, 1850–1930
Aina Marti

Manufacturing Female Beauty in British Literature and Periodicals, 1850–1914
Michelle Smith

New Media and the Rise of the Popular Woman Writer, 1820–60
Alexis Easley

For a complete list of titles published visit the Edinburgh Critical Studies in Victorian Culture web page at www.edinburghuniversitypress.com/series/ECVC

Also available:
Victoriographies – A Journal of Nineteenth-Century Writing, 1790–1914, edited by Diane Piccitto and Patricia Pulham
ISSN: 2044-2416
www.eupjournals.com/vic

The Sculptural Body in Victorian Literature

Encrypted Sexualities

Patricia Pulham

EDINBURGH
University Press

Edinburgh University Press is one of the leading university presses in the UK. We publish academic books and journals in our selected subject areas across the humanities and social sciences, combining cutting-edge scholarship with high editorial and production values to produce academic works of lasting importance. For more information visit our website: edinburghuniversitypress.com

© Patricia Pulham, 2020, 2022

Edinburgh University Press Ltd
The Tun – Holyrood Road, 12(2f) Jackson's Entry, Edinburgh EH8 8PJ

First published in hardback by Edinburgh Univeristy Press 2020

Typeset in 11/13 Adobe Sabon by
IDSUK (DataConnection) Ltd

A CIP record for this book is available from the British Library

ISBN 978 0 7486 9342 9 (hardback)
ISBN 978 1 3995 0459 1 (paperback)
ISBN 978 0 7486 9343 6 (webready PDF)
ISBN 978 0 7486 9344 3 (epub)

The right of Patricia Pulham to be identified as the author of this work has been asserted in accordance with the Copyright, Designs and Patents Act 1988, and the Copyright and Related Rights Regulations 2003 (SI No. 2498).

Contents

List of Illustrations	vi
Series Editor's Preface	viii
Acknowledgements	x
Introduction	1
1. Nineteenth-Century Pygmalions: The Sexual Politics of Tactility	29
2. Artworks in Marble: Capturing Venus in Durable Form	65
3. 'Of marble men and maidens': Sculptural Transformations	104
4. Statuephilia and the Love of the Impossible	147
5. Between Death and Sleep: Libidinal Entombments	183
Bibliography	200
Index	220

List of Illustrations

Figures

I.i The *Townley Discobolus*, after Myron. Roman, second century, marble (British Museum, London). — 6

I.ii The *Townley Venus*, Roman, first–second century, marble (British Museum, London). — 6

2.1 Aphrodite, known as the *Venus de Milo*, c.130–100 BCE, marble (Musée du Louvre, Paris). — 72

2.2 *Cnidus Venus*, Roman copy after a Greek original of the fourth century BCE, marble (Ludovisi Collection, Roman National Museums, Palazzo Altemps, Rome). — 78

3.1 The *Medici Venus*, Hellenistic copy after original by Praxiteles c.370–330 BCE, Roman, first century, marble (Galleria degli Uffizi, Florence). — 105

3.2 The *Dying Gladiator*, also known as the *Dying Gaul*, Roman copy of a Greek original of the late third century BCE, marble (Capitoline Museums, Rome). — 110

3.3 William Wetmore Story, *Cleopatra*, 1858, marble (Metropolitan Museum of Art, New York). — 111

3.4 Harriet Hosmer, *Beatrice Cenci*, 1857, marble (Art Gallery of New South Wales, Sydney). — 113

3.5 *Faun*, Roman copy of a Greek original by Praxiteles, fourth century BCE, marble (Capitoline Museums, Rome). — 115

3.6 Statue known as the *Apollo Belvedere*, copy after Greek bronze original of the fourth century BCE, marble (Vatican Museums and Galleries, Vatican City). — 117

4.1	Sir Hamo Thornycroft, *The Mower*, 1888–90, bronze (Tate Gallery, London).	148
4.2	Braschi Antinous, second century CE, marble (Musée du Louvre, Paris).	166
5.1	The *Capitoline Venus*, Roman copy of a Greek original by Praxiteles, fourth century BCE, marble (Capitoline Museums, Rome).	185
5.2	Funerary monument to Ilaria del Carretto by Jacopo della Quercia, fifteenth century, marble and stone (Cathedral of San Martino, Lucca).	188

Plates

1   Edward Coley Burne-Jones, *The Godhead Fires*, from the 'Pygmalion and the Image' series, 1868–70, oil on canvas (private collection).

2   John Gibson, *The Tinted Venus*, c.1851–6, marble (Walker Art Gallery, National Museums, Liverpool).

3   Warrington Wood, *Keats Memorial*, 1875 (Protestant and non-Catholic cemetery, Rome).

4   Edward Onslow Ford, *Shelley Memorial*, 1892, marble with bronze base (University College, Oxford).

Series Editor's Preface

'Victorian' is a term, at once indicative of a strongly determined concept and an often notoriously vague notion, emptied of all meaningful content by the many journalistic misconceptions that persist about the inhabitants and cultures of the British Isles and Victoria's Empire in the nineteenth century. As such, it has become a by-word for the assumption of various, often contradictory habits of thought, belief, behaviour and perceptions. Victorian studies and studies in nineteenth-century literature and culture have, from their institutional inception, questioned narrowness of presumption, pushed at the limits of the nominal definition, and have sought to question the very grounds on which the unreflective perception of the so-called Victorian has been built; and so they continue to do. Victorian and nineteenth-century studies of literature and culture maintain a breadth and diversity of interest, of focus and inquiry, in an interrogative and intellectually open-minded and challenging manner, which are equal to the exploration and inquisitiveness of its subjects. Many of the questions asked by scholars and researchers of the innumerable productions of nineteenth-century society actively put into suspension the clichés and stereotypes of 'Victorianism', whether the approach has been sustained by historical, scientific, philosophical, empirical, ideological or theoretical concerns; indeed, it would be incorrect to assume that each of these approaches to the idea of the Victorian has been, or has remained, in the main exclusive, sealed off from the interests and engagements of other approaches. A vital interdisciplinarity has been pursued and embraced, for the most part, even as there has been contest and debate amongst Victorianists, pursued with as much fervour as the affirmative exploration between different disciplines and differing epistemologies put to work in the service of reading the nineteenth century.

Edinburgh Critical Studies in Victorian Culture aims to take up both the debates and the inventive approaches and departures from convention that studies in the nineteenth century have witnessed for the last half century at least. Aiming to maintain a 'Victorian' (in the most positive sense of that motif) spirit of inquiry, the series' purpose is to continue and augment the cross-fertilisation of interdisciplinary approaches, and to offer, in addition, a number of timely and untimely revisions of Victorian literature, culture, history and identity. At the same time, the series will ask questions concerning what has been missed or improperly received, misread, or not read at all, in order to present a multi-faceted and heterogeneous kaleidoscope of representations. Drawing on the most provocative, thoughtful and original research, the series will seek to prod at the notion of the 'Victorian', and in so doing, principally through theoretically and epistemologically sophisticated close readings of the historicity of literature and culture in the nineteenth century, to offer the reader provocative insights into a world that is at once overly familiar, and irreducibly different, other and strange. Working from original sources, primary documents and recent interdisciplinary theoretical models, Edinburgh Critical Studies in Victorian Culture seeks not simply to push at the boundaries of research in the nineteenth century, but also to inaugurate the persistent erasure and provisional, strategic redrawing of those borders.

Julian Wolfreys

Acknowledgements

This book is moulded out of my own love of literature and sculpture and has entailed numerous enjoyable expeditions to galleries in London, Florence, Naples, Paris and Rome with favourite friends and family members, as well as visits to significant exhibitions such as 'Sculpture Victorious' held at Tate Britain in 2015. However, much of it was written during a time of personal and professional upheaval that thwarted a clear trajectory for its completion and it has often felt as if its textual body were embedded, like one of Michelangelo's 'Prisoners', in a block of marble, never fully to emerge. Many wonderful people have helped me regain the energy and will to chisel it out of its marble cell and I am truly grateful for their kindness. Among these are my partner, Bran Nicol, and my sons, Joe and Sam Pulham, whose constant love and encouragement have meant so much. Along the way, I have also been heartened and inspired by friends and mentors whose career advice and support have been invaluable. Special thanks go to Carol Barker, who so readily offered her time to read a full draft and provide thoughtful annotations; to Ana Vadillo for so generously sending me an advance copy of her chapter on sculpture in *Michael Field: Decadent Moderns* (2019); and to Danielle Dove whose excellent research assistance towards the end of this project was so vital in bringing it to completion. I am also indebted to all those colleagues on the Executive Committee of the British Association for Victorian Studies and at the University of Surrey who listened patiently to my ideas as they developed and who offered reassurance in moments of doubt.

In terms of practical support, I would like to thank the School of Literature and Languages at the University of Surrey for funding research assistance and image acquisitions and permissions, and my former department at the University of Portsmouth for funding archival research in the Arthur O'Shaughnessy Manuscript Collection at Queen's University, Belfast. Some of the chapters in this book contain sections that were originally published elsewhere; in most cases these have been substantially rewritten, augmented and recontextualised, alongside new research, to accord with the monograph's overall thesis. The William Hazlitt material in Chapter 1 originally appeared as part of a longer essay, 'The New Pygmalions: Idealism and Disillusionment in Hazlitt's *Liber Amoris* and Vernon Lee's *Miss Brown*' in *Legacies of Romanticism: Literature, Culture, Aesthetics* (2012); parts of the Thomas Hardy sections in Chapter 2 featured in 'From Pygmalion to Persephone: Love, Art, and Myth in Thomas Hardy's *The Well-Beloved*' in the *Victorian Review*, 34: 2 (2008b); some of the Hawthorne sections in Chapter 3 were formerly published in '"Of marble men and maidens": Sin, Sculpture, and Perversion in Nathaniel Hawthorne's *The Marble Faun*', in *The Yearbook of English Studies*, 40: 1–2 (2010); and Chapter 4 includes some material that originally appeared in the following articles, 'Tinted and Tainted Love: The Sculptural Body in Olive Custance's Poetry', published in *The Yearbook of English Studies,* 37: 1 (2007) and 'Eyes that trace like fingers: Keats, Wilde, and Victorian Statue Love' in *La Questione Romantica*, 5: 1–2 (2016a). My thanks to the publishers concerned for granting me permission to use relevant extracts in *The Sculptural Body in Victorian Literature: Encrypted Sexualities*.

For
Bran, Neve, and my beautiful boys

Introduction

The association between sex and statues has an established cultural history. In *The Power of Images: Studies in the History and Theory of Response*, David Freedberg shows how people have always been 'sexually aroused' by sculptures (1989: 1) and examines the slippage between the desire to possess the subject depicted in art, and desire for the representation itself. He argues that sculpture features prominently in historical examples, citing instances of statue love that range across cultural, temporal and geographical borders, including tales from ancient Iran and Greece, the Byzantine lives of saints, as well as numerous versions of the 'Venus and the Ring' and Pygmalion myths that span several centuries (1989: 323–42). In his analysis Freedberg suggests that in charting arousal by image, such examples offer us a means by which we might 'examine the issue of repression most clearly' and contends that in fearing 'the body in the image, we refuse to acknowledge our engagement with it', denying recognition of 'those aspects of our own sexuality that it may seem to threaten or reveal' (1989: 12).

In *The Sculptural Body in Victorian Literature: Encrypted Sexualities*, I argue that, in Victorian literature, transgressive desires that cannot be openly acknowledged – whether these be homosexuality, pygmalionism, necrophilia or paedophilia – are often embedded and encrypted in sculptures. The three-dimensionality of the sculptural body, its ubiquity in Victorian popular culture, its increasing visibility in public galleries, and the full or partial nudity of the classical statues on display are some of the key reasons that underpin this phenomenon. For David Gaimster, it is in the museum, 'rather than in the literary sphere, that we can best trace the origins of public delicacy towards the erotic and the development of the strict division between legitimate and illegitimate culture' (2001: 126). However, as I aim to show, the Victorian texts I discuss are locked in a symbiotic relationship with museum culture; they are both informed by the access to sculpture public museums provide, and negotiate the tensions between morality and eroticism that are implicit in the prohibition of touch in such spaces.

In the eighteenth and nineteenth centuries, public exposure to sexual images stimulated debates 'about obscenity, censorship and immorality' and the 'erotic appeal of sculptural art', and provoked 'intense anxieties about its reception and display' (Funke and Grove 2019: 16). Nude or scantily draped antique statues were of particular concern; 'the way in which the classical male nude came to be associated with male same-sex practices caused alarm to some critics', and 'unclothed or partially dressed male, female and sexually ambiguous statues' were considered to evoke the 'paganism and sexual licentiousness associated with antiquity' (2019: 16). As Walter Kendrick observes, this period was 'the great age' of museums, when the private collections of rich 'virtuosos' like the antiquary Charles Townley (1737–1805), which included 'obscene artifacts' as well as antique *objets d'art,* were sold or bequeathed to such institutions (1987: 69). The availability of such objects to the general public prompted unease regarding the effect of troubling images on 'morally vulnerable audiences, especially women, children and the lower classes' (Funke and Grove 2019: 16).[1] To accommodate these collections proved problematic and the excavation of sexually explicit sculptures from important sites, such as Pompeii, encouraged curators to seek solutions, to restrict access to such objects. Following these discoveries, the 'priceless obscenities' of Pompeii had to be 'properly managed': they were 'systematically named and placed'; labelled 'pornography'; and locked away in the *Gabinetto Secreto* or 'Secret Museum', a locked room in what was then known as the 'Museo Borbonico', and is now the National Archaeological Museum of Naples (Kendrick 1987: 11). At the British Museum, a similar fate befell such artefacts which were removed to its 'Secretum', a 'secret museum' that had expanded gradually as museum publics changed, but was officially created in 1865 in response to the Obscene Publications Act of 1857 (Gaimster 2001: 132).[2] Yet, as is clear from accounts of public engagement with those statues that remained on open display, and the erotic potential of classical sculptures and their contemporary counterparts exploited in Victorian literature, sexual responses to the sculptural body were not limited to pornographic objects. I would argue, however, that in such literature, sculpture often functions as a form of textual 'Secretum', a repository for forbidden love, whose eroticism is available to those 'in the know'; a form of 'crypt' or 'tomb' in which the Victorians' lost objects of transgressive desire, impossible to acknowledge in the moral climate of the nineteenth century, are incorporated yet hidden in cultural production.

In '*Fors*: The Anglish Words of Nicolas Abraham and Maria Torok', Derrida's foreword to Abraham and Torok's *The Wolf Man's Magic Word: A Cryptonomy*, he explains the nature of the crypt in its psychoanalytic context. Drawing on the work of Sándor Ferenczi, Derrida observes that love is intrinsically narcissistic, that to love an object is to adopt that object as part of the Self, that love is a form of introjection (1986: xvi). He further notes that in Maria Torok's view, such introjection 'includes not only the object, but also the instincts and desires attached to it' (1986: xvi). According to Torok, when that object is 'lost' (either literally or figuratively), and cannot be introjected, it is 'incorporated' and hidden within the Self in a form of crypt, 'a hidden place, a disguise hiding the traces of the act of disguising, a place of silence' (1986: xvii). The 'crypt' becomes the object's 'monument' or 'tomb', and functions as 'the vault of a desire' (1986: xvii). The aesthetic and funereal connotations of statuary permit sculptural bodies to become the vaults in which Victorian writers 'encrypt' and 'quarantine' their knowledge of sexual proclivities that cannot be fully accommodated, that they are reluctant to recognise or name. As Derrida argues, 'the cryptic place is also a sephulcher . . . The inhabitant of a crypt is always a living dead, a dead entity we are perfectly willing to keep alive, but *as* dead' (1986: xxi; original emphasis), a fitting counterpart to the sculptural figure that is always positioned in a liminal existence between life and death. In Victorian literature, I suggest, such encrypted desires become manifest through sensory signification, through literal and metaphorical forms of tactility: through a magic touch, rather than a magic word.[3] The significance of literary 'touch' will be explored in more detail towards the end of this introduction, but I would like to begin by considering the various ways in which the Victorians accessed and engaged with sculpture in both public and private spheres.

Cultures of Collecting

As Giles Waterfield writes in *The People's Galleries: Art, Museums, and Exhibitions in Britain, 1800–1914*, the nineteenth century, and especially the period between 1850 and 1914, saw 'the blooming of museums and galleries all over England and Scotland (and to a lesser extent Ireland and Wales), and the creation of a whole range of new museum types' (2015: 12). This growth in art galleries and museums resulted in the founding of central and regional museums that included the British Museum, the National Gallery, and the South Kensington Museum, as well as six important civic galleries in Birmingham, Glasgow, Leeds, Liverpool, Manchester and Nottingham that brought museum culture to the regions (Waterfield 2015: 1).[4] According to Waterfield, the museum was 'neither a palace nor a temple'; instead it was a site for practical, artistic, intellectual, and moral education (2015: 227). Moreover, the success of museums in the nineteenth century was shaped by a developing relationship in Western culture between art and industry. As Waterfield observes:

> Within twelve years, Europe and the United States witnessed the Great Exhibition of 1851; the Exhibition of Art-Industry in Dublin and the Exhibition of the Industry of All Nations in New York, both in 1853; the *Exposition Universelle des produits de l'Agriculture, de l'Industrie et des Beaux-Arts de Paris*, shown in the purpose-built *Palais de l'Industrie* in 1855; and the International Exhibition of the Industrial Arts and Manufacturers, and the Fine Arts of All Nations, held in a vast new building in South Kensington in 1862. (2015: 87)

Although there had been earlier instances of industrial display, Waterfield highlights the importance of the Great Exhibition of 1851 located in Hyde Park in London, which 'transformed the genre', attracting over six million visitors, and creating 'a new phenomenon, the visual spectacle aimed at a mass audience' (2015: 87). At the Great Exhibition of 1851 and, later, at the Crystal Palace in Sydenham which opened its doors to the public in 1854, visitors encountered Greek and Roman Courts inhabited by the casts of ancient statues, as well as Modern Sculpture Courts exhibiting works from England, France, Italy and Germany. Following the closure of the Great Exhibition in October 1851, the Crystal Palace Company bought, extended and reconstructed the building itself in Kent. The company's aims were to offer 'amusement and recreation, instruction and commercial utility to an audience of all social classes' (Nichols 2013: 25). Sculptures were organised in an approximately chronological fashion and those who were inspired by their beauty could purchase statuettes in Parian ware to adorn their own parlours.

This combination of high art and popular entertainment suggested a democratisation of cultural access that prompted a contemporary journalist to comment: 'the artisan who will pay hereafter his shilling and pace these splendid galleries, will see more of the fine arts of Europe than any nobleman who goes "the grand tour" at the cost of thousands' (qtd in Nichols 2015: 115). However, the artisan, unversed in culture, seemingly needed guidance. For sixpence visitors to the Crystal Palace could purchase *A Handbook to the Courts of Modern Sculpture* (1854) by Anna Jameson, a guide that defines the technical meaning of 'sculpture'; explains distinctions in the fine arts between '*standing*', '*seated*' or '*recumbent*' statues; differentiates between levels of sculptural relief; and identifies sculpture as both 'a *thought* and a *thing*' (1854: 3–4; original emphases). Jameson also stresses that one of the 'first considerations of sculpture' is the material from which it is formed and warns viewers that they should bear in mind variations between the originals and exhibited copies:

> All the specimens of sculpture here (both ancient and modern), are casts made in gypsum (plaster of Paris), and the hard, opaque plaster is so different in effect from the delicate semi-transparent marble, which under the master-hand seems actually to soften into life, that, in judging of some admired works, this difference must be taken into consideration. (1854: 5)

It appears, therefore, that while ordinary viewers might indeed see more of the fine arts at the Crystal Palace than the gentleman on his cultural tour of the continent, the quality of the sculpture to which they are exposed must necessarily be of a lower order. Despite this difference, *Routledge's Guide to the Crystal Palace and Park at Sydenham* (1854) expects the ordinary visitor to recognise the most famous antique sculptures. 'The Grecian Courts' section of the guide points to copies of particular statues, and notes that we may judge 'the extent to which the originals have suffered' from the following instances:

> [T]he left arm of the Apollo Belvedere is modern, and the right arm and foot have been badly mended; both the arms and the beautiful hands of the Venus de Medici are new . . . the hand and part of the foot of the Dying Gladiator are also modern additions . . . the beautiful Venus of the Capitol has a false nose; and the right arm of the Laocoon [sic] is one which did not originally belong to him. The Discobolus . . . has been fitted with a new head, and the charming Townley Venus owes her left arm and right hand to a modern sculptor. (Macdermott 1854: 43–5)

These figures are referred to with the kind of familiarity reserved for household names. The *Discobolus* (Figure I.i) and the *Townley Venus* (Figure I.ii) may have been known to many visitors from personal

Figure I.i The *Townley Discobolus*, after Myron. Roman, second century, marble (British Museum, London). © The Trustees of the British Museum

Figure I.ii The *Townley Venus*, Roman, first–second century, marble (British Museum, London). © The Trustees of the British Museum

experience of the Townley Marbles collection housed in the British Museum. In contrast, their recognition of the other statues mentioned would have been less likely due to direct contact with the originals, than to the circulation of engravings and copies of them seen elsewhere. The *Apollo Belvedere*, the *Laocoön*, the *Medici Venus* and the *Dying Gladiator* had become particularly celebrated due to the enduring influence of Johann Joachim Winckelmann's *History of the Art of Antiquity* (first published in 1764). The 'lyrical descriptions' of these that first appeared in the *History* were among his 'best-known' writings and were often quoted in tourist guidebooks and works on antique art, influencing a new wave of collectors (Potts 2000: 16).

We owe Britain's acquisition of collections such as the Townley Marbles to the 'culture for collecting' that emerged at the end of the eighteenth and early part of the nineteenth century (Coltman 2009). While a tradition of collecting had long existed in Italy, it began in earnest in Britain in the eighteenth century when, guided in part by Winckelmann's theories, classical works were acquired by wealthy young men while on the Grand Tour and brought home. Such collectors were able to capitalise on the dispersal of certain Roman collections, and on the archaeological excavations taking place during this period in and around Rome and elsewhere in Italy (Cook 1985: 9). Their inclination to possess them was also fostered by the intellectual engagement with classical culture that informed educational programmes followed in Britain. These wealthy tourists were evidently already familiar not only with the mythical characters often depicted in statuary, but also with images of the figures themselves. On seeing the statues in the Belvedere Courtyard in the Vatican, an eighteenth-century traveller, Edward Wright, comments that they are already well known to him from prints, casts and models which he has seen in England (qtd in Coltman 2006: 123). Echoing Wright's sentiments, another tourist, Arthur Young, having seen 'numberless casts' of the *Medici Venus*, writes that he is keen to rush to the Tribune in Florence's Uffizi Gallery 'for a view of the dangerous goddess' (qtd in Coltman 2006: 126). Encounters with the busts of ancient emperors, writers and philosophers also brought British travellers 'face to face with material presentations of their schoolboy heroes' (Coltman 2006: 151–2). Yet, as is clear from Young's eager desire to see the 'dangerous' *Medici Venus*, such experiences also brought them into contact with mythical objects of desire, arousing a passion for collection and possession that brought ancient sculpture physically into public and private domains and stimulated the Anglo-American cultural imagination. Exhibited in galleries such as the Boston Athenaeum, copies of classical sculpture became increasingly accessible to view in America where, in the early nineteenth century, the professional artistic gaze, initially at least, turned towards Europe. When the Pennsylvania Academy of Fine Arts was formed in 1805, and artists' training was formalised, its object was 'to promote the cultivation of the Fine Arts in the United States of America, by introducing correct and elegant copies from the works of the First Masters in Sculpture and Painting' (Fernie 2011: 45). Horatio Greenough, a young sculptor, was the first of many American artists who travelled to Rome in search of inspiration and tuition, and his statue of George Washington (1840), dressed in classical garb, is testament to the influence of Roman antiquity (2011: 23). In his wake followed other American artists and writers who, coming to Europe in increasing numbers in the nineteenth century, found themselves inspired to create works that remained in dialogue with the classical world.

As Gail Marshall has observed, in the nineteenth century Western culture was 'imbued with new possibilities for the proliferation of sculpturally informed aesthetic judgements and criteria', prompted by the expansion of museums in Britain, France and America that imported 'what were to become the best-known examples of Classical sculptures' (1998: 8). These statues contributed to 'a canon of artistic values' embodied in specific works of antiquity which were used as 'touchstone[s] by artists, art lovers, collectors and theorists alike for the gauging of taste and quality' (Haskell and Penny 1981: 6). Such values were based on Winckelmann's influential treatises on classical sculpture which developed a new kind of art history, one that offered a historical model based on the decline and fall of the antique ideal. His ideas persisted throughout the Victorian period despite the challenges posed by archaeological findings, such as the Elgin Marbles, that undermined Winckelmann's schema. According to Alex Potts, Winckelmann's theories endured even in the face of contradictory evidence; following short-lived alternatives offered during the first two decades of the nineteenth century, 'archaeological scholars tended to accept the basic logic of Winckelmann's model, and the attempt to constitute a new history generically different from his was effectively abandoned' (2000: 15).

In the late eighteenth and early nineteenth century, Winckelmannian aesthetics additionally informed contemporary politics and intellectual thought both in Britain and in Europe, particularly in revolutionary France and during the Napoleonic era that followed. In France, 'the classical aesthetic' promoted by Winckelmann in his writings on antique art was appropriated by artists such as David and Ingres 'in the service of the revolutionary cause' (Coltman 2006: 8).[5] Moreover, the classical education taught throughout the French system of *collèges*, and experienced in youth by revolutionaries such as Robespierre, Desmoulins and Danton, contributed to a sense that, juxtaposed with the golden age of a Roman republican past, their own present seemed repressive and unenlightened; the Roman republic's 'dual devotion to country and liberty spoke volumes to the French revolutionary generation' (2006: 14). Emerging from that revolutionary generation, Napoleon clearly shared its investment in classical antiquity. His post-revolutionary world offered a model on which to build the new France, and French culture was to become 'the true culmination and continuation of the great classical traditions of the past' (Potts 2000: 30).

Imaginary Museums

Given Napoleon's intention to revive French culture along classical lines, it is unsurprising to find that he, too, should desire to amass his own collection of antiquities, albeit one created from the spoils of war. The Napoleonic government assimilated the classical tradition, seizing from Italy all the most notable antique sculptures that represented 'the embodiment' of this tradition and transported them to Paris (Potts 2000: 30). The Treaty of Tolentino, signed between France and the papacy in February 1797, ensured the surrender of key works of art from the Vatican and Capitoline Museums (McClellan 1994: 121). In 1802, Dominique-Vivant Denon (1747–1825) became director of the Musée Napoléon (now the Louvre) and oversaw the display of looted artworks that included the *Laocoön*, the *Apollo Belvedere*, the *Medici Venus*, the *Dying Gladiator* and the *Capitoline Venus* (1994: 140). The widely reported theft and subsequent repatriation of these statues following Napoleon's fall in 1815 contributed to their increasing presence in literary works. In Mme de Staël's *Corinne, ou L'Italie* (first published in 1807), the improvatrice's drawing room is 'adorned with plaster copies of Italy's finest statues, Niobe, Laocoön, the Medici Venus and the dying gladiator' (2008: 37). In 1810, *The Dying Gladiator*, now also known as *The Dying Gaul* and *The Dying Galatian*, was the subject of Oxford's Newdigate Prize, a prize awarded to the most successful ekphrastic poem written each year on a specified subject. Two years later, the *Apollo Belvedere* was the topic and in the same year, Felicia Hemans published her own poem on 'The Statue of the Dying Gladiator'. Hemans would later discuss the *Laocoön* and the *Medici Venus* in *The Restoration of the Works of Art to Italy* (1816), sculptures which, along with the *Apollo Belvedere* were famously apostrophised by Byron in Canto IV of *Childe Harold's Pilgrimage* (1812–18). Keats mentions the *Apollo* and the *Medici Venus* in his 1816 poem, 'I stood tiptoe upon a little hill', and although the *Medici Venus* does not appear in Shelley's *Notes on Sculptures in Rome and Florence* (1879), the *Laocoön* and *Niobe* receive his attention. These writers were of course celebrated by many Victorians and the sculptures in question 'belonged to a select group of several dozen [statues] so well known that writers could depend on readers' visual memory of them' (Haley 2003: 179). Moreover, the commercialisation of photography in 1839 and its rising popularity throughout the nineteenth century facilitated access and personal 'possession' of such treasures.

As Patrizia Di Bello demonstrates in her essay 'Photography and Sculpture', the evolution of photography is closely bound up with the sculptural image; from its inception, those who wished to 'fix' the image formed by the camera obscura experimented with statuary (2010: 19). In his efforts 'to perfect the daguerreotype before announcing it to the Académie des Sciences', Louis Daguerre (1787–1851) photographed plaster of Paris casts on a window ledge in his studio and, while developing his salted paper and calotype processes, Henry Fox Talbot (1800–77) photographed a bust of Patroclus and a statue of Venus (Di Bello 2010: 19–20). The reason for sculpture's popularity among photographers is made clear by Fox Talbot in *The Pencil of Nature* (published in six parts between 1844 and 1846): 'Statues, busts, and other specimens of sculpture are generally well represented by the Photographic Art; and also very rapidly, in consequence of their whiteness' (1844: 23). But, as André Malraux argues in *Museum without Walls* (*Le musée imaginaire*) first published in 1947, the advent of photography also had interesting and enduring consequences for the cultural power of the traditional museum:

> At one time, the student visited the Louvre and some subsidiary galleries and memorized what he saw as best he could. We, however, have far more great works available to refresh our memories than even the greatest of museums could bring together. A museum without walls has been opened up to us, and it will carry infinitely farther that limited revelation of the world of art which the real museums offer us within their walls: in answer to their appeal, the plastic arts have produced their printing press. (1967: 12)

For Malraux, the freedom afforded by this imaginary alternative centred on the evolution of the museum from 'a real space where a specific history could be authenticated by objects recalling it' into 'a virtual space' (Blanchard 2000: 681). Such spaces permitted 'unpremeditated juxtapositions' that would challenge existing historical trajectories and test 'new, interhistorical arrangements of objects' that had never been previously compared or seen together (2000: 681). Photographs, in Malraux's view, functioned as 'virtual sites for moveable displays' and forged a new relationship between the collection and consumption of art which democratised access to cultural objects, and undermined the structures of patronage and power that had informed museum formation and development in the nineteenth century (2000: 682). Anticipating Malraux by some twenty years, between 1926 and 1929 the German art historian, Aby Warburg, created his own 'imaginary museum', the *Mnemosyne Atlas*, composed of seventy-nine panels displaying a total of around 2,000 black and white photographs, featuring reproductions of artworks in varying media (statues, engravings, illustrations) that were to form, in his words, 'an art history without text' (qtd in Angel 2011: 266). The eventual composition of Warburg's encyclopaedic project is a mystery that died with him in 1929, but the panels that still exist have been described as 'the surviving artifacts of a never-completed, encyclopaedic effort to represent the West's cultural legacy'; in particular, he aimed to show 'how antiquity's art-historical and cosmological currents flowed through the Renaissance' (Johnson 2012: ix).

What is clear is that both Warburg and Malraux advocate personalised acts of visual curation that disrupt the conventional patterns of textual history and established power. Given that the curator is often seen as an 'imparter of value' (Balzer 2015: 9), and that the act of curation is necessarily dependent on personal or institutional ideologies, Malraux's investment in the democratic liberation implied by the imaginary museum may now seem naive. Yet, in some sense, we have all now become curators of our own imaginary museums, or indeed Mnemosyne Atlases. As Griselda Pollock notes in *Encounters in the Virtual Feminist Museum*, 'our slide collections or databases of jpegs' like the 'picture atlas of the nineteenth century' function as 'extensions of the museum' (2007: 16). We organise them into our own galleries, creating our own narratives to share with others on websites such as Pinterest, Instagram or Facebook. While such sharing facilities were of course unavailable to the Victorians, literature did provide Victorian writers with one means by which to circulate their own imaginary museums, composed of words rather than images, featuring certain statues or setting classical, renaissance and Victorian sculptures alongside one another for effect. Inspired perhaps by what Catriona Macleod calls the 'exalted *musée imaginaire*' represented in Winckelmann's own influential writings (2014: 4), works such as George MacDonald's *Phantastes* (1858), Nathaniel Hawthorne's *The Marble Faun* (1860), Henry James's *Roderick Hudson* (1875) and Thomas Hardy's *The Well-Beloved* (1897) are prime examples, and found in the company of numerous poems that feature sculptors and statues, including the 'Thoughts in Marble' series that appeared in Arthur O'Shaughnessy's *Songs of a Worker* (1881) and Thomas Woolner's twelve-book poem, *Pygmalion* (1881), one of various Victorian texts that engaged with the myth directly or tangentially throughout the nineteenth century. In addition, statues make a brief, but famously important appearance in George Eliot's *Middlemarch* (1871–2), and sculptural metaphor is utilised in many Victorian works including Emmeline Stuart-Wortley's *Lillia Bianca* (1841), Elizabeth Barrett Browning's *Aurora Leigh* (1856), Mary Elizabeth Braddon's *Lady Audley's Secret* (1862), Vernon Lee's *Miss Brown* (1884) and George Du Maurier's *Trilby* (1895).

Artefactual Corpses

Given that the word 'museum' means a place or home for the muses, it is only natural that it should inspire literary, as well as other forms of artistic production. Hardy literalises this effect in 'Rome: The Vatican: Sala delle Muse', written during a visit to Italy in 1887 and later published in *Poems of the Past and Present* (1902), in which the speaker debates the call of the arts with a speaking statue, an animated muse. However, in a letter to Edmund Gosse dated 31 March 1887, he writes, 'I am so overpowered by the presence of *decay* in Ancient Rome that I feel it like a nightmare in my sleep' (Hardy 1978a: 1, 163; original emphasis). His comment expresses an unease that is notably shared by Dorothea Brooke in *Middlemarch* who, exposed for the first time to the Vatican's 'long vistas of white forms whose marble eyes seemed to hold the monotonous light of an alien world', feels the 'weight of unintelligible Rome' pressing upon her senses (Eliot 2003: 193). For Eliot and Hardy, the sculptural remnants of classical antiquity suggest death, ruin and decay.

Albeit in a somewhat different context, a key aspect of this response is anticipated and shared by Antoine Quatremère de Quincy (1755–1849) who considered the removal of antique statues to the museum space as a form of cultural 'death'. Quatremère, an armchair archaeologist and art critic, took exception to Napoleon's looting of Italian treasures, and to the removal of works of art from their original locations. In *Letters to Miranda* (1796) he writes, 'What mean these images which retail nothing but their substance? What signify these mausoleums without graves, these cenotaphs doubly empty, these tombs which death animates no longer?' (qtd in Haley 2003: 16).[6] As Bruce Haley observes, Quatremère's 'model for the artifactual corpse is an emblematic tomb figure, lifeless as the body it is supposed to honor, an allegory arousing no "emotion" for the viewer' (2003: 16). Like Quatremère, Malraux equates the museum with the graveyard but argues that photography enables 'a world of sculpture far different from that of the museum'; while the museum without walls cannot restore statues to their original contexts, 'the temple, the palace, the church, or the garden they have lost', he argues that the imaginary museum delivers them 'from the Necropolis' (1967: 110). Whether or not this is true remains debatable, but the same argument could be made of the 'imaginary museums' we find in literature, albeit in complex and seemingly contradictory ways. In his broad study of ekphrasis that examines examples from Homer to John Ashbery, James Heffernan suggests that the entire collection of ekphrastic poetry addressed in his book might be described as 'a museum of words—a gallery of art constructed by language alone' (1993: 8) and in his discussion of Keats's ekphrastic writing, Grant F. Scott refers to ekphrasis as 'the trope of museums and galleries par excellence' (1994: xi). Yet, as Scott notes, the relationship between visual and verbal arts is not simple. While ekphrasis appears to 'translate the arrested visual image into the fluid movement of words', it is 'equally the *topos* of stillness ... [it] is that which quickens as well as that which stills life' (1994: xi; original emphasis). For Heffernan, ekphrasis is 'essentially *paragonal*, a struggle for dominance between the image and the word' (1993: 8; original emphasis). However, if one extends Heffernan's analogy to include the variety of ways in which literature engages with statuary beyond the confines of ekphrastic writing, one opens up an interesting dynamic that moves beyond paragonal competition and allows us to explore the liminal spaces between movement and stillness, life and death and what these might mean in the context of the Victorians' negotiation of sexual desire.

Sculpture in Victorian Culture

The tension between animation and stasis is one of my key concerns in this study of literary statues as is the role sculpture plays in Victorian culture where it co-existed in the realms of high and popular entertainment. In part, the rise of Victorian interest in sculpture was inspired by the nineteenth-century's investment in past civilisations, prompted to a significant extent by archaeological findings. As Michael Booth writes, although 'archaeological excavation and the stimulus of ancient cultures' did not begin with the reign of Queen Victoria, the Victorian public 'responded enthusiastically' to a whole series of important discoveries:

> The Elgin Marbles were placed in the British Museum in 1816, and the next really significant impact of ancient architecture upon the public was the discoveries by Layard and Rawlinson at Nimrud and Nineveh in Assyria between 1845 and 1855 . . . After Nineveh came Pompeii in the 1860s, Ephesus in the sixties and seventies, Schliemann's Troy and Mycenae in the 1870s – each one a further stimulus to exhibitions, entertainments, learned treatises, and the arts, and each one creating a further demand for pictorial realisation. (1981: 19)

Classical sculpture was particularly prominent in such popular spectacles. At Astley's Amphitheatre and on tour during the 1820s, one might see Andrew Ducrow's 'living statues' performance in which he posed 'in the precise attitudes of classical statuary', and by the 1830s similar *tableaux vivants* had become part of public entertainment and music hall culture (Booth 1981: 18–19). In the mid-nineteenth century, the minor theatres included 'Professor' Keller's 'Poses Plastiques' and *tableaux vivants*, bringing Canova's *Three Graces* and Thorwaldsen's *Baths of the Dianes* to the London stage, while Madame Wharton offered theatre-goers 'A Night with Canova and Flaxman', such performances characterised by 'the amount of bare flesh the originals depicted' (Altick 1978: 346–7).[7] Towards the end of the nineteenth century, such poses were appropriated by the bodybuilder Eugen Sandow (1867–1925) for the expression of manly beauty and health. As Michael Hatt explains, Sandow 'effectively turned himself into a sculpture: he posed like a statue, complete with plinth and fig-leaf, and dusted himself with white powder to give an effect of marble' (2001: 48).

Such *poses plastiques* no doubt had their origins in the famous 'Attitudes' of Emma Hart (later Hamilton) that gained considerable fame in the early nineteenth century. In *Italian Journey* (first published in 1816–17), Goethe recalls Hart – Nelson's mistress-to-be – whose patron, at that time, Sir William Hamilton, was a diplomat, archaeologist and antiquarian who later married her in 1791. By the time Goethe visited Naples, her 'Attitudes' had become the stuff of legend and comment, and a 'must-see' for any visitor. Relating his visit, Goethe writes:

> Sir William Hamilton, who is still living here as English ambassador, has now, after many years of devotion to the arts and the study of nature, found the acme of these delights in the person of an English girl of twenty with a beautiful face and a perfect figure. He has had a Greek costume made for her which becomes her extremely. Dressed in this, she lets down her hair and, with a few shawls, gives so much variety to her poses, gestures, expressions etc., that the spectator can hardly believe his eyes. He sees what thousands of artists would have liked to express realized before him in movements and surprising transformations – standing, kneeling, sitting, reclining, serious, sad, playful, ecstatic, contrite, alluring, threatening, anxious, one pose follows another without a break. (1970: 208)

As Coltman notes, through this 'rapid succession of staged poses' Emma Hart 'inverted the Pygmalion myth by metamorphosing into a series of sculpted and painted artifacts as well as examples of historical, mythological, and literary heroines' (2006: 66). Hart's ability to transform herself into works of art concretised her status as Hamilton's possession; Goethe suggested that, in Emma, Hamilton 'had found all the antiquities, all the profiles of Sicilian coins, even the Apollo Belvedere' (1970: 208), and another viewer, Lady Palmerston, noted that Hamilton could not help but idolise Emma, so 'magnificent a marble, belonging so entirely to himself' (qtd in Connell 1957: 276). Coltman comments that '[l]ife and art were inextricably combined in Sir William Hamilton's relationship with Emma'; when performing her famous attitudes, Emma was essentially 'a living incarnation of her collector-husband's affair with antiquity' (2006: 66). For Carrie Preston, Emma's attitudes serve a dual purpose; they 'fulfill the Pygmalionesque longing for a statue to melt into a living woman and for a beautiful woman to solidify into a work of art' (2011: 33). As Marshall explains, due to Emma Hamilton's exemplary performances, 'the statuesque, Classical register' was adopted by actresses 'in a variety of types of theatre', and the implicit dynamics of 'a recognisable Pygmalion-Galatea trope' were later embraced by the legitimate Victorian stage (1998: 43).

The lure of the classical world also informed other forms of entertainment that took place in England in the first decades of the nineteenth century. London saw several exhibitions of anatomical 'Florentine' Venuses whose body shapes and poses were based on the *Medici Venus* (Altick 1978: 339). Naked and often adorned with jewels, such Venuses, though ostensibly shown for educational purposes, clearly drew undesirable attention; in 1825, the *Literary Gazette* called one example, 'a large disgusting Doll . . . as indecent as it is wretched' (Altick 1978: 339), but public interest continued. In the decades that followed various anatomical venuses were shown at several London addresses: 'at the Cosmorama Rooms, Dubourg's Saloon of Arts, and in the Strand opposite Exeter Hall, which occupied the site of Exeter Change', as well as at addresses in Oxford Street, Piccadilly and Leicester Square; in 1832, Louis Auzoux (1797–1880) exhibited his 'anatomical Antinous', and in 1839 anatomical versions of Venus and Adonis became the draw at an exhibition that took place at 27 Margaret Street (Altick 1978: 339–40). While promoted as a way to view anatomical specificity without the discomforts of putrefaction, it is evident that such shows also offered what Richard Altick refers to as 'the tantalizing hint of forbidden knowledge', tacitly acknowledged by the provision of private showings for women to avoid accusations of impropriety (1978: 339).

Sculptural Nudes

The prevalent nudity of classical sculpture and the disturbing revelation that statues had originally been polychromatic elided the boundary between ideal sculpture, anatomical figures, and the living bodies of the *poses plastiques*. As Hatt comments in his introductory essay to *Exposed: The Victorian Nude*, given that the Victorians are commonly labelled prudes and that our familiarity with Victorian art often centres on painting (particularly, perhaps, on the Pre-Raphaelites), the ubiquity of the Victorian sculptural nude whether in 'plaster, marble, bronze or stone . . . may seem surprising' (2001: 37). But, as he points out, 'Greek art was still widely viewed as the greatest that had ever been produced', and the classical nude considered the epitome of beauty; rather than 'an embarrassment or an abomination', the sculpted nude was 'the very model of perfection' (2001: 37).

Despite the sculptural body's association with purity and perfection, viewers' reactions, whether in the art gallery or the music hall, were clearly ambivalent. Citing the example of Hiram Powers's *The Greek Slave* exhibited at the Great Exhibition of 1851, Hatt notes that some, such as William Peters who 'appealed to the fathers of England to protect their children and their womenfolk from such appalling spectacles' objected to Powers's work, while others defended the statue 'on the grounds that her nudity was a sign of her purity and chastity' (2001: 38). Depicting a naked young girl, the statue invites us to assume that she stands before the gaze of a lascivious master and Powers's slave drew the sympathy of Elizabeth Barrett Browning who, in a sonnet inspired by the statue begs the image: 'Appeal, fair stone,/From God's pure heights of beauty against man's wrong!' (1995: 375, ll. 10–11). Yet, in viewing the young girl's naked body, it is difficult to distance oneself from the licentiousness of the male gaze which we inevitably inhabit even as we reject it. Hatt acknowledges the problematic nature of an ideal sculpture such as this in an accessible three-dimensional form; sharing the viewer's space, its very materiality can threaten its purity (2001: 38). Furthermore, while ideal sculpture, like the anatomical Venus, 'transforms the body, disavowing the messy interiority of the human form' (2001: 38), it nevertheless represents that body. Similarly, while the removal of bodily processes is 'matched by the absence of psychic processes, such as sexual desire, carnal appetites', the projection of the viewer's fantasies often supplies that which should be missing (2001: 38). As these examples suggest, such invocations of an erotic physicality in ideal form are particularly disturbing when colour is applied and the question of whether statues could be tinted and yet remain ideal, was widely discussed:

> From early in the nineteenth century scholars across Europe debated the question of whether the Greeks painted their sculptures. Archaeological evidence, supported by the re-examination of certain writers such as Pliny, seemed to prove that, unlike the purely formal white bodies so worshipped by the moderns, Greek sculpture was polychromed. (2001: 38–9)

Stone figures were usually painted in red and blue; limestone figures were often coloured a reddish-brown; and in those fashioned in marble, details such as hair, lips, eyes and possibly some part of the drapery were discreetly tinted (Beazley and Ashmole 1966: 15). Taking his inspiration from the Greeks, John Gibson produced *The Tinted Venus* (1851–6), using coloured wax to stain the marble, which he exhibited in London at the International Exhibition in 1862. Though marginally more modest, Gibson's Venus shares her stance with the *Cnidian Aphrodite*, a statue that had long elicited erotic responses, and similarly clutches her robe, caught perpetually between the acts of dressing and undressing, the golden apple she holds in her hands marking her success in the Judgement of Paris.

In an article published in *The Era* in May 1854, a journalist commenting on works to be displayed in the sculpture galleries of the new Crystal Palace dismisses the prudish attitude of those demanding that nude statues should be covered to preserve the modesty of wives and daughters. Arguing against the concerns raised by 'Bishops and nobles' that some 'dreadful violation of decency had been threatened', he points out that they are unlikely to see any cast that is more shocking than any they have already seen in 'private houses or at public exhibitions' in the company of their wives and daughters, and maintains that to cover these figures with 'aprons' is 'the very way to make the mass of spectators feel shame' (Anon. 1854: 9). Warming to his theme, the journalist asks:

> What will the reverend dignitaries, who are so shocked at Sydenham, say at Windsor, when they see there, in possession of Queen Victoria, the tinted Venus of Gibson, which has just been finished at Rome, and which represents, as nearly as possible, not only 'nude' form, but 'nude' flesh! (1854: 9)

Yet, unaccustomed to such nudity, some viewers of sculpture did indeed experience a sense of shock.

Sculptural Erotics

In his memoir, *Father and Son* (first published in 1907), Gosse recalls an incident involving Susan Flood, a young female member of the Plymouth Brethren,[8] which occurred when she accompanied relatives to the original Crystal Palace exhibition in London's Hyde Park:

> [I]n passing through the Sculpture Gallery, Susan's sense of decency had been so grievously affronted, that she had smashed the naked figures with the handle of her parasol, before her horrified companions could stop her. She had, in fact, run amok among the statuary, and had, to the intense chagrin of her uncle and aunt . . . been arrested and brought before a magistrate, who dismissed her with a warning to her relations that she had better be sent home to Devonshire and 'looked after'. (2004: 147)

This account is preceded in the text by Gosse's own experience of statuary as a thirteen-year-old boy prior to which he 'had never seen so much as a representation of a work of sculpture' (2004: 146). His first encounter comes in the form of several steel engravings of statues he discovers in 'a gaudy gift-book' belonging to his mother and it is evidently a key moment in his intellectual and sexual development. 'These attracted me violently', he writes, 'here for the first time I gazed on Apollo with his proud gesture, Venus in her undulations, the kirtled shape of Diana, and Jupiter voluminously bearded' (2004: 146). Having unwittingly angered his father by asking him about these 'old Greek gods', he is told that they are 'the shadows cast by the vices of the heathens' and that there was nothing in the myths of 'these gods, or rather devils, that it is not better for a Christian not to know' (2004: 146). This exchange marks a pivotal, if as yet unspoken, rupture in Gosse's relationship with his father. 'I did not accept his condemnation of the Greeks', he tells us, and privately continues to view the engravings concluding that 'they were too beautiful to be so wicked' as his father insisted, noting that, due to these images, the 'dangerous and pagan notion that beauty palliates evil budded in [his] mind, without any external suggestion' (2004: 146). While this incident clearly sets up a conflict between his family's evangelical Christianity and Gosse's growing pagan aestheticism, his passionate response to statuary – 'These attracted me violently' – suggests an unacknowledged sexual frisson that resurfaces later in Gosse's life through his relationship with the sculptor Hamo Thornycroft in which sculpture functions as a medium of tacit desire. What is also clear is that Gosse is strongly stimulated both by the images themselves and by the sculptures that function as the engravers' models.

On one level, the teenage Gosse's reaction to pictures of naked figures is instantly recognisable. However, the sublimation of his desire into aesthetic response deserves greater attention and has interesting implications for the Victorians' investment in classical statuary. In Victorian writings, the tension between sculpture's eroticism and its ideal purity frequently surfaces in literary negotiations designed to bury its threatening nature. The reactions to classical and neoclassical nudes discussed above point to the Victorians' dynamic relationship with ancient civilizations, especially with the Greeks. Yet, as Frank Turner has remarked, in order to accommodate unacceptable aspects of ancient Greek culture, the Victorians needed 'to find the Greeks as much as possible like themselves and to rationalize away fundamental differences', resulting in false parallels where 'Greek subjects were made to conform to contemporary categories of thought, culture, and morality' (1981: 8). An example of this can be found in *Routledge's Guide to the Crystal Palace and Park at Sydenham* (1854). In response to the furore surrounding sculptural immodesty, the author, Edward Macdermott, quotes Anna Jameson who had elsewhere argued that '[t]he Greeks and other great designers gave into this practice (of representing the figure undraped) in order to show, in its full extent, the idea of character they meant to establish' (1854: 58). For Jameson, nudity is vital for the full depiction of beauty, strength and agony, but what her argument deliberately ignores is the erotic charge of the naked statue, and the sexual expression and transgression often implicit in sculptures and associated with their mythical counterparts.

My book suggests that such apparent attempts to remould perceptions of classical sculpture hide the fundamental role played by ancient statues and related myths in the Victorians' negotiation of their own sexualities. In doing so, it contributes to a field of interest in nineteenth-century literature and the visual arts that has grown over the last twenty-five years. During this time, a number of scholars have explored the significance of the sculptural body in a variety of contexts. These works vary in coverage: some are broad in scope, covering a variety of media (Gross 2006; Stoichita 2008) or a wide chronological span (Joshua 2001; Hersey 2009); others are primarily historical (Funke and Grove 2019) or art-historical (Getsy 2004; Edwards 2006; Davis 2010); and some, like my own, engage with nineteenth-century literature, but centre on a specific author (Fernie 2011; Østermark-Johansen 2011), genre (Marshall 1998) or country's production (Aspley et al. 1999; MacLeod 2014).

At the core of my own study is the interrelationship between aesthetics, sexuality and sensory responses to sculpture, and it builds on the work of critics who have explored the eroticism of statuary and sculptural metaphor. Among these is Gail Marshall who, in *Actresses on the Victorian Stage: Feminine Performance and the Galatea Myth*, argues that the performances and relationships of Victorian actresses – on and off stage – were always informed by the power negotiations implicit in the Pygmalion myth. Given Marshall's seminal coverage of sculptural bodies in Victorian theatre, my own book focuses instead on the poetry and fiction of the period and, while Pygmalion is necessarily important to any book on literary statues, I move beyond the myth to consider other forms of interaction with the sculptural body. The eroticism of sculpture is also discussed at length in George Hersey's *Falling in Love with Statues: Artificial Humans from Pygmalion to the Present*, which explores statue cults in the ancient world and the significance of sculpture in the Cypriot cultures that gave birth to the Pygmalion myth, and the sexual allure of statues features in Jason Edwards's *Alfred Gilbert's*

Aestheticism: Gilbert Amongst Whistler, Wilde, Leighton, Pater and Burne-Jones, which partly considers the codification of homosexuality in the works of Oscar Wilde and Walter Pater. The intersections between sculpture, aesthetics and sexual desire examined in Whitney Davis's *Queer Beauty: Sexuality and Aesthetics from Winckelmann to Freud and Beyond* are closest to my own interests. However, while Davis focuses primarily on male homosexuality, and engages with his material from an art-historical point of view, my own work additionally examines other forms of desire and considers the texts discussed from a literary-critical perspective. Furthermore, I focus on the ways in which direct tactile contact and metaphors of tactility in the texts discussed provide a means through which to elide the boundaries between touch and vision in the experience of statuary and permit implicit expressions of transgressive sexual proclivities.

Touching Statues

Touch is, of course, at the heart of the Pygmalion myth that resonates so strongly in any erotic engagement with statuary and, while not all who view sculptures are budding Pygmalions, the 'desire to touch is typically part of our encounters with sculptures' (Kenaan 2014: 45). As Constance Classen has discussed, the function of touch in the appreciation of sculpture has been a matter of historical and aesthetic debate. In Renaissance Italy, she observes:

> Some critics found such tactile interaction with sculpture too coarsely sensuous. Sixteenth-century art theorist Vicenzo Borghini denounced the practice of touching and kissing statues as vulgar ... Benedetto Varchi, by contrast, suggested that the particular value of touch in relation to sculpture was that it alone could appreciate the artifice involved in sculpted work ... Referring to an ancient statue known as the Hermaphrodite, Lorenzo Ghiberti commented that 'there was the greatest refinement, which the eye would not have discovered, had not the hand sought it out'. (2012: 132)

Whatever the differences in opinion, it is evident that, at this time, touch was 'common practice' in the experience of sculpture (2012: 132). Yet as Classen explains, the sixteenth century saw what she describes as 'a backlash' against such practices. The Protestant Reformation in sixteenth-century Europe considered the touching and kissing of religious images a form of idolatry and frowned upon sensuality, affecting attitudes to touch, 'the most apparently sensuous of the senses', and later concepts of aesthetic response (Howes and Classen 2014: 19). While the original definition of 'aesthetic' was developed from the Greek term 'aisthetikos' relating to bodily sense perception (*Oxford English Dictionary* n.d.), in the eighteenth century Alexander Gottlieb Baumgarten (1714–62), best known for naming the discipline we now call 'aesthetics', redefined its meaning and posited a relationship between sensual response and rational cognition that became newly associated with the perception and appreciation of taste and beauty (Carroll 2006: 70). Later in the century Immanuel Kant (1724–1804) was to revise Baumgarten's aesthetics in *The Critique of Judgment* (1790), in which he disembodied the sense of taste and developed instead a 'disinterested' appreciation and judgement of beauty based on reason that would proceed to dominate modern aesthetics (Howes and Classen 2014: 19).

Many eighteenth-century theorists favoured sight over touch, but among those who contested the primacy of sight in the appreciation of the plastic arts, was Johann Gottfried Herder (1744–1803) whose treatise, *Sculpture: Some Observations on Shape and Form from Pygmalion's Creative Dream* was first published in 1778. Herder privileged touch over sight in the perception of sculptural aesthetics and it was an argument he developed from personal experience. Although Herder did not visit Rome until 1788 and therefore did not see many of the original sculptures he considered in his treatise, he did in fact have access to copies of such sculptures both in the Louis XIV collection at Versailles, and in the Johann Wilhelm collection, eventually housed in the Mannheim Drawing Academy, both of which he visited in 1769 (Gaiger 2002: 2–3). For Herder, the eye offers only a fragmented perception of the sculptural figure. Requiring a continual shift in perspective as one circles a statue, a sense of the sculpture's unity can only be determined by imaginatively combining such partial views. Moreover, unlike touch, vision cannot provide us with a sense of the statue's texture, mass or volume (Herder 2002: 19). According to Herder, when one looks at sculpture, one must deploy vision differently. Gathering impressions, the eye that looks at painting and 'sees a depiction on a surface', becomes instead 'a hand, the ray of light becomes a finger and the imagination becomes a form of immediate touching' (2002: 19). Herder goes on to propose two further arguments for the importance of this form of imaginative touch: first, it allows us to appreciate sculpture by replicating the artist's own experience of shaping the object; secondly, it allows us to 'understand' the statue's unity and its expressive quality through a form of identification with the statue. As he explains:

> Because (a sculpture) presents a *human being*, a fully *animated body* . . . it seizes hold of us and penetrates our very being, awakening the full range of responsive human feeling . . . [I]t possesses the power to virtually *transpose* our soul into the same sympathetic *situation*. . . . [W]e find ourselves . . . embodied in the nature before us, or the nature in question is enlivened by our own soul . . . Nothing must be merely *observed* and treated as if it were a surface; it must be touched by the gentle fingers of our inner sense and by our harmonious feeling of sympathy, as if it came from the hands of the Creator. (2002: 80–1; original emphases)

The aesthetic linkage between sculpture and touch has a long history; most notably represented in the *paragone* of the Italian Renaissance that pitted sculpture, the art of touch, against painting, the art of vision (Dent 2014: 14). The association is an enduring one and still active in the twentieth century in Herbert Read's concept of sculpture as 'an art of palpation'; for Read, sculpture, as opposed to painting, 'gives preference to tactile sensations as against visual sensations, and it is precisely when this preference is clearly stated that sculpture attains its highest and its unique aesthetic values' (1956: 70). However, in eschewing the role played by vision in the perception of sculpture, Read subscribes to 'a division of the senses which corresponds to an analogous division of the arts' making a 'clear-cut distinction between touch and sight' that 'finds its correlation in the distinction between sculpture and painting' (qtd in Kenaan 2014: 46). In doing so, he fails to examine the vital interrelationship between vision and touch in this process. As Hagi Kenaan observes:

> [S]culpture does not address our tactile sensibilities independently of vision; on the contrary, its tactility manifests itself precisely within the confines of what the eye reveals in us. Hence, instead of debating whether sculpture is closer to touch or to vision, the question that needs to be asked should be one that invites us to explore an intersection, a double proximity, a tactility whose resonance is visual, and a visuality whose inner pulse is the desire to touch. (2014: 46)

In making this point, Kenaan draws on Maurice Merleau-Ponty's theories of perception to argue that 'seeing' cannot be considered independently of the body that sees. As Kenaan explains, for Merleau-Ponty 'seeing is not an event that can occur inside an independent or virtual mind; it is not a relation between an ideal viewer and an image, but a real condition of our moving about in the world'; instead it is what Merleau-Ponty calls an 'intersection' between the eye and the body (Kenaan 2014: 53). This suggests that when we view sculpture, 'our body is always an issue'; inhabiting the same physical space as sculpture, vision is not fully disassociated from touch as tactile connection is always a possibility (2014: 53–4).

Such a possibility necessarily has erotic potential; the line between sculpture and flesh becomes significantly blurred, an elision of boundaries to which Goethe subscribed in his *Roman Elegies*. Caressing his lover's curves, he claims that to 'See with an eye that can feel, feel with a hand that can see' enhances his experience of sculpture, and helps him to 'appreciate marble' for the first time (1996: V, 52).

The implicit tension between touch and vision identified by Merleau-Ponty becomes increasingly charged when touch is forbidden. In *Art, Museums and Touch*, Fiona Candlin observes that, in the nineteenth century, touch becomes increasingly prohibited in museums; 'parliamentary records, newspaper reports and museum minutes document the growing disapprobation of touch in a museum context and the correlative restrictions on touch', though handling artefacts remained 'a necessary and highly valued skill for curators and connoisseurs' (2010: 2). In *Ways of Sensing: Understanding the Senses in Society*, David Howes and Constance Classen note that it was in the nineteenth century that the museum became 'the eyes-only space it is known for being today' (2014: 19). As Howes and Classen argue, there was a practical aspect to this shift from tactuality to visuality, deemed necessary for the purposes of conservation; as the number of museum visitors rose, the chances of theft and damage also multiplied (2014: 19). However, as they point out, there were 'larger cultural forces' at work behind this shift than 'mere concern for preservation' and the fact that the 'no touching' policy required a 'long process of public education concerning correct museum comportment', suggests that people were reluctant to abide by the new rules (2014: 19). Where the experience of sculpture is concerned, this study suggests that one of the 'larger cultural forces' at work concerned sexual response. As the examples given in this introduction imply, access to the sculptural body was fraught with potential impropriety, and the viewing, let alone touching, of sculpture was charged with sexual tension. In such circumstances, I would argue that literature becomes a crucial 'safe' space in which such tensions are explored and in which the viewer's encrypted desire, embedded in sculpture, surfaces for circulation and interpretation, facilitated by the 'magic touch' expressed at the intersections between visual, tactile and, in this case, readerly encounters with the sculptural body.

A Literary Gallery

This book contains a literary gallery of sculptures. Here you will find Venuses and Apollos, marble fauns and hermaphrodites, as well as tomb sculptures and sarcophagi. What they share is an insistent presence in Victorian literature, peopling the writings of both established and neglected authors. As sculptural metaphor is employed liberally in Victorian literature, this book centres specifically on works which feature the physical presence of sculpture, be it in the form of statues, tomb effigies or bas-reliefs, reflecting the experiences of the Victorian public who, as the century progressed, were permitted close encounters with classical, renaissance and Victorian examples. The following chapters follow a route through a literary statue gallery that takes the reader on a journey from animation through to stasis and entombment. Chapter 1, 'Nineteenth-Century Pygmalions: The Sexual Politics of Tactility', addresses the prevalence of the Pygmalion myth in Victorian fiction, considering works that have received comparatively little critical attention: George MacDonald's *Phantastes* (1858), William Morris's 'Pygmalion and the Image' from *The Earthly Paradise* (1868), and Thomas Woolner's *Pygmalion* (1881).[9] Opening with a discussion of Ovid's Pygmalion and its influence on Romantic and late-Romantic writing, this chapter focuses on the ways in which the aesthetic and sexual concerns it raises inform and complicate negotiations of heterosexual desire and the 'purity' of the artist in the Victorian texts discussed. Demonstrating the slippage between living and sculpted women in such expressions of eroticism, this chapter explores the tensions between touch, animation and stasis that are at the heart of the book. Chapter 2, 'Artworks in Marble: Capturing Venus in Durable Form', begins by emphasising the role played by Venus Aphrodite in the animation of Galatea. It considers the prevalence of Venus sculptures in Arthur O'Shaughnessy's 'Thoughts in Marble' series, which appears in *Songs of a Worker* (1881), and in Thomas Hardy's *The Well-Beloved* (1897). In this chapter, I examine these writers' conflation of creativity, aesthetics and eroticism through metaphors of moulding and sculpting, before focusing on the role played by sculpture in the memorialisation of the dead in their texts. Chapter 3, '"Of marble men and maidens":

Sculptural Transformations',[10] takes as its starting point the fact that the British edition of Hawthorne's novel, *The Marble Faun: Or, The Romance of Monte Beni*, was published under the title *Transformation* (1860) and examines the connections between Hawthorne's work and Henry James's early novel *Roderick Hudson* (1875). Drawing on both writers' relationships with Anglo-American circles of sculptors, artists and writers in Rome, this chapter considers the mediation of desire between protagonists in *The Marble Faun* and *Roderick Hudson* through key sculptural figures and metaphors of touch that contribute to the recognition, and eventual burial, of unruly desires. In Chapter 4, 'Statuephilia and the Love of the Impossible', I consider how sculpture channels Gosse's homoerotic desire for the sculptor Hamo Thornycroft, enabling the memorialisation of their relationship in his poetry and prose. This chapter then proceeds to explore how sculpture facilitates complex vortices of libidinal energies in poems by Oscar Wilde and Olive Custance. I argue that Wilde's 'Charmides' (1881a) enables a phantasmatic congress between Wilde and his dead 'beloved', the poet John Keats, and that a similar process is at work in Olive Custance's statue poems, which are in dialogue with Wilde's own life and poetry. Drawing on the work of French and English Parnassian poets, Custance's poems additionally develop a sculptural aesthetic that expresses a complicated negotiation of her ambiguous sexuality. In my concluding chapter, 'Between Death and Sleep: Libidinal Entombments', I focus on the role played by funerary monuments in the mediation of sexual expression and repression. Here, I consider the tomb of Ilaria del Carretto by Jacopo della Quercia, and its importance in the writings of John Ruskin and Michael Field, before going on to explore the broader significance of entombment in the literary texts discussed in the preceding chapters.[11]

The ubiquity of the sculptural form and sculptural metaphor in the literature of the period means that this literary gallery is necessarily a personal one; it is composed of works from across the nineteenth century which nevertheless form what, in my view, is an illustrative selection of texts that engage with classical, renaissance and Victorian sculpture. Many other imaginary museums remain to be visited in our search to understand the complexities of gender and sexuality at the intersections of literature and sculpture, not least those where race and national identity play significant roles; these are beyond the scope of my book, but it is hoped that this study will prompt new avenues for investigation and play its part in stimulating fresh lines of future research.

Notes

1. As Victoria Donnellan notes, Townley was part of a circle of antiquarians, including Pierre-François Hughes, known as 'Baron Hancarville', and Richard Payne Knight, who 'were interested in the interpretation of ancient art as part of a system of primitive universal theology, exploring the idea of a single generative force shared across ancient cultures', a theory that 'focussed on artefacts with sexual themes' (2019: 155).
2. Donnellan's essay explores the reception and display history of Townley's nymph and satyr, an explicit sculpture that shows the figures in the act of copulation. She argues that removal of this artefact from public view may have been due to a relaxation in admissions policy. When the Gallery of Antiquities opened at the British Museum, members of the public were only admitted as part of guided tours; in March 1810, however, these arrangements were relaxed and, while visitor numbers doubled as a result, Donnellan considers that 'the greater freedom of access for a wider audience instituted in 1810 may well have prompted curators to remove these objects from display at this time' (2019: 162). Gaimster notes that the Secretum at the British Museum became official following the donation of 'four hundred and thirty-four diverse objects' described as 'Symbols of the Early Worship of Mankind' by Dr George Witt which included erotic artefacts from 'Classical, medieval European, Oriental and contemporary cultures' (2001: 132).
3. Abraham and Torok revisit the problematic case of Russian aristocrat, Sergei Pankejeff (1886–1979), one of Sigmund Freud's case studies in 'From the History of Infantile Neurosis' (1918). Given the name 'Wolf Man' to disguise his identity, Pankejeff was treated by Freud for psychological problems that included deep bouts of depression, and physical symptoms, such as the need to have enemas to pass bowel movements. Freud's analysis focused on Pankejeff's childhood dream of several white wolves perching in a walnut tree which, together with his patient's bowel problems, he interpreted as a response to Pankejeff's witnessing of a primal scene as a young child in which his parents were copulating *a tergo*. Abraham and Torok's analysis of the Wolf Man case complicates Freud's interpretation and explores the other multiple readings available through gaps in linguistic signification.
4. The British Museum was founded in 1753; the National Gallery in 1824; the South Kensington Museum, originally known as the 'Museum of Manufacturers' was founded in 1852 and later renamed the 'Victoria and Albert Museum' in 1899; the Walker Art Gallery, Liverpool opened in 1860, the Nottingham Caste Museum and Art Gallery opened as the first municipal art gallery outside London in 1878, the Birmingham Museum and Art Gallery in 1885, the Leeds Art Gallery and the Manchester Museum in 1888, and the Kelvingrove Art Gallery and Museum in 1901.

5. Jacques-Louis David (1748–1825) was a significant French artist who painted in the neoclassical style and whose history paintings are of particular note; David was a supporter of the French Revolution. Jean-Auguste-Dominique Ingres (1780–1867), a French neoclassical artist, was best known for his detailed portraits.
6. It is worth noting, however, that, as Dominique Poulot has observed, Quatremère de Quincy supported the removal of the Elgin Marbles to the British Museum, ignoring 'the rights of the Greeks or the identity of a putative Greek nation'; Poulot argues that he may have distinguished between the classical Greece of ancient glories, and a contemporary Greece he perceived as 'wretched' (2012: 13).
7. Antonio Canova (1757–1822) was an Italian neoclassical sculptor whose notable statues include *Psyche Revived by Cupid's Kiss* (1787–93), and a colossal statue, *Napoleon as Mars the Peacemaker* (1802–6), which can be seen at Apsley House in London. John Flaxman (1755–1826) was a British neoclassical sculptor who produced important works such as *The Fury of Athamas* (1790–4), but who is now often best known for the classical designs he produced for the Wedgewood potteries. Bertel Thorwaldsen (1770–1844) was a Danish sculptor in the neoclassical style, often seen as Canova's successor; *Jason with the Golden Fleece* (1803) is one of his best-known sculptures.
8. The Plymouth Brethren are an evangelical, non-conformist protestant sect to which Edmund Gosse's parents belonged. His father, the naturalist Philip Henry Gosse (1810–88), was strongly committed to the sect and his son's rejection of it led to a family rift.
9. See Pulham (2016b) for a discussion of the Pygmalion myth in nineteenth-century women's writing.
10. John Keats, 'Ode on a Grecian Urn' (1988: 345, l. 42).
11. Variants of Ilaria's name include 'del Carretto', 'di Caretto' and 'Del Carretto'. In this book, I use 'del Carretto' unless quoting directly.

Chapter 1

Nineteenth-Century Pygmalions: The Sexual Politics of Tactility

The myth of Pygmalion as it appears in *Metamorphoses* (composed between AD 1 and 8) is reputedly 'the earliest version of cultural importance' (Joshua 2001: 2). However, Ovid's story of statue love has its genesis in earlier, similar, tales that either complicate the worship of statuary or consider Pygmalion's treatment of his statue as a form of sexual violation. In her invaluable survey of the myth and its transformations across time and genres, Essaka Joshua observes that mythographers such as Arnobius and Clement of Alexandria employ the story as a form of parable: 'Clement warns that pagan statue-worship is wrong; Arnobius argues that it is impossible for gods to dwell in statues' (2001: 1).[1] In each of these cases, the statue worshipped is of Venus Aphrodite: in Clement's version, Pygmalion, a Cypriot, falls in love with and embraces a naked ivory statue of Aphrodite; in Arnobius's account Pygmalion, now elevated to king, falls in love with the statue of a Roman Venus. In referring to the myth, both draw on the writings of Philostephanus of Cyrene, a writer of the early Hellenistic period who produced a now lost cycle of stories about the history of Cyprus, *Cypriaca*, which included the legend of Pygmalion (Salzman-Mitchell 2008: 292). Philostephanus's concern with religious rites suggests that his account offers an example of the hierogamy between the King of Cyprus and the island's goddess, Aphrodite.[2] In Philostephanus's version, Pygmalion is not a sculptor; instead we are told that he 'fell in love, as if she were a woman, with an image of Venus'; that he treated the statue 'as if it were his wife'; and that, lifting 'the divinity to the couch, kissing and embracing her, he used to have intercourse with her and do other vain things, carried away by his foolish and lustful imagination' (qtd in Salzman-Mitchell 2008: 292). But Arnobius and Clement also relate the Pygmalion story to another myth, one in which Aphrodite is violated by a Cnidian youth. In Arnobius's version, the young man is a nobleman whose love leads him to perform 'lewd' acts with the statue, while in Clement's version, it is the beauty of the craftsmanship, rather than the body, that bewitches the viewer (Joshua 2001: 1–2).

In these related but differing explanations of statue love, we find the beginnings of the conflict between lewdness and purity that afflicts the story from its earliest incarnations, simultaneously titillating yet providing a 'chaste permission' to desire (Marshall 1998: 51). From its inception, the story of Pygmalion sets up a tension between purity and impurity that later informs perceptions of statuary and versions of the myth in the eighteenth and nineteenth centuries. Writing of nineteenth-century responses to 'naked, or only partially draped' classical statues, Marshall observes that, in this period, the 'Classical body becomes a signifier both of the Fall and of a state of innocence' (1998: 10). Yet, as Clement's retelling suggests, the Pygmalion myth is not concerned with sexuality alone, and may sometimes focus on 'craftsmanship' rather than desire. Combinations of such concerns emerge in the four nineteenth-century texts examined in this chapter: William Hazlitt's, *Liber Amoris, or The New Pygmalion* (1823); George MacDonald's *Phantastes: A Faerie Romance for Men and Women* (1858); William Morris's poem, 'Pygmalion and the Image' from *The Earthly Paradise* (1868–70); and Thomas Woolner's twelve-book poem, *Pygmalion* (1881).

These works engage in interesting ways with the myth and highlight how it gives rise to complex interactions between the real and the ideal, nature and art.

The Pygmalion Myth

At the heart of the Pygmalion story lies a rejection of public wantonness that may well have resonated with a Victorian public increasingly concerned with prostitution, that 'Great Social Evil' that dominated debates surrounding women's bodies and culminated in the Contagious Diseases Acts of 1864, 1866 and 1869.[3] Book X of Ovid's *Metamorphoses* features the punishment of the immoral Propoetides, women of Amathus in Cyprus. Having refused to acknowledge Venus's divinity, they are chastised by the goddess who makes them 'the first/Strumpets to prostitute their bodies' charms' (2008: X, l. 290). Having lost any sense of shame and their power to blush, we learn that 'their cheeks grew hard' and that 'They turned with little change to stones of flint' (2008: X, ll. 244–7). Ovid here plays with his readers' knowledge that Cyprus was 'a famous centre of sacred harlotry' (2008: 434, n. 240), where the worship of Venus Aphrodite gave birth to 'cults of sacred marriage and sacred prostitution'.[4] Horrified by the Propoetides' sexual excesses, Pygmalion sculpts his own perfect woman. Carving 'his snow-white ivory/With marvellous triumphant artistry', he gives it 'perfect shape, more beautiful/Than ever woman born' (2008: X, ll. 53–6).[5] Enthralled by his own 'masterwork', he becomes 'Fired . . . with love' for a statue that seems 'to be alive' (2008: X, ll. 56–7). Pygmalion's art appears to equal or outdo nature.[6] Inspired to love by his own handiwork, Pygmalion increasingly desires the body he has sculpted, explores it for signs of imagined life and engages in erotic fantasies:

> With many a touch he tries it – is it flesh
> Or ivory? Not ivory still, he's sure!
> Kisses he gives and thinks they are returned
> He speaks to it, caresses it, believes
> The firm new flesh beneath his fingers yields,
> And fears the limbs may darken with a bruise.
> (2008: X, ll. 254–9)

Following the Feast of Venus at which he prays for a bride who will be the 'living likeness' of his 'ivory girl' (2008: X, l. 281), he returns home to find that Venus has granted his wish. Kissing his statue, he observes that 'she seemed warm' and caressing her breast feels the flesh grow soft 'beneath his touch', 'its ivory hardness vanishing' and yielding in his hands 'as in the sun/Wax of Hymettus softens and is shaped/By practised fingers into many forms' (2008: X, ll. 288–93).

In her essay, 'Some Versions of Pygmalion', Jane Miller argues that, while seeming to differentiate between Aphrodite and Pygmalion's 'ivory girl', Ovid's language implies a conflation between the goddess and Pygmalion's creation:

> Pygmalion rejects nature's women and creates his own ideal out of ivory. He is obviously a great craftsman for the statue possesses a beauty *qua femina nasci/nulla potest* . . . which no woman ever born could have. It is noteworthy that Ovid specifically declares this beauty unattainable by any woman born. Aphrodite was the goddess who personified ideal female beauty and was like no woman born in two senses: she was a goddess and therefore supernatural, but she was also born, according to legend, from the sea-spume, not from male and female. The suggestion could be, therefore, that the statue represents the goddess, as in Philostephanus' aetiology. (1988: 206)

The sexual nature of Pygmalion's reaction to the statue once completed is evident in Ovid's choice of words: '*operisque sui concepit amorem* ('and he falls in love with his own work')', especially as the word '*concepit* is a sexual metaphor' (Miller 1988: 206). Despite Ovid's erotic response, and the statue's life-like quality, it is nevertheless a statue, though Pygmalion seems reluctant to believe this. Translating Ovid's text, Miller highlights the 'fleshly quality' of Pygmalion's desire: 'Pygmalion is full of admiration and burns with love for this semblance of a body' and often 'lifts his hands to the work to test whether it is flesh or ivory', refusing to 'admit it is ivory' (1988: 206). Ovid tells how Pygmalion 'kisses and fondles it, believing his kisses to be returned'; 'he flatters his statue and brings it little presents, just as any other lover would court his mistress'; and, more tellingly perhaps, he lays the statue on his bed and calls her his '*tori sociam*, the partner of his bed' (1988: 206–7). While not explicitly mentioned, Ovid suggests that, as in some of the accounts on which his narrative draws, Pygmalion is in fact the King of Cyprus. 'There is a hint', Miller writes, 'that Pygmalion is more than a simple sculptor'; on Venus's feast day, 'he approaches Venus' altar with his own gift of incense, an act which may imply kingship' (1988: 207). In Miller's view:

> Ovid appears to have remythologised the story reported by Clement and Arnobius. The first element of his narration deals with the story of a man on Cyprus who falls in love with a statue and has a sexual relationship with it. In the second, the man is revealed as Pygmalion, the King of Cyprus, and the statue is Venus, their union being the *hieros gamos* probably described by Philostephanus. The two aspects cannot be divided and are therefore told more or less concurrently. (1988: 208)

Whether or not the statue is meant to be Venus Aphrodite, by loving and caressing his statue while still in sculptural form, Pygmalion initially appears to be what might be classified by sexologists as an 'agalmatophiliac', a term that identifies those who find themselves sexually attracted to statues.[7] Such amorous engagements with the sculptural body have been a matter of clinical interest since the inception of sexology: in *The Sexual Instinct and its Morbid Manifestations* (first published in 1886), Benjamin Tarnowsky cites ancient and modern examples of such cases, and in the fourth volume of *Studies in the Psychology of Sex* (first published in 1905), Havelock Ellis explains that 'Pygmalionism, or falling in love with statues, is a rare form of erotomania founded on the sense of vision and closely related to the allurement of beauty' (1936: 188).[8] Writing much later, in the mid-twentieth century, clinicians A. Scobie and A. J. W. Taylor attempted to differentiate between two forms of statue love: 'pygmalionism' and 'agalmatophilia':

> Agalmatophilia is the pathological condition in which some people establish exclusive sexual relationships with statues. The condition is neither to be confused with pygmalionism nor with fetishism, although confusion sometimes arises about these three different manifestations of immature sexuality . . . The myth of Pygmalion can apply only to those who actually bring statues to life, and not to those who use statues for their own sexual purposes without bringing them to life . . . An agalmatophiliac . . . establishes a personal relationship with a complete statue as a statue. He does not bring the statue alive in his fantasy as would a pygmalionist.[9] (1975: 49)

Despite Scobie and Taylor's attempts to distinguish between the agalmatophiliac and the pygmalionist, there is evidently a fine line to be drawn between the lover who desires a statue in its sculptural form, and the lover who, in his imagination, animates the rigid statue he desires. As we have seen above, Ovid's story of Pygmalion itself seems to stem from tales of what Scobie and Taylor would call 'agalmatophiliacs'. Yet his relationship with the ivory statue is here 'normalised' in congress with a living statue who is moulded by Pygmalion into his wife and becomes the mother of his child.

William Hazlitt: the Critic as Artist

Such fantasies of female passivity and masculine control clearly resonated with nineteenth-century Pygmalions. Implicit in Romantic and Victorian adaptations and appropriations of the myth is the construction of pure and ideal femininity. According to Marshall, Victorian Pygmalions responded 'to contemporary anxieties about women and their ability to "metamorphose" into unprecedented professional and intellectual forms', and she notes how, in contrast to Ovid's ending, where the statue bears Pygmalion's child, most Victorian versions of the myth enact a reverse pygmalionism that returns their Galateas to stone (1998: 24). In this formulation, the eventual immobility of the woman–statue functions as both a reification of the body into art object, and a simultaneous immurement of vital life that conjoins 'both admiration and admonition' (1998: 25).

Focusing on stage adaptations, Marshall shows how Victorian actresses, embodying what she calls 'the Galatea-aesthetic' fulfilled 'the role of the isolated and desirable spectacle which was Galatea's first incarnation' (1998: 30–1). For Marshall, the Pygmalion myth is concerned primarily with the objectification and silencing of women. While this is clearly the case in the examples from the Victorian stage that Marshall employs, I would argue that the Victorian appropriation of the Pygmalion myth and especially the return to stasis that characterises nineteenth-century versions of the myth are part of a wider cultural phenomenon that entombs and encrypts desire in Victorian culture. It is particularly important to recognise, as I aim to show in later chapters of this book, that in Victorian literature it is not only women who are silenced and deadened in sculptural form. For now, however, I want to consider the treatment of the myth in William Hazlitt's *Liber Amoris, or The New Pygmalion* (1823).

In Hazlitt's novella, the only physical sculpture is a little image of Napoleon that functions as the conduit of desire, purchased no doubt from one of the many Italian street sellers of plaster figurines.[10] Hazlitt's own Pygmalion is informed by Jean-Jacques Rousseau's popular one-act play, *Pygmalion* (1771) which was widely translated and performed (Joshua 2001: 37). While Rousseau's play had been less well received in Britain in the aftermath of the Napoleonic Wars, Leigh Hunt produced an English translation in 1820, and the name 'Galatea', meaning 'she who is milk-white' was popularised by Rousseau whose play may be responsible for the appropriation of the name and its ubiquity in British literature (Joshua 2001: 34).[11] Hazlitt's novella, additionally inspired by Rousseau's *Julie, ou La Nouvelle Héloïse* (1761) and *Confessions* (1782), appeared shortly after, and was informed by Hunt's translation.[12]

Since its publication, Hazlitt's text has defied categorisation. Set alongside Rousseau's *Confessions*, one might read it as 'a "straight" Romantic autobiography' (Butler 1984: 214). Yet, read in the context of Hazlitt's aesthetic philosophy and, in particular, his championing of the Elgin Marbles, it takes the form of a self-conscious and ironic comment on questions of the aesthetic ideal in addition to depicting a troubling instance of unwanted sexual attention. Hazlitt's narrative is underpinned by his extensively documented obsession with a lodging-house maid. Living in London in 1820 having separated from his wife, Hazlitt became infatuated with Sarah Walker, a daughter in the family from whom he rented a room at 9 Southampton Buildings, Chancery Lane. There is no doubt that *Liber Amoris* has its genesis in real events: published anonymously three years later, it presents the story of unrequited love between H-, an educated writer, and S.L., his landlord's lower-class daughter, who also serves as a maid and to whom he refers as 'the statue'. The advertisement that precedes the narrative notes that the names and characters 'are so far disguised . . . as to prevent any consequences resulting from the publication, farther than the amusement or sympathy of the reader' (Hazlitt 1998a: 3). Nevertheless, Hazlitt's albeit weak efforts at disguise proved fruitless. Within a month of the novella's appearance, the publication in the *John Bull* magazine of an actual letter written by Hazlitt to Sarah Walker unmasked the protagonists (Barnard 1999: 183).

Told predominantly from H-'s viewpoint, *Liber Amoris* has often been read as a damaging self-revelation, but it may also be read as an ironic, self-conscious fiction. This reading is suggested within the text itself by H-'s shift in tone in the note that follows his impassioned first letter to a friend, C. P.,[13] in which he acknowledges:

> I have begun a book of our conversations (I mean mine and the statue's) which I call Liber Amoris. I was detained at Stamford and found myself dull, and could hit upon no other way of employing my time so agreeably. (Hazlitt 1998a: 26)

This implies that the letters were written with 'at least half an eye to publication' (Butler 1984: 216) and that the affair is essentially 'fictionalized as it happens' (Barnard 1999: 184). However, H-'s reference to S.L. as 'the statue' suggests that Hazlitt's text is self-consciously literary, functioning as a witty repositioning of the Pygmalion myth in his own period. The question is why did Hazlitt choose the Pygmalion myth, in particular, as the background to his story of unrequited love? In doing so, Hazlitt draws on an anonymous transmutation of the Pygmalion myth, *Ovide Moralisé* (1309–20), a French poem from the early fourteenth century that seeks 'Christian and moral truths in the *Metamorphoses* by reinterpreting the stories' (Miller 1988: 208). As Miller explains:

> The first interpretation put forward in the *Ovide Moralisé* . . . is a kind of aetiology expressed in demythologised terms which has clear parallels with the Cinderella story. Pygmalion is interpreted as a great lord who has in his household a serving girl, dirty and uneducated but nonetheless beautiful. Such a lord might take this girl and groom her until finally she is to be his wife. (1988: 208)

The most famous example of this version of the myth is, of course, George Bernard Shaw's play *Pygmalion* (first performed in 1913) in which, through lessons in elocution and social comportment, the flower-girl Eliza Doolittle is trained to pass as a duchess.[14] However, Shaw's social comedy offers only a more overt example of interactions that are more subtly characterised not only in Morris's 'Pygmalion and the Image' but also in Woolner's *Pygmalion*. In Hazlitt's version, as in Shaw's, Galatea is sculpted not in ivory, like Pygmalion's statue, but in language; but whereas sex is occluded in Shaw's play, sexual politics play a significant part in Hazlitt's novella. In the latter, H- presents an image of S.L. that vacillates between virgin and whore. At times she is 'divine' (Hazlitt 1998a: 9), 'heavenly-soft, saint-like' (1998a: 11); at others 'a practised, callous jilt, a regular lodging-house decoy' (1998a: 71). In art, she is equally difficult to define and contain; the figure of 'Guido's or Raphael's' whom she resembles is identified as both a 'Madona' [sic] and 'a Magdalen' (1998a: 7). Like Pygmalion's statue, formed to belie the nature of women manifested in the Propoetides, S.L. must contain within her perfection the imperfection of her sex. Moreover, H- expresses a desire to educate his Galatea. As Barnard comments, 'H-'s project is clear; in Pygmalion fashion (more like Shaw's than Ovid's), he will bring out S.L.'s sensibility and educate her through continental travel' as well as introducing her to literature and art through his gift of books and aesthetic discussions (1999: 192).[15]

For John Barnard, H- 'is a victim of the Romantic ideology' that places 'aesthetics above ethics', one who 'persistently tries to transform S.L. into a womanly ideal' drawn from literature and art (1999: 183–4). But I would argue that Hazlitt's representation of H-'s aestheticism is more complex and informed by Hazlitt's own discussions of art and sculptural aesthetics. It is worth noting that *Liber Amoris* was published in 1823, shortly after Hazlitt's extended essays on the Elgin Marbles which appeared in the *London Magazine* in 1822. As Stephen Larrabee has observed, in the second decade of the nineteenth century Hazlitt began to establish himself as a serious art critic, commenting on aspects of painting and sculpture:

> As early as 1814 [Hazlitt] was writing on the fine arts ... [and] his work for *The Champion* firmly established him as a critic of art. Early in the following year, when the hearings in regard to the purchase of the Elgin Marbles began before a Parliamentary Committee, Hazlitt gladly entered the lists, joining Haydon in his attacks on the connoisseurs who preferred the familiar Greco-Roman antiques such as the Apollo Belvedere. ... By 1817 Hazlitt was so deep in aesthetic criticism that references to the fine arts began to appear in his literary criticism. (1941: 78)

More recently, in his foreword to *William Hazlitt, On the Elgin Marbles*, Tom Paulin suggests that Hazlitt's training as an artist gave his critiques a certain form of insight. For Paulin, Hazlitt is 'the critic as artist' (2008: viii). While Hazlitt may have had a special understanding of painting, Larrabee claims that he was 'unaccountably slow in arriving at an appreciation of sculpture' and notes that the Elgin Marbles were the first works of sculpture to excite his interest (1941: 80). Nevertheless, the Elgin Marbles clearly triggered a response that prompted Hazlitt to challenge traditional perceptions of sculptural perfection informed by Winckelmannian aesthetics and disseminated by the Royal Academy of Arts. This 'perfection' was epitomised by late-Hellenic statuary which, according to Winckelmann, exuded a 'noble simplicity' and 'quiet grandeur' (qtd in Mallgrave 2006: ix).

In a lecture delivered to students of the Royal Academy on 14 December 1770, Sir Joshua Reynolds draws attention to the Greek ideal as an intellectual concept. Referring to the 'poets, orators, and rhetoricians' of antiquity, Reynolds argues that 'all arts receive their perfection from an ideal beauty, superior to what is to be found in individual nature', that the ideal can never be found in nature, because nature is always imperfect (1891: 82). In his essays on the Elgin Marbles, Hazlitt contests Reynolds's argument privileging the real over the ideal. As he asserts, the 'master-excellence' of the Elgin Marbles lies in the fact that 'they do not seem to be the outer surface of a hard and immovable block of marble, but to be actuated by an internal machinery and composed of the same soft and flexible materials as the human body' (Hazlitt 1998b: 82–3). For Hazlitt, the qualities exhibited by these magnificent marbles oppose what he calls 'the fashionable and fastidious theory of the *ideal*' (1998b: 77; original emphasis). According to Hazlitt, this ideal is represented by Greek statues that are 'marble to the touch and to the heart', whose beauty raises them 'above the frailties of passion or suffering', and seem 'to have no sympathy with us, and not to want our admiration' (1818: 21–2). S.L., the object of H-'s unrequited love, the 'statue' in *Liber Amoris*, possesses precisely those properties that we might associate with this 'ideal'. Allusions to her sculptural counterpart are employed to laud her grace and condemn her callous nature. She is described as 'pale and beautiful' (Hazlitt 1998a: 7); following a perceived act of emotional cruelty, she resembles 'some graceful marble statue, in the moon's pale ray' (1998a: 11); separated from her, H- imagines her face 'constantly before [him], looking so like some faultless marble statue, as cold, as fixed and graceful as ever statue did' (1998a: 48); and on his return from a journey to Scotland, in a letter to a friend he compares her to 'a Greek statue' (1998a: 56). Situated in the context of Hazlitt's art criticism, such allusions prompt a reconsideration of *Liber Amoris*, asking us to question the apparent simplicity of its autobiographical genesis.

For Barnard, H-'s 'alternating idealization and demonization of S.L. taps into the ambiguous psychic responses to women's sexuality in Regency England' (1999: 187), responses which continue, as we know, into the Victorian period, becoming a matter of increasing tension as the century progressed. Interestingly, S.L. often resists H-'s perception of her, albeit that this resistance is always expressed via H-'s report of her direct speech. In the opening dialogue between them, he shows S.L. the picture of a woman, and asks: 'Don't you think it like yourself?', to which she replies that she does not, and points out that the sitter's complexion is fair as opposed to her own which is dark (Hazlitt 1998a: 7). Similarly, when during a quarrel H- accuses her of deceiving him, of being a 'common lodging-house decoy, a kissing convenience', she counters: 'I never have, Sir. I always said I could not love' and affirms, 'I deceive no one Sir' (1998a: 14). In reconciliation, H- gives her a little statue of Napoleon, his idol, an image which, in S.L.'s eyes, bears a likeness to a former lover to whose memory she claims to be faithful.[16] The transfer of the 'little image' – as it is referred to by both H- and S.L. – from his possession to hers functions as a form of erotic exchange; it is only through the little image that any communion can take place for here, the 'God' of his 'idolatry' is also 'like her idol' (1998a: 19). However, the little image also doubles for H-'s image of S.L. who is his own heart's idol. Later, when S.L. avoids H- and spurns his request to speak with her for the sake of the little image, she refuses him. In rejecting the figurine, she refuses both H-'s desire and his construction of her, choosing to remain fixed in her own image. Significantly, in his angry response to her rejection, H- smashes not only the statuette, but also a symbolic image of Sarah's affection, a locket she had given him which contains her hair and metonymically represents her. In the process both items are destroyed: he tramples on the locket and then dashes the 'little Buonaparte' to the ground before stamping on it. When Sarah has the little image mended for him, she tells H- that 'they had been obliged to put some new pieces to it' (1998a: 67), suggesting a reconstruction of the image that forces an acknowledgement of her independence. Faced with S.L.'s agency, H- is seemingly powerless.

Read in the context of Hazlitt's biography, *Liber Amoris* is simply the record of unrequited love across class boundaries. However, read alongside his art criticism, one might consider it a meditation on the tension between art and nature, the ideal and the real. S.L.'s refusal to be H-'s ideal and the destruction of the latter's romantic and political idols point to a preference for 'nature' that is evident in Hazlitt's rejection of the Greek ideal revered by Royal Academicians in favour of sculptures which, in his view, excel because they parallel the physical (and natural) movements of the human body. Describing the Elgin Marbles, he writes:

> It seems here as if stone could move: where one muscle is strained, another is relaxed, where one part is raised, another sinks in ... and all this modulation and affection of the different parts of the form by others arises from an attentive and co-instantaneous observation of the parts of a flexible body, where the muscles and bones act upon, and communicate with, one another like the ropes and pulleys in a machine, and where the action or position given to a particular limb or membrane naturally extends to the whole body ... put a well-formed human body in the same position, and it will display the same character throughout; make a cast from it while in that position and action, and we shall see the same bold, free, and comprehensive truth of design. (1998b: 78)

For Hazlitt, the perfection of the Elgin Marbles lies in the fact that they appear to be 'copied from nature, and not from imagination', that they, like his own fictional text, have 'the appearance of absolute *facsimiles* or casts taken from nature' (1998b: 75; original emphasis). Viewed from this perspective, *Liber Amoris* becomes a form of literary tribute to the Elgin Marbles, and this privileging of the natural in art would later have a significant impact on John Ruskin and the Pre-Raphaelites whom Ruskin championed. In his discussion of nineteenth-century art criticism, William C. Wright observes that Ruskin's critiques contain 'certain ideas and views already expressed by Hazlitt' and that 'it is quite possible that Ruskin was more indebted to Hazlitt at this early point in his career than has been generally acknowledged' (1974: 509–10). Writing more recently, Uttara Natarajan remarks on how the second edition of the first volume of *Modern Painters* was published with 'a new "Preface," in which Ruskin propounds for the first time, and to silence his critics, a theory of the ideal, formulated in retrospect to justify the principles of criticism already set out in his text'; in doing so, she argues, 'he draws substantially – although without acknowledgement – on Hazlitt's theory of the ideal', expressed in two essays: 'On the Fine Arts' and 'On the Elgin Marbles' which had recently appeared in the first volume of *Criticisms on Art* (1843) (Natarajan 2002: 493–4).

Ruskin's rejection of the 'ideal', as proposed by Royal Academicians such as Joshua Reynolds, and his emphasis on natural detail was also to influence William Morris, whose awareness of the Pre-Raphaelites came from his reading of the Edinburgh Lectures in which Ruskin expressed his approval of the Pre-Raphaelite Brotherhood's attention to 'absolute uncompromising truth . . . obtained by working everything, down to the most minute detail, from nature' (1855: 227–8). In his own 1877 lecture, later published as 'The Lesser Arts' in 1882, Morris emphasised the importance not only of nature, but of history, telling his audience that 'Nature and History' must be their 'teachers', stating: 'I do not think that any man but one of the highest genius could do anything in these days without much study of ancient art, and even he could be much hindered if he lacked it' (1882: 19–20).[17] As Peter Faulkner notes, while 'the Pre-Raphaelite respect for nature was embodied in Morris's early decorative work', his 'indebtedness to earlier historical traditions became equally important' (2012: 51). These tensions and intersections between nature, history and art surface in 'Pygmalion and the Image', a poem that is one of the twenty-four stories in *The Earthly Paradise* told over a twelve-month period by a group of Norsemen who flee the plague in their own land to seek a haven across the seas.[18] Each month, the tales are related in pairs; 'Pygmalion and the Image' is told in August, 'the month of fruition which also marks the end of the "year's desire"' (Miller 1988: 212).

Divine Interventions: Morris's Reluctant Agalmatophiliac

Dedicated to his wife, Jane Morris, at a time when their marriage was falling apart due to her affair with Dante Gabriel Rossetti, *The Earthly Paradise*'s celebration of love in 'Pygmalion and the Image' could be read as an ironic comment on a relationship in which the artwork and the woman had become very much conflated.[19] In the 'Argument' that precedes 'Pygmalion and the Image', we are told that 'in the end [Pygmalion] came to love his own handiwork as though it had been alive: wherefore, praying to Venus for help, he obtained his end, for she made the Image alive indeed, and a Woman, and Pygmalion wedded her' (Morris 1888: 588). The relationship between William and Jane Morris resonates with that of H- and S.L. in *Liber Amoris*. Though not a lodging-house maid, Jane, like Sarah Walker on whom S.L. is modelled, was also a working-class woman whose natural beauty was transformed into art, and whom, unlike

H-, Morris succeeded in moulding into a middle-class wife (Parkins 2013: xi). Grzegorz Zinkiewicz suggests that Morris's disenchantment with women is evident in the work's female characters most of whom are 'cold, withdrawn, aloof, and deprived of feelings' (2017: 148, n. 13), and certainly, in Morris's version, Pygmalion is a disillusioned figure whose engagement with the Propoetides leads to a heavy heart rather than anger, and who bewails his lonely existence and his commitment to inert and unresponsive figures, exclaiming, 'For what to him was Juno's well-wrought hem,/Diana's shaft, or Pallas' olive stem?' (1888: 589), thus questioning the value of his art in a life without love and human companionship.

While in Ovid, Venus Aphrodite emerges only when Pygmalion prays to her to bring his statue to life, in Morris's poem the goddess is involved in sculpting the image, guiding Pygmalion's hand with 'godlike mastery' (1888: 590). Moreover, Morris's Pygmalion is self-conscious, disturbed by and aware of the 'strange and strong desire he could not name' that enters his heart as he contemplates his handiwork (1888: 591). Unsettled by his libidinal response to an inanimate statue, he seeks refuge in nature, taking 'his quiver and his bow' to 'the mountain slopes' (1888: 592). Here, he is among natural life and movement: the scythe sweeps; 'the swallow fleet' flies over him; a partridge stirs, and a brown bee whirs, yet he rejects this, asking: 'what do I midst this stir and noise?/What part have I in these unthinking joys' and returns to his workshop (1888: 592–3). On the way, he asks himself what he will do if 'she were gone', then realises that he is speaking of his statue as if it were alive, 'and therewithal/ In turn great pallor on his face did fall' (1888: 593). As he enters his studio, this sensitive Pygmalion who finds his statue still 'motionless and white and cold' (1888: 593) sheds tears and feels mocked by his own desire for the object. Yet amid his exhortations to the image, there is an acknowledgement that others are also enamoured of inanimate sculptures: 'I know indeed/That many such as thou are loved of men,/Whose passionate eyes poor wretches still will lead/Into their net, and smile to see them bleed' (1888: 594). But, he argues, these were made by the gods, and he wishes that she, who is made by his own hands would speak to him (1888: 594). He then stops for a moment to assess his creation:

> Then from the image did he draw aback
> To gaze on it through tears: and you had said,
> Regarding it, that little did it lack
> To be a living and most lovely maid;

> Naked it was, its unbound locks were laid
> Over the lovely shoulders; with one hand
> Reached out, as to a lover, did it stand,
>
> The other held a fair rose over-blown;
> No smile was on the parted lips, the eyes
> Seemed as if even now great love had shown
> Unto them, something of its sweet surprise,
> Yet saddened them with half-seen mysteries,
> And still midst passion maiden-like she seemed,
> As though of love unchanged for aye she dreamed.
> (1888: 594–5)

In this ekphrasis, the statue is a strange mix of innocence and sexual knowledge: her 'unbound locks' suggest wantonness; one hand is outstretched in a beckoning motion that invites a lover's touch while in the other she holds an over-blown rose that speaks of love consumed; her lips are parted with desire; and her eyes seem to know of love (1888: 594–5). Yet, despite her erotic allure, she seems 'maiden-like' (1888: 595). Like Ovid's Pygmalion, Morris's sculptor lays his statue down upon his bed, but the oddity and material reality of such an action is made manifest in Morris's poem where 'Strong men' are called in from the street to 'bear the ponderous, moveless feet' of the statue into Pygmalion's bedchamber (1888: 595). Here, like Ovid's Pygmalion, he adorns his statue with jewels, placing precious gems around her neck, fingers and arms, and sets a 'little altar' at her feet at which he prays (1888: 596).

When he wakes the next morning to find his statue still and unmoving, his attention is diverted to the streets beyond his home where a procession of young men and women, 'in wonderful attire' bear in their midst an image of Venus Aphrodite, the 'Mother of Desire/ Wrought by his hands' whose sculptural body has been covered in a flame-coloured, gem-encrusted garment for a tri-annual festival in the goddess's honour (1888: 599). Following the crowds, Pygmalion finds himself in her temple where he watches as the statue of Aphrodite is stripped of her attire to display 'the ivory limbs his hand had wrought' (1888: 601). We learn that during the ritual, the ground is strewn with 'summer flowers' and that 'Lydian music' and a 'dancer's cry' can be heard in the 'far-off halls' of the temple (1888: 602). The event described here resonates with Hellenistic rituals associated with statue love and sacred marriages. Referring to the Homeric *Hymn to Aphrodite*, George Hersey remarks that the poet describes how Aphrodite's lover, Anchises, removes 'her bright jewelry of pins and twisted brooches and earrings and necklaces', and how he 'loosed her wrap, and stripped her of her bright garments' (2009: 67). He goes on to observe that 'Aphrodite dressing (or undressing) and Aphrodite bathing are major themes in sculpture relevant to the cults of statue love' and discusses how such rituals are also 'associated with sacred marriages between a mortal and the goddess's statue' (2009: 88–9). However, while in the temple, Morris's Pygmalion prays to Venus but never fully articulates his desire; rather he lets the goddess intuit it.

Although Morris seems at pains to minimise the nature of Pygmalion's sexual play with the statue, there is a quiet acknowledgement of such activity when he returns to his home and stands in his bedchamber where we learn that 'for very shame/Of all the things he had done before' he 'Still kept his eyes bent down upon the floor/Thinking of all that he had done and said/Since he had wrought that luckless marble maid' (1888: 606). When he raises his eyes, he finds that his statue has come alive, and that though she is exactly as he made her, she is now 'arrayed/In that fair garment that the priests had laid/Upon the goddess on that very morn' (1888: 607). This indicates not only Aphrodite's hand in bringing his marble maiden to life, but also a conflation between the goddess and the statue who, as Pygmalion approaches, says the words Aphrodite has bade her say: '*Pygmalion,/My new-made soul I give thee to-day*', and invites him to feel her breath, touch her breast and sweep her hair around his neck (1888: 608; original emphasis). In contrast to Ovid's Pygmalion, where the moment of animation is experienced as the sculptor caresses his statue and feels her soften beneath his touch, Morris's poem stages an encounter between the statue and Venus Aphrodite which the former (now brought to life) recounts:

> 'My sweet,' she said, 'as yet I am not wise,
> Or stored with words, aright the tale to tell;
> But listen: when I opened first mine eyes
> I stood within the niche thou knowest well,
> And from mine hand a heavy thing there fell,
> Carved like these flowers, nor could I see things clear,
> And but a strange, confused noise could hear.
>
> At last mine eyes could see a woman fair,
> But awful as this round, white moon o'erhead.
> So that I trembled when I saw her there,
> For with my life was born some touch of dread,
> And therewithal I heard her voice, that said,
> "Come down, and learn to love and be alive,
> For thee, a well-prized gift, to-day I give."

> Then on the floor I stepped, rejoicing much,
> Not knowing why, not knowing aught at all,
> Till she reached out her hand my breast to touch;
> And when her fingers thereupon did fall,
> Thought came unto my life, and therewithal
> I knew her for a goddess, and began
> To murmur in some tongue unknown to man.
>
> . . .
>
> With that she said what first I told thee, love,
> And then went on: "Moreover, thou shalt say
> That I, the daughter of almighty Jove,
> Have wrought for him this long-desired day;
> In sign whereof these things that pass away,
> Wherein mine image men have well arrayed,
> I give thee for thy wedding-gear, O maid."
>
> Therewith her raiment she put off from her,
> And laid bare all her perfect loveliness,
> And, smiling on me, came yet more anear,
> And on my mortal lips her lips did press,
> And said, "Now herewith shalt thou love no less
> Than Psyche loved my son in days of old.
> Farewell. Of thee shall many a tale be told."'
> (1888: 610–11)

In this exchange, the animated image resembles Condillac's statue in *Traité des sensations* (1754) which gradually gains the five senses in succession, and the movement from stasis to animation is figured by the drop of the over-blown rose wrought in marble, suggesting a reset to a state of innocence.[20] Moreover, here, it is Venus Aphrodite whose touch brings the statue to life, and whose kiss gives it the power to love, thus converting Pygmalion's sexualised touch into a moment of divine intervention. But most important is the conflation that occurs between the statue and the goddess: both are products of Pygmalion's art and the conferment of the ritual garment on his statue turns the latter into Aphrodite's double.

Stefanie Eck has argued that, in nineteenth-century versions of the Pygmalion myth, the emphasis shifts from a focus on Pygmalion as artist, to Pygmalion as educator (2014: 5). She cites Morris's Pygmalion as an example and notes how his animated statue states that she is 'yet . . . not wise', and is advised by Aphrodite that she 'still wilt wiser grow', thus implying that 'the awakening statue needs instruction and a guiding hand' and that the goddess has 'given her into Pygmalion's care "as his love and wife"' that he might take on 'the role of the educator' (2014: 10). Yet Morris also appears concerned with what Miller calls, 'the problem of Time's destructiveness and how to achieve immortality', a problem which, she claims, informed *The Earthly Paradise* more broadly (1988: 212). She contends that:

> Morris is clear that art, no matter how perfect, cannot replace real life; the statue cannot replace a living girl as an object of love. To convey this, he has to use the elaborate technique of relieving Pygmalion of his unnatural obsession so that it can be replaced by normal human love when the maiden comes to life. In Ovid passion is simply transferred, but for Morris there can be no question of the two objects or the feelings they inspire being interchangeable. (1988: 212)

Thomas Woolner's twelve-book poem, *Pygmalion*, explores similar issues, although, here, it is the sculptor who is 'educated' as the poem progresses and made to look beyond his art for love.

Educating Pygmalion

The 'Prelude' to Woolner's poem claims that it aims to show 'How passion deep, and Aphrodite's aid,/Resolved to life that wondrous Maid,/Pygmalion wrought in marble, by the stress/Of worship, to pure loveliness' (1881: 2). This suggests that the poem will conform to the classical Ovidian version of the story. However, this is not quite the case. Woolner's Pygmalion is not a solitary artist; he exists in a domestic space along with his mother and her twelve maids, and his initial aim is not to sculpt an ideal woman to overcome his aversion to the Propoetides, but 'To bring the Gods' own language, sculpture,/down/For mortal exaltation' (1881: 3). He muses that 'Men made in marble look but men, no more', but that 'Gods in sculpture are immortal powers/To whom we kneel helplessly lost in awe' (1881: 3).[21] In Woolner's poem, the twelve maids who are his mother's companions become important to the plot and model for his sculptures. These 'maids' are unmarried noblewomen who learn home management from Pygmalion's mother, who are being tutored to be good wives to 'heroes' and will 'rear/A race of children bold and beautiful' (1881: 6). Education, here, is provided not by Pygmalion, but by his mother, the mistress of the home in which he lives and works.

Woolner's Pygmalion, like Morris's, seeks refuge from art in nature: he swims, and ranges 'the forest solitudes' to seek inspiration. For this Pygmalion, however, nature is also a gateway to art:

> These lapses from close labour nerved his will,
> Which, quickening half-born dreams and thoughts obscure
> To living truths, gave him the strength he craved
> Whereby to animate the forms he wrought
> With nature's varied movement; pause and play
> Of impulse: complex outwardly in strain
> And laxity alert. Armed with this power
> The damp impressible clay glanced into light
> Along the tendons' length; hardened to bone;
> And tightened straightway into comely shape
> Beneath his certain touch. Hard marble changed,
> In softened shadows rounding tenderly
> To firm elastic life: and what anon
> Was but as chaos beamed a new delight
> More lasting than all beauty born of man.
> (1881: 12–13)

As in the Elgin Marbles, the life in this Pygmalion's statues seems copied from nature. Pygmalion's turn 'To living truths', give him the strength 'Whereby to animate the forms he wrought/With nature's varied movement; pause and/play/Of impulse', recalling Hazlitt's declaration that the 'chief excellence' of the Marbles 'depends on their having been copied from nature, and not from imagination', that they are like 'human figures petrified', having the 'appearance of absolute *facsimiles* or casts taken from nature' (Hazlitt 1998b: 75; original emphasis). Yet Woolner's tale revolves around Pygmalion's work on a series of sculptural compositions described in Book II of the poem where each ekphrastic sequence ends with the same refrain: 'And this in pure immortal marble he/Laboured to show; bound by those rules of/Art/The Wise had found inexorably fixed' (1881: 17, 24, 29, 39), suggesting those rules of ideal sculpture that Woolner had learned at the Royal Academy.[22] Therefore, the poem's subtext appears to engage with questions relating to sculptural 'craft' which, I would argue, are never fully resolved as there is a constant slippage between the primacy of the sculptural ideal and the importance of the natural body.

The sculptural scenes Pygmalion creates feature the gods: Aphrodite, Dionysus, Prometheus and Zeus, and he uses Ianthe, one of his mother's maids, as the model for Hebe, Zeus's daughter, cupbearer of the gods, and one of Aphrodite's retinue.[23] Consumed by his work, Pygmalion is oblivious to Ianthe who brings him food and wine each day, and whom he only notices as an image useful for his art, regarding her only 'as a beauteous shape/Aiding him in the Godlike counterfeit' and 'Unconscious what she felt' (1881: 45–6).[24] Though she models well for him and transforms herself into a living statue for the purpose, not flinching 'at tingling nerves and throbbing pulse' though often 'dizzy from the continual strain/Of keeping motionless' (1881: 45-6), Pygmalion is unable to capture her natural beauty and her grace:

> The gracefulness
> And pride of her long rounded throat, his hands
> Changed into awkwardness by mimicry.
> The arches of her shoulders! Could he touch
> On curves so exquisitely drooped, their sheen
> Of movement tremulous?
> (1881: 46)

Obsessed by his efforts, Pygmalion, like Prometheus, seeks 'The spark to flash his Hebe into life' and feels doomed to failure 'if unaided now/By gracious favour of immortal love' (1881: 52). Eager for others' thoughts on his work, Pygmalion asks his mother's maids to offer their opinions of his Hebe sculpture. While some speak, others' unvoiced thoughts note how the statue seems more a representation of Ianthe than a statue of Hebe: to Clytie, 'The statue seemed more like Ianthe than/A Statue' and the narrator agrees that 'the statue looked/Ianthe, but without her charm'; to Aglaia, 'Instead of Hebe serving Zeus', the statue looks more like 'Ianthe pouring for Pygmalion' (1881: 56–7). When Ianthe is asked whether the statue should bear Hebe's name or her own, she answers modestly that only Pygmalion would know his aim, 'and if his efforts struck or missed'; that her role was to model for him and to serve him; and that 'neither gave her claim/To take from Hebe, an Olympian God,/Her name, and glorify herself therewith' (1881: 59).

Frustrated by the statue's lifelessness, Pygmalion worships Aphrodite in her temple, seeking the goddess's help to bring that 'spark divine', that 'throbbing touch of pulse,/To touch all other pulses as Her own' to his statue of Hebe (1881: 68). In answer, Aphrodite appears to Pygmalion in a vision that reinforces both her immortal and erotic power; 'shedding azure radiance from Her eyes' and 'brightly clad' in a diaphanous 'tissue sunbeam-wove' which barely conceals her charms, she promises him that Hebe will have 'life and immortality' (1881: 69–71). But, she warns, he must pay a price for this: his name will be tainted unfairly and he will have to contend with the hatred of some, and the censure of others. As the tale progresses, Pygmalion's friend, Orsines, declares his intention to ask for Ianthe's hand in marriage, and asks his permission. At this news, Pygmalion becomes pale and feels a pain in his heart, yet does not understand why, but duly makes his friend's case to Ianthe who rejects the suit. Her spirited refusal makes him realise that it is she whom he loves, and he reveals his feelings to her, while calling her both 'Ianthe' and 'Hebe' (1881: 108–9). As he bends to kiss her, he sees 'the glow' of her breast 'Rose pointed, proud, with glimmering azure laced,/ Too fair for touch or even mortal glance', while 'splendour like a garment covered her' (1881: 109), charms that echo those barely concealed beneath Aphrodite's diaphanous garb. Released from his hold, Ianthe steps up on the platform on which she has often posed for him, adopting Hebe's stance and, when they declare their love in his mother's presence, Pygmalion exclaims: 'O mother, I/Have found her! Hebe She is come to life!' [*sic*] (1881: 112). Pygmalion, now, with renewed passion, works on his statue of Hebe and we learn of his pleasure in doing so:

> Great his joy
> To raise the wonder in her brows. To make
> The shadows dark within her upward eyes;
> In those fine nostrils breathing purity.
> Pressing the mouth to longer droop of curves
> Above the prow of her imperial chin.
> These now in his fierce energy were but
> As trifles. Chisel edge could scarcely touch
> Ere the obstruction vanished as a cloud.
> (1881: 119)

He works on her to perfect 'the grace/Of Hebe or Ianthe' (1881: 120). On completing the statue, Pygmalion is asked, by his father's friend, Crito, to show it to the public who eagerly await a view of it. Aware of Pygmalion's solicitation to Aphrodite, Ianthe proposes that her statue be given as a 'sacred offering to the Goddess' and 'placed within her Temple for all time' and Crito 'With utmost reverence' believes Aphrodite to have spoken through Ianthe (1881: 125). The final three books of Woolner's poem realise Aphrodite's warning and cover the ways in which Pygmalion's reputation is defiled, chart how he regains it – partially through martial glory – and ends in his being chosen by the Lord of Council to be King of Cyprus.

Noli mi tangere

In this poem, Woolner appears to 'purify' the interactions between Pygmalion and his statue; his is a domesticised Pygmalion who is publicly lauded for his sculpture, becomes a Cypriot king and gains the love of a real woman, thus eschewing any perverse amatory encounter between the sculptor and his statue. In his *Pygmalion*, Aphrodite helps the sculptor by revealing his love for the statue's model and double, Ianthe, and permitting his desire for the maid to imbue his statue with a life-likeness that is within the bounds of conventional art, thus omitting the need for any direct erotic experience with the statue itself. It is this chaste rendering of the myth that won Woolner praise from the reviewer who wrote in the *St James's Gazette*, on Tuesday 7 February 1882, that though none but his 'most cordial admirers' would 'scarcely pronounce him a first-rate poet', Woolner had nevertheless 'handled his theme with delightful freshness and originality' (Anon. 1882b: 6). An earlier reviewer in *The Spectator*, 7 January 1882, was even more effusive in his praise:

> Ma. WOOLNER has understood the true poetry in the legend of Pygmalion better than most of his predecessors, either Greek or English. He sees that the physical magic in the story – the actual bringing to life of the statue, and the marriage with the maker of it – is a degenerated form of its true meaning, which is simply that it is love which gives life to the artist's work, and that nothing less than love will make it truly live. (Anon. 1882a: 25)

Similarly, Morris's 'Pygmalion and the Image' avoids any direct illustration of sexual contact between the sculptor and the statue. While such congress is implied when he experiences 'shame', on returning to his home after his visit to Aphrodite's temple, 'for all the things he had done before' (1888: 606), it is Aphrodite's, rather than Pygmalion's, touch that brings his image to life.

As Amelia Yeates has shown, this reluctance to engage with the explicit eroticism of Ovid's Pygmalion is equally present in Edward Burne-Jones's *Pygmalion and the Image* series which 'has its basis in the illustrations undertaken for Morris's poem' (2018: 108). In

William Morris and Edward Burne-Jones: Interlacings, Caroline Arscott traces the 'close interconnections in theme, allusion and formal strategy' between Burne-Jones's work and Morris's own, their mutual interests informing a friendship that 'was one of the defining features of both their lives' (Arscott 2008: 9). Writing of *The Earthly Paradise*, Arscott notes that Burne-Jones originally planned to contribute 'up to 500 wood-engraved illustrations' to a richly illustrated edition of Morris's work (2008: 17). She explains that, while 'the illustrated edition was never completed, and the poem came out with just two woodcuts in 1868-70', Burne-Jones had nevertheless 'made dozens of compositional sketches' and that his 'work on the illustrations' inspired 'a number of Burne-Jones's elaborate projects in watercolour or oil, preoccupying him for decades, notably the *Cupid and Pysche* series and the *Pygmalion* series' (2008: 17). Commenting on the two sets of finished paintings (1868–70 and 1875–8) that make up Burne-Jones's *Pygmalion* series, Yeates notes that the first set 'was a commission for Euphrosyne Cassavetti, the wife of an Anglo-Greek merchant, Demetrios Cassavetti, living in London', and mother of Burne-Jones's model and lover, Maria Zambaco, 'whilst the second set was exhibited at the Grosvenor Gallery in 1879' (2018: 107).

The series is composed of four paintings: *Pygmalion and Galatea I: The Heart Desires*; *Pygmalion and Galatea II: The Hand Refrains*; *Pygmalion and Galatea III: The Godhead Fires*; and *Pygmalion and Galatea IV: The Soul Attains*. As Yeates acknowledges, Burne-Jones's *Pygmalion* series is often read as an expression of his passionate, and fraught, affair with Zambaco but, she argues,

> there is every possibility that Burne-Jones had already worked out the designs for his *Earthly Paradise* illustrations before he had met Zambaco, in which case the works were not biographical in origin even if they received a biographical inflection as they developed. (2018: 108)[25]

For Yeates, the *Pygmalion* series is far more than the expression of a troubled lover, and needs to be understood 'within more complex debates concerning the shared exploration of desire and romantic love by Burne-Jones and Morris' (2018: 108). Yeates argues that, while Morris 'relies on the same signifiers of masculinity as Ovid' to represent Pygmalion as 'libidinous and virile', the former demonstrates 'a degree of reticence about Pygmalion's desire for Galatea' (2018: 112); this reticence is equally in evidence in Burne-Jones's *Pygmalion* series. Drawing on a detailed contemporary review of

Burne-Jones's paintings, that appeared in the *Athenaeum* in 1879, Yeates observes:

> Of *The Heart Desires*, the author writes that Pygmalion's eyes are 'fixed in thought and hardly yet fully stirred by passion' . . . Of the final painting in the series, *The Soul Attains*, the *Athenaeum* reviewer observes, 'There is speculation now in her [Galatea's] eyes, hardly yet moved by passion' . . . the anticipated passion of this dramatic love story clearly not palpable for the reviewer. (2018: 114–15)

She adds that 'in *The Soul Attains* . . . Pygmalion returns to find Galatea already alive, a process which has started in *The Godhead Fires* where Venus breathes life into the statue' (Plate 1) and that Burne-Jones's narrative here 'corresponds with Morris's poem where Pygmalion returns from praying to find Galatea already transformed' (2018: 115). Moreover, she contends that 'the removal of Pygmalion from the moment of physical transformation is a crucial aspect of Morris's and Burne-Jones's depictions', and observes that, omitting this dramatic moment, that is in most depictions sexually charged, 'considerably affects the erotic tenor of the scene' (2018: 115–16). What appears to be prohibited in each case is the direct representation of erotic touch between artist and statue that one finds in the Ovidian version of the myth. In Morris's and Woolner's works this prohibition is implicit; however, it is far more direct in George MacDonald's *Phantastes*.[26]

Now often best remembered for a few of his fairy tales and fantasies, including *At the Back of the North Wind* (1871), *The Princess and the Goblin* (1872) and *Lilith, A Romance* (1895), in his own lifetime MacDonald attained a distinct measure of fame if not fortune and counted writers and poets such as John Ruskin, Lewis Carroll, the Brownings, the Morrises, the Rossettis and the Pre-Raphaelite artist, Arthur Hughes, who illustrated *Phantastes*, among his friends and acquaintances. According to Colin Manlove (2005), MacDonald's *Phantastes*, which combines medievalism and classicism, may have been influenced by Morris's prose romances which had appeared two years earlier in 1856, and he notes that *Phantastes* shares with Morris's romances 'an interest in medievalism, in dreams and dream structures, in the relation of the reader or dreamer to art and life, and in such topics as death, sex, impulsive passion and the after-life'.[27] For MacDonald, *Phantastes* is 'a sort of fairy tale for grown people' (Page 2008: 14), but the subtitle, *A Faerie Romance for Men and Women*, might easily be read as an allusion to Robert Browning's *Men and*

Women, published in 1855, a collection of poems that also deals with the complexity of human relationships and, in some works, explores the tensions between art and life.[28]

The hero of MacDonald's story is 'Anodos' who on his twenty-first birthday inherits the family estate and the keys to an old desk within which he discovers a portal to a fairy kingdom where he meets a fairy-woman who tells him that he will find his way to fairy-land the following day. What follows is a series of episodic trials and adventures like those prevalent in medieval romance narratives that lead Anodos from self-centredness to humility. Structured around 'repetition and reflection', the story is reminiscent at times of *Sir Gawain and the Green Knight* (*c.*1400) where self-interest is pitted against the 'trouthe' and 'gentilesse' demanded of chivalric behaviour, and the name 'Anodos', which can mean both 'upwards' and 'pathless' (Page 2008: 15), points to the fact that the hero's successful completion of his spiritual journey is often in jeopardy.[29] As Nick Page explains, 'The "main" story of Anodos contains many events which repeat, rework or reflect one another. And his story is mirrored in the poems, ballads and stories embedded within the text' (2008: 15). Given the story's maze-like structure, and allusive intricacy, MacDonald's 'fairy tale' for grown-ups is far more complicated than his description might suggest; it may be read alternatively as a spiritual biography, a Romance quest narrative or a form of *Bildungsroman*, and its symbolic nature has attracted a variety of Freudian, Jungian and Kristevan psychoanalytic readings.[30] Yet, as Albert Pionke has observed, there is comparatively 'little modern criticism devoted to *Phantastes*' (2011: 21). While since the 1990s MacDonald's other works have received increasing critical attention, *Phantastes* remains relatively unexplored.[31] The reasons for this are difficult to fathom, particularly as it resonates with other well-known texts by MacDonald's friends and contemporaries, including John Ruskin's *King of the Golden River* (1851), Christina Rossetti's 'Goblin Market' (1862) and Lewis Carroll's *Alice's Adventures in Wonderland* (1865).[32] This scholarly disinterest is even less explicable when one finds that many of its themes engage with issues and ideas that are 'of central concern to MacDonald's Victorian contemporaries, including medievalism, Romanticism, and aestheticism' (Pionke 2011: 21).

If the medievalism in *Phantastes* has received only cursory notice, the aesthetic dimensions of MacDonald's work have been almost entirely neglected. With the notable exception of Helen Sutherland's essay, 'Pictures on a Page: George MacDonald and the Visual Arts' (2013) and Pionke's article 'The Art of Manliness: Ekphrasis and/as Masculinity in George MacDonald's *Phantastes*' (2011), little interest has been shown in MacDonald's engagement with the arts. Yet, one of the main repeated motifs in *Phantastes* is the Pygmalion myth. The fairy-lady Anodos first meets by the portal to the fairy kingdom is described as a 'tiny woman-form, as perfect in shape as if she had been a small Greek statuette roused to life and motion' (MacDonald 2008: 43). Later, while embarked on his journey, Anodos rests in a 'rocky cell' in which 'all the angles [were] rounded away with rich moss, and every ledge and projection crowded with lovely ferns' (2008: 81) where, following a brief reverie, he becomes aware of a 'strange, time-worn bas-relief' that he recognises as a representation of Pygmalion awaiting his statue's animation (2008: 81). Shortly afterwards he notices that the block of rock on which he has been lying is 'marble, white enough and delicate enough for any statue' and, using his knife as a form of chisel, finds that the rock is in fact alabaster (2008: 82). Enclosed within it is 'the form, apparently in marble, of a reposing woman' whom he brings to life with his song, and who, following her release, gleams 'away toward the woods' and is lost to him (2008: 82–6).

The final allusion to the Pygmalion myth occurs towards the end of the text following Anodos's arrival at a fairy palace. Here, he discovers twelve halls divided by crimson curtains which contain within them 'an innumerable assembly of white marble statues, of every form, and in multitudinous posture' that stand 'upon pedestals of jet black' (2008: 175–6). One of the halls is lit by the glow of a great lamp around which is written 'the two words – TOUCH NOT!' (2008: 176). After dreaming that his marble lady is in the tenth hall, one night he seeks her there and finds an empty pedestal where she stood in his dream. Looking more closely he sees that her white feet have appeared on the pedestal 'vaguely revealed as if through overlapping folds of drapery' (2008: 179). Reasoning that his song might bring her to life once more, he takes a harp from one of the statues, and begins to sing. The song he sings is reproduced in the text in poetic form and functions as a cross between a striptease and a blazon, each verse successively, and suggestively, revealing parts of her body (2008: 182–4):

> Feet of beauty, firmly planting
> Arches white on rosy heel!
> Whence the life-spring, throbbing, panting,
> Pulses upward to reveal!
> Fairest things know least despising;
> Foot and earth meet tenderly;
> 'Tis the woman, resting, rising
> Upward to sublimity.

Rise the limbs, sedately sloping,
   Strong and gentle, full and free;
Soft and slow, like certain hoping,
   Drawing nigh the broad firm knee.
Up to speech! And up to roses
   Pants the life from leaf to flower,
So each blending change discloses,
   Nearer still, expression's power.
. . .
Sudden heaving, unforbidden
   Sighs eternal, still the same—
Mounts of snow have summits hidden
   In the mists of uttered flame.
But the spirit, dawning nearly,
   Finds no speech for earnest pain;
Finds a soundless sighing merely—
   Builds its stairs, and mounts again.
. . .
All the lines abroad are spreading,
   Like the fountain's falling race,
Lo, the chin, first feature, treading,
   Airy foot to rest the fact!
Speech is nigh; oh, see the blushing,
   Sweet approach of lip and breath!
Round the mouth dim silence, hushing,
   Waits to die ecstatic death.
. . .
With a presence I am smitten
   Dumb, with a foreknown surprise;
Presence greater yet than written
   Even in the glorious eyes.
Through the gulfs, with inward gazes,
   I may look till I am lost;
Wandering deep in spirit mazes,
   In a sea without a coast.

Windows open to the glorious!
   Time and space, oh, far beyond!
Woman, ah! thou art victorious,
   And I perish, overfond.
Springs aloft the yet Unspoken
   In the forehead's endless grace,
Full of silences unbroken;
   Infinite, unfeatured face.
. . .

Sideways, grooved porches only
  Visible to passing eye,
Stand the silent, doorless, lonely
  Entrance-gates of melody.
But all sounds fly in as boldly,
  Groan and song, and kiss and cry,
At their galleries, lifted coldly,
  Darkly, 'twixt the earth and sky.

Beauty, thou art spent, thou knowest;
  So, in faint, half-glad despair,
From the summit thou o'erflowest
  In a fall of torrent hair;
Hiding what thou has created
  In a half-transparent shroud:
Thus, with glory soft-abated,
  Shines the moon through vapoury cloud.
(2008: 182–4)

Anodos's song in MacDonald's *Phantastes* anticipates elements of Morris's 'Pygmalion and the Image', suggesting an osmotic exchange between the writers' works: both create a naked statue–woman through poetic art, whose unbound hair signals sexual availability, and the artist in each text responds to his creation with intense desire expressed in the 'ever-burning, unconsuming fire' of Morris's Pygmalion (Morris 1888: 595), and by the young Anodos who finds himself 'smitten' and 'overfond' (MacDonald 2008: 184) as he summons his Galatea into being. As Pionke argues, this song 'achieves a sexually supercharged enargeia as it minutely describes every feature [of] her body from her "Arches white on rosy heel" up through the "half-transparent shroud" of her unbound hair' (2011: 32), a sexual charge that, I would add, is already present at the beginning of Anodos's song, which speaks of 'the life-spring, throbbing, panting' (MacDonald 2008: 182) that pulses from the firmly planted arches of her beautiful feet.[33]

While the poem suggests that Anodos's song brings into life a breathing, living image, Anodos's narrative appears less certain:

Ever as I sang, the veil was uplifted; ever as I sang, the signs of life grew ... But I cannot tell whether she looked more of a statue or more of woman; she seemed removed into that region of phantasy where all is intensely vivid, but nothing clearly defined. At last, as I sang of her descending hair, the glow of soul faded away, like a dying sunset. A lamp within had been extinguished, and the house of life shone blank in a winter morn. She was a statue once more – but visible, and that much was gained. (2008: 185)

Yet, it is worth noting that it is only when she has once again become a statue that Anodos can no longer control his desire: 'I sprang to her . . . flung my arms around her, as if I would tear her from the grasp of a visible Death, and lifted her from her pedestal down to my heart' (2008: 186). While his touch animates her, she does not fall into his arms, but flees instead, crying 'You should not have touched me! . . . you should have sung to me; you should have sung to me!' and once more disappears (2008: 186–7).

For Pionke, such incidents 'confirm ekphrasis as one of the key organising motifs of *Phantastes*' and reveals art as an 'ethical-aesthetic basis for gentlemanly masculinity' (2011: 34). As Pionke puts it, MacDonald's model indicates that 'how a man reacts to art reveals the quality of his manhood . . . if he perceives . . . art with clarity and humility . . . and returns to work without excessive self-consciousness, then he is a true gentleman akin to Carlyle's hero-as-man-of-letters' (2011: 34). Yet, Anodos's encounter with the statue seems far more complex than Pionke's reading would suggest in that it also permits a direct desire for the statue as statue and therefore engages in an illicit love that is then occluded by the living woman's rejection of his touch. What interests me about this experience, however, is the way in which *Phantastes* operates for MacDonald as a form of imaginary museum in which the tensions between the conception, realisation and eroticisation of the artwork are explored.

Sculpture Palaces

The allusive nature of MacDonald's *Phantastes* has been extensively discussed, and his deployment of epigraphs from medieval, Romantic and Shakespearean sources have been noted. The Pygmalion episodes are prefaced by references to Thomas Lovell Beddoes, 'Pygmalion, or The Cyprian Statuary' (1825), Shakespeare's *A Winter's Tale* (1623) and Friedrich Schiller's 'Das Ideal und das Leben' ('Life and the Ideal', written in 1796).[34] However, I would argue that what situates MacDonald's tale in the context of contemporary Victorian culture is the gallery setting. While the encounter with the marble lady in the 'rocky cell' resonates with the medieval legend of Venus and

Tannhäuser,[35] the long galleries peopled with statues in the later chapters are more akin to the crimson-curtained avenues of the Great Exhibition, or the marble halls of the sculpture galleries in the British Museum. It is worth noting that the MacDonald family, including the author himself, were admirers of the Great Exhibition of 1851, and were among the millions of visitors who visited its halls that year. Indeed, Lesley Willis Smith argues that the Koh-i-Noor jewel, presented to Queen Victoria following the British conquest of the Punjab in 1849 and displayed at the Great Exhibition, may have influenced MacDonald's decision to give the name 'Diamond' to the child protagonist of *At the Back of the North Wind* (2015: 14). While Smith makes no specific mention of MacDonald's responses to the sculpture courts at the exhibition, one might conjecture, given the descriptions of the marble halls in *Phantastes*, that these made an equally significant impression on him. The Great Exhibition featured galleries of statues in its Italian, Greek and Turkish courts; casts of famous sculptures in its Cast Courts; and neoclassical offerings by contemporary artists in the Fine Arts Court such as John Gibson's *The Greek Huntsman* and Hiram Powers's *The Greek Slave* (Challis 2008: 178).

As indicated in my introduction, the line between erotic response and aesthetic appreciation is particularly fine when the statue viewed is nude, and Powers was sufficiently conscious of his sculpture's lascivious appeal to provide a narrative context intended to exculpate the statue's nudity and did so long before *The Greek Slave* was displayed at the Great Exhibition. As Joy Kasson observes, 'When Powers sent *The Greek Slave* on a tour of American cities in 1847, he made sure the sculpture was accompanied by texts that would instruct and direct the viewers' gaze' and, by 1848, his agent was able 'to compile a booklet that could be republished for every city where *The Greek Slave* was displayed' (1992: 179). Part of the narrative, which had appeared earlier in Charles Edwards Lester's study of Powers' work, read:

> The Slave has been taken from one of the Greek Islands by the Turks, in the time of the Greek Revolution ... She is now among barbarian strangers, under the pressure of a full recollection of the calamitous events which have brought her to her present state; and she stands exposed to the gaze of the people she abhors, and awaits her fate with intense anxiety, tempered indeed by the support of her reliance upon the goodness of God. Gather all these afflictions together, and add to them the fortitude and resignation of a Christian, and no room will be left for shame. (qtd in Lester 1845: 88)

As Kasson remarks, while Powers may have been at pains to minimise the statue's sensuality, exhibitors seemed 'to recognize at least tacitly the erotic potential of the statue' for during Powers's American tour 'it was sometimes displayed with special viewing times for women and children' (1992: 181). Moreover, Mark Miller notes that representations of Powers's sculpture 'entered pornographic economies' centred on the dual axes of sex and race:

> Popular English illustrations parodied the sculpture by presenting a similarly posed black woman as an object of sexual desire, and a less widely circulated 1840s US daguerreotype evoked amalgamationist fears by surrounding the white statue with three leering dark-skinned men in turbans. (2016: 156)

Commenting on his own experience of nude statuary, Powers explains, 'History and nature both require nudity. The Slave is compelled to stand naked to be judged of in the slave-market; – this is an historical fact' (qtd in Lester 1845: 85). But, despite excusing the slave's nudity on the grounds of historical accuracy, Powers confesses to experiencing a sexual frisson when sculpting the bodies of women, speaking not only for himself, but for his fellow artists:

> And here I will make a remark that will be confirmed by all artists who have worked after naked models. Whatever temptation they have experienced while so engaged, has been while the model was partially draped, either dressing or undressing. And I have heard many say, and I can testify from my own experience, that he who can resist the allurements of a modern *belle*, dressed *à-la-mode*, is steel-proof against all the temptations of naked models, statues, and pictures. (qtd in Lester 1845: 86)

While clearly meant to flatter fashionable women of his acquaintance, and to assure the reader that he experiences desire only as his models undress, the conflation between them and their naked sculptural counterparts is not fully avoided. Here, as in the tales of fictional artists to be found in Morris's 'Pygmalion and the Image', Woolner's *Pygmalion* and MacDonald's *Phantastes*, there is an undoubted slippage between the sculpted figure and the living woman. However, while Powers's desire centres on vision, the artists in the texts I have discussed battle with the urge to touch. In Morris's poem, the artist's tactile congress with the statue as statue is obscured, and the sensual process of animation experienced by Ovid's Pygmalion is replaced by Venus's which sparks the statue into life. Similarly, Woolner's Pygmalion relies on Venus Aphrodite's 'throbbing touch of pulse,/To touch all other pulses as Her own' to bring life to his statue of Hebe (1881: 68). While touch in each case is displaced onto the goddess of love, what separates Morris's and Woolner's Pygmalions from MacDonald's Anodos is the gallery setting in which touch is explicitly prohibited and where that prohibition is transgressed. What all three texts share, however, is the doubling of poetic craft and sculptural production. In all three texts there is a focus on art as well as love, as expressed in the renarration of the myth by Clement of Alexandria where craftsmanship and desire are of equal concern.

In *Phantastes*, the importance of the imagination and sensory desire is experienced by Anodos in the 'rocky cell' in which he first sees the Pygmalion bas-relief and his marble lady. Here, he engages in 'a delicious reverie for some time; during which all lovely forms, and colours, and sounds seemed to use [his] brain as a common hall, where they could come and go, unbidden and unexcused', an 'assembly of forms and spiritual sensations, which yet were far too vague to admit of being translated into any shape common to [his] own and another mind' (MacDonald 2008: 81). Anodos's consciousness becomes a 'hall' or gallery of the senses and by implication the arts. This experience is repeated in the fairy palace, where he finds his soul suffused with song, though no external music can be heard, and where he is conscious of the statues dancing though he initially sees no movement. In one of the halls he sits for hours giving himself up to the pleasures of song and 'to a succession of images of bewildering beauty, which passed before [his] inward eye, in a long and occasionally crowded train', aware that 'only in the marble cave, before [he] found the sleeping statue, had [he] ever had a similar experience' (2008: 174). After this, Anodos returns every morning to the same hall, where sometimes he sits and dreams. At others he acts within himself 'a whole drama' or pursues a 'whole epic of a tale'; sometimes he sings and is astonished at the beauty of his voice or hears 'something like the distant sound of multitudes of dancers . . . moving their rhythmic motion, that within [him] blossomed in verse and song' (2008: 175). The ethereality and internal nature of Anodos's experience is key. The external halls of the fairy palace mirror the creative museum of words and song in his mind. As soon as the membrane between imagination and reality is broken through touch, Anodos's sensual world collapses. While he may sculpt his marble lady with song, and indulge in the sexual reverie his poetry permits, he may not touch: 'Touch Not' is the command written on the lamp that lights the palace halls.

Such an injunction is perhaps related to the fact that, due to its intrinsic connection with the body and purported distance from the '"higher" cognitive functions', touch has been considered 'a sense incapable of affording aesthetic experience' (Zuchert 2009: 285). In her introduction to *The Deepest Sense: A Cultural History of Touch*, Constance Classen reinforces the point that for Victorian scholars, 'touch was typed . . . as a crude uncivilized form of perception' (2012: xii). Yet in deploying the Pygmalion myth, and including the injunction 'Touch Not!', MacDonald draws attention to the significance of touch, particularly erotic touch. As we know from Ovid, Pygmalion lovingly touches his statue long before she comes to life, and the statue's stillness and three-dimensionality invites uninhibited touch. As David Getsy argues, 'people take liberties with sculpture all the time . . . They respond; they want to touch it, to feel it . . . Under the guise of exploration or appreciation, they probe and caress the sculptural body' (2014: 11). It is because of this that in our own museums, as in MacDonald's imaginary gallery, the injunction is: 'Touch Not!' In the scene in which Anodos creates his marble lady, he is mirroring not only Pygmalion but Ovid whose poetry brings Pygmalion's statue to life, anticipating those Victorian Ovids: Morris and Woolner. In addition, he plays with the suggestion posited coterminously by Gautier, and later adopted by the Parnassian poets, that 'the whole secret of sculpture, like that of poetry, is that it expresses thought in material form', but for MacDonald the artist must remain free from fleshly taint (Scott 2006: 141).[36] While the Pygmalion passages in *Phantastes* resonate with the aestheticism and eroticised medievalism and classicism of literary contemporaries such as Rossetti and Swinburne, MacDonald pulls back. His Galatea does not stay to indulge in Anodos's poetic and/or physical caresses. She belongs to another, and exists in an ethereal rather than a material world. While the erotic concept of the Pygmalion myth appeals, the realisation of that concept in Anodos's song raises powerful desires that must be suppressed for the purity of MacDonald's art. In focusing on the artistic imagination and its expression of thought in material form, MacDonald also anticipates two significant engagements with sculpture, desire and the creative imagination that I will discuss in Chapter 2: Arthur O'Shaughnessy's poetic series, 'Thoughts in Marble' which appeared in *Songs of a Worker*, published posthumously in 1881, and Thomas Hardy's *The Well-Beloved* (1897). In these texts, as in MacDonald's, touch proves equally problematic.

Notes

1. Arnobius of Sicca (d. *c*.330) was a Christian apologist during the reign of the Roman emperor, Diocletian (284–305); Clement of Alexandria (Titus Flavius Clemen, *c*.150–*c*.215) was a Christian convert who was influenced by Greek philosophers such as Plato and the Stoics.
2. Philostephanus of Cyrene's (third century BCE) geographical works included fables and myths associated with the Greek world. Most of his writing is now lost.
3. The first Act was passed to police epidemics of venereal diseases in the armed forces. Women suspected of prostitution in garrison towns and ports could be arrested, examined and, if found to be infected, placed in lock hospitals until they reached the end of their sentence or were seemingly cured; the 1866 Act enabled police to incarcerate women in such towns for up to three months, and extended police powers over civilian populations. The 1869 Act permitted the incarceration period to be extended to one year. 1869 saw the formation of the National Association for the Repeal of the Contagious Diseases Act and the Ladies National Association for the Repeal of the Contagious Diseases Act led by Josephine Butler. The Acts were finally repealed in 1886.
4. Sacred marriage, also known as sacred prostitution, is generally understood to mean marriage between two divinities, between a divinity and a mortal, or between two mortals, one of whom is temporarily invested with divinity, and was common in the Near East, notably in Babylonia and Syria. Hersey explains that in Paphos, in Cyprus, 'the sacred-marriage system applied to the town's entire population of young unmarried females, rich and poor. The women were forced to sit on the benches in the temple gardens, offering themselves to the first comers' (2009: 79). Due to the notoriety of such practices, the words 'Paphian' and 'Cyprian', 'became euphemisms for prostitute – and not the sacred kind – in many languages' (2009: 79, n. 23).
5. For an interesting discussion of the inherent problems in creating a full-size statue from ivory, see Salzman-Mitchell (2008).
6. Kennedy notes that in 'Pygmalion', Ovid expresses 'one of his favourite ideas, the power of art to equal or indeed outdo nature' (2008: 434, n. 252). As I will show, this focus on the rivalry between craft and nature remains implicit in nineteenth-century manifestations of the myth.
7. The word 'agalmatophilia' is composed of the word 'agalma' meaning 'statue', and 'philia' meaning 'love' and relates to those who are sexually attracted not only to statues, but also to dolls or other such inanimate figures.
8. Tarnowsky refers to the story of Clysophus who, enamoured of a marble statue but thwarted by its marble hardness, pressed a piece of meat against the statue's genitalia in order to fulfil his desire. He also alludes to another Greek who fell in love with a statue of Cupid in the temple of Delphi and committed a pederastic act on it. More contemporary

examples include a case, reported in the French papers of 1877, of a gardener who fell in love with a representation of the *Venus de Milo* in a park, and the case of a young man living in St Petersburg who desired the statue of a nymph he had seen at a country house (Tarnowsky 1898: 85).

9. More recently, the term 'objectum sexuality' or 'objectophiles' has been used to classify people who experience a romantic attachment to objects, encompassing statues, cars, buildings and so on. For a useful article on this topic, see Marsh 2010.
10. Itinerant, Italian figure makers began to come to England in large numbers following the fall of Napoleon; see 'Italian figure makers in the 19th century'. Available at <https://www.npg.org.uk/research/programmes/plaster-figure-makers-history#italian> (last accessed 28 September 2018).
11. The discovery of the *Venus de Milo* in 1820 and its subsequent display in Paris in 1821 may have also reignited popular interest in the Pygmalion myth.
12. *Julie, ou La Nouvelle Héloïse* written in epistolary form, charts the tension between feeling, authenticity and morality; its popularity led to seventy editions between 1761 and 1800. *Confessions* is Rousseau's autobiography; it centred on a life experienced through feeling and includes instances of humiliation and punishment.
13. Patrick George Patmore (d.1855) was a periodical writer in the 1820s and, later, Coventry Patmore's father.
14. It has been suggested that the Pre-Raphaelite Brotherhood's penchant for working-class women – Jane Morris among them – who could be transformed into idealised forms in art and educated beyond their social origins may have informed Shaw's *Pygmalion*. Certainly, Jane Morris appears to have been the inspiration for Vernon Lee's *Miss Brown* (1884), a satirical *roman-à-clef*, in which the Pre-Raphaelite 'stunner', Anne Brown, is elevated by her guardian and eventual husband, the poet Walter Hamlin. For a discussion of the relationship between Hazlitt's and Lee's version of Pygmalion, see Pulham (2012).
15. Following a quarrel and separation, H- sends S.L. three novels of sensibility: Oliver Goldsmith's *The Vicar of Wakefield* (1766), Henry Mackenzie's *The Man of Feeling* (1771) and Elizabeth Inchbald's *Nature and Art* (1796).
16. Hazlitt, along with other 'radicals and reformists' idolised Napoleon and saw him as a 'secular spirit of liberty', a challenge to the stagnation of European '*anciens regimes*' (Moores 2018: 263).
17. Lecture delivered by Morris to the Trades' Guild of Learning.
18. William Morris's 'Pygmalion and the Image' appeared in *The Earthly Paradise* which was originally published in three volumes between 1868 and 1870. Volume 1 consists of two parts; therefore, the full collection consists of four parts in total.

19. In *Jane Morris: The Burden of History*, Wendy Parkins argues that whether or not the affair was consummated is open to interpretation, and argues that, while Rossetti's love for Jane was indisputable, her own feelings remain unconfirmed (2013: 23). Jane Morris was the model for numerous paintings by Dante Gabriel Rossetti, most famously perhaps for *Proserpine* (1874) and *The Day Dream* (1880). She also modelled for Morris's *La Belle Iseult* (1858). The painting is sometimes referred to as *Queen Guinevere*.
20. Étienne Bonnot de Condillac (1714–80) was a French philosopher and psychologist who, in his treatise, imagines a statue animated by a soul that has never encountered any ideas or any experience of the senses. Chapters in *Traité des sensations* include: 'Of the Ideas of a Man limited to the Sense of Smell', 'Of a Man limited to the Sense of Hearing', 'Of Smell and Hearing combined', 'Of Taste by itself, and of Taste combined with Smell and Hearing' and 'Of a Man limited to the Sense of Sight'.
21. Woolner's twelve maids resonate with those in Penelope's household in Homer's *The Odyssey* (c. eighth century BCE). Like Penelope's maids, Woolner's function as a form of chorus, though, unlike hers, they are not disloyal, nor do they suffer a violent end.
22. Thomas Woolner was admitted to the Royal Academy as a student on 16 December 1842; became an Associate Member of the Royal Academy in 1871; a Royal Academician in 1874; and was Professor of Sculpture there from 1877 to 1878.
23. In the *Homeric Hymn to Apollo*, for example, Aphrodite dances with the Charites, the Horae, Harmonia and Hebe (Breitenberger 2007: 125).
24. In ignoring the live model in favour of his art, Woolner's Pygmalion appears to be in the tradition of the artists in Poe's 'The Oval Portrait' (1842) and Christina Rossetti's 'In an Artist's Studio' (composed 1856, published posthumously in 1896) who paint at the expense of their model's well-being. Poe's model dies, while Rossetti's fades away.
25. See Yeates for a detailed discussion of Zambaco's significance in the context of Burne-Jones's *Pygmalion* series. Yeates notes that 'Richard Jenkyns sees Galatea as a personal, erotic expression of Burne-Jones's feelings for Zambaco. Galatea, for Jenkyns, is a "smoothed" Maria. Similarly, Stephen Kern claims that Burne-Jones "projected his frustration [at the affair] into this [the Pygmalion] myth"' (2018: 110). In this, one might argue, he resembles Hazlitt who appears to use the myth, at least in part, for similar purposes. See Richard Jenkyns (1996) and Stephen Kern (1996).
26. George MacDonald (1824–1905), a Scottish poet, author and ordained minister whom Roderick McGillis described as 'one of the great Victorians', produced between 1851 and 1897 over fifty works including novels, plays, essays, sermons, poems and fairy tales. In 1872 he engaged in a successful tour of the United States where he addressed

his lectures to packed houses. In the early twentieth century, his worth was acknowledged by W. H. Auden who named MacDonald 'one of the most remarkable writers of the nineteenth century', as well as by C. S. Lewis who regarded him as his 'master', and the influence of his fairy tales on the world of Tolkien's *Lord of the Rings* has been widely recognised. Nevertheless, following his death in 1905, MacDonald's work rapidly fell out of print and favour. See Frederick Buechner's foreword to Hein (1993: xvii); Page (2008: 27); and Gaarden (2005: 20).

27. Morris wrote seven early prose romances, all of which were set in a medieval context, and many of which involved dream narratives. MacDonald's biographer, William Raeper, notes that *Phantastes* 'derives its name from Phineas Fletcher's poetic allegory *The Purple Island* of 1633' in which 'Phantastes or Fancie is one of the three counsellors of the mind' (1987: 144).
28. See for example, 'Fra Lippo Lippi' in Vol. 1 and 'Andrea del Sarto' in Vol. 2 (Browning 1855).
29. For a discussion of the importance of 'trouthe' and 'gentilesse' in medieval contexts, see Amtower and Vanhoutte (2009).
30. See Wolff (1961) (Freudian reading); Reis (1962) (Jungian reading); Gray (1996) (Kristevan reading).
31. See McGillis (2008), Gray (2011), and MacLachlan et al. (2013).
32. The 'Advertisement' to the first edition of *King of the Golden River* refers to the book as a 'Fairy Tale', one that, like MacDonald's, illustrates the triumph of love, kindness and goodness over evil (Ruskin 1851). However, like MacDonald's text, it is also complex and might be characterised variously as a fable, a constructed origin myth and a parable.
33. The focus on the foot's arch anticipates Freud's discussion in 'Delusion and Dream in Jensen's *Gradiva*' (first published in 1907 as 'Der Wahn und die Träume in W. Jensen's *Gradiva*' and later as 'Delusions and Dreams in Jensen's *Gradiva*' (1955)), a psychoanalytical reading of the novel which features a conflation between a sculpted and living woman.
34. See Docherty (1990) and Prickett (1990).
35. According to this legend, the knight and poet, Tannhäuser, finds the Venusberg (the underground home of the goddess Venus), and becomes so enamoured that he spends a year with her and worships her. Once he leaves the Venusberg, he travels to Rome to seek absolution for his sins.
36. My translation; original text: 'pour Gautier, tout le secret de la sculpture, comme celui de la Poésie, ramène à exprimer par suggestion la pensée immanente à la forme matérielle'.

Chapter 2

Artworks in Marble: Capturing Venus in Durable Form

In an unpublished poem entitled 'Pagan', dated 5 November 1867, Arthur O'Shaughnessy (1844–81) designs palaces dedicated to the senses that resonate with the marble halls and galleries in MacDonald's *Phantastes*.[1] His speaker imagines himself a pagan king, who will for each sense 'build up a palace ... Chamber on chamber immense and vast', and explains how he proposes to inhabit these cavernous spaces:

> I shall enter a new one every day
> As the conscious soul without halting or haste
> Moves onward & lights to a [potent] display
> All the being possesses & holds all fast
> Till I blaze from each window in full array
> Till all fill the whole palace with [one at] last.
> (O'Shaughnessy n.d.a: 100)

The poem includes an apostrophe to the arts that suggests frustrated creativity and a yearning for freedom from daily cares:

> Oh painting! oh sculpture, oh melody
> What are ye? strange mystical deities
> Having keys of whole worlds that belong to me
> Where my sense inborn in a slumber lies
> How shall I woo ye to set me free
> Of all [rid]
> I would be all things I was born to be
> Fill all my worlds see all my [skies].
> (O'Shaughnessy n.d.a: 95)

The poem might be read as a poignant displacement of the conflicts inherent in O'Shaughnessy's working life; while he aspired to poetic glory, by day he worked as an entomologist and herpetologist in the Zoological department of the British Museum writing poetry in his spare time. As Jordan Kistler has shown, the 'apparent incongruity of zoology and poetry' seems to be one of the main tensions at the heart of O'Shaughnessy's life and she notes that biographical accounts almost always discuss 'the absurdity of a poet working as a zoologist', identified as a 'distinctly unpoetic career' (2016: 9).[2] While his first volume of poetry, *An Epic of Women* (1870), brought him recognition and admittance into elevated literary and artistic circles that included Ford Madox Brown, the Rossettis, William Morris and Algernon Charles Swinburne, neither this, nor his subsequent volumes, *Lays of France* (1872) and *Music and Moonlight* (1874), were sufficiently successful to bring O'Shaughnessy the financial independence he craved.[3] While often referred to as a 'Pre-Raphaelite poet', Kistler points out that O'Shaughnessy rather 'fell into the category of the "young men" of the movement, a generation behind its founders' (2016: 9). However, as she observes, the epithet is not entirely incorrect given that O'Shaughnessy's volumes appeared in 1870 alongside Rossetti's *Poems* and in the wake of Swinburne's *Poems and Ballads, First Series* published in 1866. Today, like many other minor poets of the late nineteenth century, his primary value seems to lie in his peripheral relationship to more important figures such as Rossetti, Swinburne and Morris. Furthermore, O'Shaughnessy's reputation has suffered because, from the start, his poetry has been considered derivative; for example, in 'The Fleshly School of Poetry' (1871), Robert Buchanan (writing under the pseudonym 'Thomas Maitland') labels him 'a second-hand Mr. Swinburne' (1871: 346–7). However, writing in the *Academy* after O'Shaughnessy's death, Edmund Gosse argues that 'By virtue of his best work, O'Shaughnessy must always hold an honourable place in the roll of Victorian poets'; finds his 'exquisite' poetry 'full of odour and melody'; and claims that it was 'essentially unlike the work of anyone else' (qtd in Chandler Moulton 1894: 13–14). The truth lies somewhere in between: certainly, O'Shaughnessy's poetry is at times 'exquisite' and 'full of odour and melody', but it is difficult to say categorically that it is 'essentially unlike the work of anyone else'. *An Epic of Women* contains 'Creation', a poem that an early biographer, Louise Chandler Moulton, describes as an 'audacious, mystical, sensuous, Swinburnian poem', while 'A Troth for Eternity' invokes 'memories of Rossetti, and also of Browning, without containing anything that could distinctly be traced to either' (1894: 13–15). Similarly, O'Shaughnessy's 'Thoughts in Marble', an incomplete sequence of twelve poems he defines as 'Poems of Form' in his final volume, *Songs of a Worker*, published posthumously in 1881, shares inspiration not only with the poetry of those 'English Parnassians', Swinburne and Rossetti, but also with that of the French Parnassian poets.[4] Indeed, Gosse credits O'Shaughnessy with being 'the first to bring us back authentic news of the Parnassians', gained during the poet's visits to France where 'he was presented to Victor Hugo and to Leconte de Lisle' and heard stories of Baudelaire from the lips of Catulle Mendès (Gosse 1925: 177).[5] Kistler contends that, during his lifetime, O'Shaughnessy was seen as being far more influenced by 'French aesthetic theory than the practices of his English contemporaries' and in her analysis of *Songs of a Worker* shows how he attempted to negotiate between the ethical art proposed by Ruskin and Victor Hugo and the seductive tenet 'Art for art's sake' propagated by Gautier and embraced by Baudelaire (Kistler 2012: 73). This negotiation is evident in the preface to *Songs of a Worker* where the poet's cousin, the Rev. Alfred Newport Deacon, quotes from a letter written by O'Shaughnessy shortly before his death in which he seems anxious to instruct his readers on how the ensuing poems should be interpreted. According to Deacon, O'Shaughnessy states:

> I wish to provide against the series of poems which I have associated with the art of sculpture being judged from an erroneous point of view . . . I have kept strictly within the lines assigned to the sculptor's art, an art in which I have as yet failed to perceive either morality or immorality. They are therefore essentially thoughts in marble, or poems of form, and it would therefore be unjustifiable to look in them for a sense which is not inherent in the purest Parian. I have been represented as saying with Baudelaire, 'Art for Art,' and laying myself open to all the unfavourable limitations which that dictum is unjustly supposed to imply. Truly, I think that a little 'Art for Art' has already done a great deal of good in England . . . but with Victor Hugo I do not say 'Art for Art,' but 'Art for humanity' and my meaning is that Art is good – is an incalculable gain to man; but art, in itself equally perfect, which grows with humanity and can assist humanity in growing – is still better. (qtd in Deacon 1881: viii)

O'Shaughnessy manages the space between Ruskin and Baudelaire by focusing on poetic labour, showing 'a commitment to the formal craft of poetry, a commitment that would transform over the course of his career into his theory of poetic *work*, enacted through the metaphor of stone work, or sculpture' (Kistler 2016: 87; original emphasis). In 'Song of a Fellow-Worker', the first poem in O'Shaughnessy's collection, the sculptor is equated with the poet. Meeting a sculptor, the speaker-poet tells us that his toil is 'fashioning thought and sound' (1881: 3, l. 2) while the sculptor's is to hew stone, that he carves 'the marble of pure thought, until the thought takes form' (1881: 4, ll. 9–15). Here, physical and intellectual labour are equated, correlating with O'Shaughnessy's view, expressed in the first stanza of the well-known 'Ode' from his earlier volume of poetry, *Music and Moonlight*, that artists are 'to be a part of the world', they must '*do* their part, to serve some purpose' (Kistler 2012: 83; original emphasis):

> We are the music makers,
> And we are the dreamers of dreams,
> Wandering by lone sea-breakers,
> And sitting by desolate streams;—
> World-losers and world-forsakers,
> On whom the pale moon gleams:
> Yet we are the movers and shakers
> Of the world for ever, it seems.
> (O'Shaughnessy 1874: 1, ll. 1–8)

In 'Ode', artists are no longer 'World-losers and world-forsakers' but 'movers and shakers'. Similarly, in 'Song of a Fellow-Worker' O'Shaughnessy synthesises his 'seemingly conflicting aesthetic theories' by 'redefining art as work' (Kistler 2012: 83). For Kistler, the 'unifying symbol of *Songs of a Worker* is stone, and she argues that O'Shaughnessy 'couches his artistic theory' in sculpture, 'the most physical of the visual arts'; 'Like a sculptor carves stone, he carves thought, both craft something new', and in 'Song of a Fellow-Worker' the poet and the stonemason become equals (2012: 85). Yet, the 'return to form' in *Songs of a Worker* is also 'a return to a celebration of poetry *as* poetry, rather than a mere method of delivering a moral' (2016: 89; original emphasis).

Crafting Thoughts in Marble

In *Songs of a Worker* more generally, and especially in the 'Thoughts in Marble' sequence, O'Shaughnessy asks readers to consider his poetry from a Parnassian perspective. Privileging craftsmanship, beauty and permanence, and subscribing to Gautier's influential precept, the Parnassian ideal often manifested itself in content which centred on 'hard' materials such as marble and gemstones, frequently used in the creation of art objects and applied to traditional prosodic forms. In her 2008 study, *Persons and Things*, Barbara Johnson notes that 'this "cult of form" or "art for art's sake" is often represented in Parnassian poetry as love for a statue' (2008: 19). This is evident in such poems as Théodore de Banville's 'Á Venus de Milo' (1842), Leconte de Lisle's 'Vénus de Milo' (1846), and Baudelaire's 'La Beauté' (1857).[6] In Gautier's poem, 'L'art' (1857), the creation of statuary is equated with the poet's art: 'Verse, marble, onyx, and enamel' are the 'rebellious' forms from which the work of art emerges, and he orders the artist to sculpt not in clay, but to 'Fight the carrara' and 'Parian marble' to seal his 'floating dream' forever in the 'resistant block' (qtd in Johnson 2008: 118).[7] For Gautier, 'the whole secret of sculpture, like that of poetry, is that it expresses thought in material form' (Scott 2006: 141). In suggesting that language or verse in some way resembles marble, a substance that one must work at as the sculptor does stone,

> Gautier posits a theoretical principle that led certain French poets ... to understand the importance of the malleable nature of language and verse, according it a plastic quality that, in poetry, manifests itself in the form of prosodic structures – meter, rhyme stanza – which inspire the poet, in addition to the themes and concepts explored. (Scott 2006: 146; my translation)[8]

The ideas posited in 'L'art' exerted 'a continuing influence on the poets of the French Parnassian movement' until the 1870s (Denommé 1972: 52). Gautier's impact is especially discernible in the work of those poets labelled the 'English Parnassians' such as Swinburne, Morris and Rossetti, as well as in that of Arthur O'Shaughnessy. For example, the correlation of poetry, form and sculpture informs Swinburne's 'Hermaphroditus' (1866) inspired by the *Sleeping Hermaphrodite* in the Louvre; it is evident in Rossetti's 'A Sonnet is a Moment's Monument' in which the sonnet can be carved in 'ivory or in ebony/As Day or Night may rule' (1881: 161); and in Morris's 'Pygmalion and the Image' the craft involved in the creation of sculpture and poetry coalesce.[9] Yet it is in O'Shaughnessy's *Songs of a Worker*, and his sequence, 'Thoughts in Marble', that we see a more sustained engagement with Gautier and the Parnassians. Nevertheless, it is also important to note that, as Deacon observes, 'Thoughts in Marble' is a series of poems inspired by physical statues, by O'Shaughnessy's 'study of the masterpieces of ancient sculpture – which he had taken up recently with great zest' (1881: vii).

As Johnson has shown, the study of classical statuary and the writing of Parnassian poetry are not mutually exclusive; indeed, the former appears to have informed the latter as is clear in the poems by Leconte de Lisle and Banville, mentioned above, that feature the *Venus de Milo*. Johnson begins her chapter on Parnassian poetry in *Persons and Things* by referring to two of the key archaeological acquisitions of the nineteenth century: the Elgin Marbles purportedly purchased for the nation in 1816 and first displayed in the British Museum in 1817, and the *Venus de Milo* discovered on the Greek island of Melos in 1820, presented to Louis XVIII and housed in the Louvre since 1821.[10] For Johnson, these two significant cultural touchstones, and the stories that accompany their removal from Greece in the wake of conflicts with the Ottoman Empire, mark a difference in the reception of classical sculpture in England and France; she writes:

> These two stories, perhaps, explain why the fate of Greek sculpture was so different in France and in England, which were, after all, at war with each other when the artifacts were 'found'. In England when Keats writes about Greek artifacts they always tell a story, possess a kind of group immortality, speak of a whole culture. In France, the figure of the female beloved was easy to see in the single stone individual. (2008: 111)

For Johnson, Leconte de Lisle's address to the *Venus de Milo* is representative of a move away from the Romantic aesthetic that privileged feeling, to a Parnassian style that privileged form; the 'Venus de Milo's stony unresponsiveness' permitting 'the unrestrained development . . . of the poet's addresses to an isolated female figure, while the frenzy of his passion turned into poetry rather than to masochism' (2008: 111).

Songs of the Museum

Clearly in dialogue with his French counterparts, O'Shaughnessy nevertheless complicates Johnson's schema, not least because the poems in the 'Thoughts in Marble' sequence that intermingle 'the ethereal (thought) with the substantive (marble)' (Kistler 2016: 104), were inspired by O'Shaughnessy's study of ancient statuary, sculpture that would have included the Elgin Marbles as well as individual statues of Venus. Although Deacon's comment suggests that O'Shaughnessy's concern for antique sculpture was a recent development, 'which he had taken up recently with great zest' (1881: vii), the poet's archive held at Queen's University Belfast indicates that his interest in antique art and archaeological artifacts was of longer standing. His 'Notes on Books' include a newspaper cutting of an advertisement for a four-volume collection of engravings: '86 GALÉRIE (La) DE FLORENCE ET LE PALAIS PITTI. Tableaux, Statues, Bas-reliefs, et Camées, dessinés d'apres Wicar et graves sous la Direction de C. L. Masquelier, avec des Explications par Mongez. 4 vols. Folio, 12l, 12s' and for 'Les collectionneurs de l'ancienne Rome. Notes d'un amateur. Aug. ... Paris 1867' (O'Shaughnessy n.d.b).[11] Moreover, during his time at the British Museum, from 1861 to 1881, he would have been privy to the repositioning and display of antique sculptures including the Parthenon Marbles and the Townley Collection. Working in the museum in the 1860s and 1870s, he would have witnessed the sharp rise of artistic interest in its antiquities. As Ian Jenkins observes:

> During the 1860s a new generation of painters turned to the Parthenon sculptures with fresh admiration for Pheidias and the art of Periklean Athens ... broken or not, whether in original or in cast, the Elgin Marbles exerted a new influence over the classical painters that would last until the great upheaval of the First World War. This new interest in classical art was accompanied by a dramatic rise in the number of students drawing in the sculpture galleries of the museum. In 1870 the annual visits stood at 2,981. As the new decade dawned, so the numbers began to rise ... until in 1879 the increase peaked at an almost incredible 15,626. (1992: 38–9)

As an employee of the British Museum and a poet who frequented artistic circles, it is unlikely that O'Shaughnessy would have been ignorant of this heightened cultural awareness of classical sculpture. In addition, although he worked in the natural history section of the museum, it is worth noting that, during O'Shaughnessy's time there, zoological and archaeological objects often shared the same space. As Jenkins notes, for most of the nineteenth century 'the two were exhibited within the same building' and the 'officers of the respective departments will have had daily contact' (1992: 70–1). Located in the same building, O'Shaughnessy would have experienced the major changes to the Elgin Rooms that took place in the late 1860s and early 1870s that resulted in the rearrangement of the Parthenon frieze and the reinstallation of the pedimental sculptures (Jenkins 1992: 98–9). Similarly, O'Shaughnessy is unlikely to have been oblivious to the Graeco-Roman statues – including the Townley Marbles – displayed in the museum's sculpture galleries whose organisation remained relatively unchanged between the 1850s and the 1930s. Here, 'the

Figure 2.1   Aphrodite, known as the *Venus de Milo*, c.130–100 BCE, marble (Musée du Louvre, Paris). Photo © Luisa Ricciarini / Bridgeman Images

sculptures were arranged by subject', the Greek and Roman deities collected together in one room (Jenkins 1992: 136). Furthermore, given the Parnassians' interest in the *Venus de Milo* (Figure 2.1) and being a frequent visitor to Paris, O'Shaughnessy would no doubt have encountered similar galleries in the Louvre where photographs from the *salles des antiquités*

> dating from as late as the 1870s indeed confirm that the *Venus de Milo* presided over a section of long gallery lined with other divinities – Venuses in the main – rather than a place populated by a heterogeneous assembly of fourth-century Greek works. (Arscott and Scott 2000: 7)

A number of the poems in the 'Thoughts in Marble' series suggest a consciousness of such statues not only as art objects, but as archaeological artefacts carved from the geological rocks of the regions from which they emerged: 'Pentelicos' recalls the pentelic marble from which the Parthenon was constructed; 'Paros' names the Greek Island whose Parian marble gave birth to the *Cnidian* and *Medici Venuses*, as well as to some of the sculptures in the Townley Collection; and 'Carrara' alludes to the Tuscan city from whose marble myriad statues have been carved. Used widely in ancient Rome, the latter is notably not only the marble from which Michelangelo's *Pietà* (c.1498–9) and *David* (c. 1501–4) were chiselled but also the material from which the Townley *Discobolus* was created.[12]

The Line of Beauty

Yet, most of the poems in O'Shaughnessy's 'Thoughts in Marble' series focus on the female form. 'The Line of Beauty', the work that precedes the poems 'Pentelicos', 'Paros' and 'Carrara' mentioned above, draws on Hogarth's chapter 'Of Lines' in his 1753 treatise, *The Analysis of Beauty*. Here, Hogarth claims that the curved, 'waving' or 'serpentine' line 'composed of two curves contrasted' is 'the line of beauty' (1772: 38). While focusing on form, such curves necessarily suggest the serpentine lines of the female body and it is therefore perhaps fitting that 'Pentelicos' and 'Paros' should focus on womanly figures. In the sonnet, 'Pentelicos', the speaker, hurt by 'Love's last deceits', attempts to avoid those 'snakelike' paths in which they 'lurk and gleam', yet finds himself inevitably drawn to an impossible desire that takes him by surprise:

> When, sometimes, mid these semblances of love,
>   Pursued with feverish joy or mad despair,
>   There flashes suddenly on my unrest
> Some marble shape of Venus, high above
>   All pain or changing, fair above all fair,
>   Still more and more desired, still unpossest.
> (O'Shaughnessy 1881: 107. ll. 9–14)

While 'Pentelicos' does not make it clear whether this unconsummated desire is fleshly or artistic, in the sonnet 'Paros' the speaker is a sculptor who, looking at a living model, takes clay with an 'eager passionate hand/Inspired by love—to mould the yielding curves/ Of all her shape consummate that deserves/Immortal in the sight of heaven, to stand' before carving her form in 'grand/Imperishable marble'; once he has done so, he observes:

>   Henceforth-seeing
>   The glory of her nakedness divine—
>   My heart is raised, I bend the knee and deem her
>   Not simply woman and not merely mine,
>   But goddess, as the future age shall deem her,
> Ideal love of man's eternal being.
> (1881: 108, ll. 9–14)

In 'Paros', O'Shaughnessy reverses the Pygmalion myth. Invoking the *Cnidian Venus,* by naming the poem after the marble from which she was carved, he simultaneously alludes to the ancient Lucianic tale of a young man's desire and sexual violation of the statue, told in *Amores* (fourth century BCE), as well as to the Pygmalion story as told by Philostephanus where the sculptor fashions a statue of Aphrodite.[13] In O'Shaughnessy's poem, however, the statue does not come to life; instead the living woman becomes a statue. Carving the 'grand/imperishable marble' with an 'eager passionate hand/Inspired by love', he captures his lover's 'yielding curves', and makes them 'immortal', forever contained by the rigidity of sculptural and poetic form. According to Kistler, this reverse pygmalionism applies to all three of the poems in the stone sequence within 'Thoughts in Marble'; the classic story of Pygmalion is inverted and art is privileged 'above all else, even human love' (2016: 106). She argues that in 'rejecting Pygmalion's wish for statue to become flesh' the poems may also reject 'accusations of immorality in art, suggesting that it is people, not art, who are immoral and false' (2016: 106). Kistler therefore reads 'Pentelicos' as a simultaneous rejection of 'the faithlessness of a mortal woman' and an acknowledgement of his desire for 'the pure type of beauty, represented by a statue of Venus' (2016: 106). Similarly, she contends that in 'Paros' O'Shaughnessy is interested in 'the actual act of creation', 'the *physicality* of that creation' and argues that 'unlike Pygmalion, the sculptor doesn't wish for the stone to actually yield to his desiring touch' (Kistler 2016: 106; original emphasis). He 'is shaping not his perfect woman, but the perfect art object'; here, Ovid's 'mythic transformation is reversed ... as the sculptor turns flesh into stone, preserving and improving upon the human form in marble' (2016: 106). Kistler makes a similar case for 'Carrara', arguing that, here, O'Shaughnessy 'denies the connection between form and sexual desire, focusing instead on the reverse pygmalionism which rejects flesh in favour of "pure" art' (2016: 107). However, 'Carrara', I suggest, is a complex poem that eschews simple interpretation; here the marble from which forms are made 'speaks' for itself and it does indeed state 'I am the body purified by fire; A man shall look on me without desire', the line on which Kistler bases her reading. Yet, the body purified by fire also suggests both the martyr burned at the stake for their faith, and the recrystallising process by which marble is formed from limestone softened by heat and pressure. It is a poem that conflates the pagan with the Christian, and both with the sculptural process, and contains images of violence and pain that point to something beyond the mere refusal of desire:

> I am the body purified by fire;
>   A man shall look on me without desire,
> But rather think what miracles of faith
> Made me to trample without fear or scathe
> The burning shares; the thick-set bristling paths
> Of martyrdom; to lie on painful laths
> Under the torturer's malice; to be torn
> And racked and broken, all-victorious scorn
> Strengthening the inward spirit to reject
> The frame of flesh, with sins and lusts infect,
> Whose punishment, like to the sin, was gross,
> And man the executioner.
> (O'Shaughnessy 1881: 109, ll. 1–12)

At first it is unclear whether the speaker is male, female or sexless, and the references to 'miracles of faith', and 'martyrdom' suggest a religious context that recalls one of the most famous statues composed of Carrara marble: Michelangelo's *La Pietà*. References to 'the torturer's malice', to being 'torn/And racked and broken' may also easily be read either as images of Christ's Passion or the embodied stone's own experience of the creation process. The lines that follow: 'I arose/Changed from those beds of pain, and shriven at last/From the whole shameful history of the past' may apply equally to Christ's resurrection and to the sculpted figure risen from the layered history of Carrara's marble strata. However, the second half of the poem makes it clear that the speaker is female:

> So I was led, a priestess or a saint,
> Robed solemnly, leaving the latest taint
> Of earthliness in some far desert cell
> Ascetic; and the hand late used to tell
> Rough rosaries, the hand for ever chilled
> With fingering the death-symbol, feels unthrilled
> With any passionate luxury forbidden
> The world's new wedlock.
> . . .
>   I am the bride
> Who clings with terror, suppliant and pale,
> And fears the lifting of her virgin veil,
> Because the shrinking form, spite of her prayers,
> Has grown to know its earthliness, and bears
> The names of sins that gave up shameful ghosts
> On antique crosses. Raised now amid the hosts
> Of living men, my effigy is grown—
> Passionless, speechless through postured stone

That holds one changeless meaning in its pose;
The murmuring myriads pass, and each man knows
And sees me with a cold thought at his heart;
For I am that from which the soul must part.
(1881: 110–11, ll. 19–44)

Being simultaneously 'priestess', 'saint', 'virgin', 'effigy' and 'postured stone', the marble figure conflates the pagan with the Christian perhaps because those effigies and 'postured' statues we find in churches and galleries are often made of the same substance – the material remains the same, though the image and purpose may change. 'Robed solemnly' the figure may be a statue of Venus Aphrodite made ready for hierogamy, or the effigy of a Madonna, adorned in garments for a Catholic Holy Week procession. What is clear in either case is that the statue represents death: 'For I am that from which the soul must part'. In 'Carrara', the marble itself makes a transition from pagan idol to religious icon, and stands as a reminder to man of death and the afterlife. As in 'Paros', the focus is on the transition from flesh and movement to marble rigidity, a transition that also reflects the ways in which the senses – sight and touch – are stimulated and then controlled by the form of each poem: 'Paros' by the use of the sonnet form; 'Cararra' by a strong deployment of rhyming couplets, both of which also work to contain desire in 'Paros' and violence in 'Carrara'.

According to Kistler, the poet's focus in 'Carrara' is 'on the act of production; the craft that has gone into the statue denies any potential prurience in the viewer' and, here, the 'mediating presence of art purifies' (2016: 108). She deems the 'Thoughts in Marble' sequence a response to the charges of 'fleshliness' laid against O'Shaughnessy, an attempt to 'set Beauty free' from shame (2016: 108). In 'Carrara', she argues, he 'attacks the hypocritical culture that takes a prurient view of artistic expression'; in his statue, 'any sin or pain that wracked the body of the actual person has been burned away by the act of creation and the art form is left pure and unburdened' (2016: 109). Yet, as Kistler acknowledges, these poems 'are no less sensuous or physical than his earlier works, despite the claims he makes in his Preface' (2016: 107) and, as Louise Chandler Moulton remarks, in the group of poems

> called by a singular misnomer Thoughts in Marble, we certainly find little of the cold chastity of sculpture. The poems are, indeed, oversensuous – going beyond even the not too rigid boundaries the author set for himself in An Epic of Women [sic]. (1894: 41)

Chandler's concerns clearly informed her choices because none of the poems from the 'Thoughts in Marble' sequence is included in her selections from O'Shaughnessy's volumes of poetry. In my view, it is telling that five of the poems in the 'Thoughts in Marble' sequence focus explicitly on Venus. If form and craft alone were O'Shaughnessy's primary concerns, why does the goddess of love, and mortal interactions with her, feature so prominently in this series of poems?

In focusing on this figure, O'Shaughnessy may have been simply following in the footsteps of Parnassian poets. As Caroline Arscott and Katie Scott have observed, in 'Vénus de Milo' Leconte de Lisle 'pitilessly divides the goddess from the impassioned literary myths of her birth, her loves, her companions in beauty', and in her Parnassian incarnation 'the divinity beneath these unworthy narrative excrescences stands alone and partakes rather of the colourless inertia of stone' (2000: 11). However, as Arscott and Scott point out in their study of Venuses in art and culture, it is necessarily difficult to disentangle Venus from her reputation and she often functions as a cover for unruly desires:

> The idea of Venus offered an alibi for sexual abandon. The seduction imagined as being perpetrated by the aesthetic, under the aegis of Venus, is the seduction of the arch-seductress. Venus is a goddess after all and her powers cannot be resisted by the mere will of mortals. The fantasy is of an irresistible, engulfing effect that sets asceticism and self-denial aside. The charms of the goddess and, by implication, aesthetic experience, are conceived of as going beyond the brutal physical realm. Arousal mingles with worship, passion with veneration. The double nature of Venus, low and high, makes the metaphorical identification of Venus with art especially durable.[14] (2000: 6)

It is this tension between art, aestheticism and desire that is explored in O'Shaughnessy's Venus poems. In 'Living Marble' the speaker is a sculptor who watches his 'wayward Venus who for days hath hid/ Her peerless, priceless beauty, and forbid,/With impious shames and child-like airs perverse' his 'great, fond soul from worshipping the sight/That gives religion to [his] day and night—That shape sublime that should be none of hers' (O'Shaughnessy 1881: 102, ll. 8–13). She lies still under his gaze having 'lollingly surrendered to the spell/ Of sleep's warm death, whose tomb is odorous/And made of recent roses', while he contemplates the 'wonder of her nakedness' noting how 'all the sweet, rebellious body, slim,/Exuberant, lay abandoned to the whim/And miracle of unabashed repose'; her 'One white hand vaguely touching one red rose,/One white arm gleaming through her thick golden hair' (1881: 102–3, ll. 3–5; 14–22). Like that of the Galatea figures in Morris's and MacDonald's works, Venus's 'thick golden hair', presumably unbound, signals sexual abandon, and the red rose she touches draws attention to her desire and her post-coital languidity. However, unlike the Victorian Pygmalions in Chapter 1, O'Shaughnessy's sculptor, piqued by his inability to capture her living beauty in art, breaks 'the marble [he] had made' and wishes 'That sleep indeed were endless, even as death' (1881: 103, ll. 22–6). The sculptor's desire, then, is for the death-like stillness of the living Venus, whose form he plans to turn to stone.

Duelling Venuses

In a later poem in the sequence, 'Dialogue between Two Venuses', O'Shaughnessy stages a debate between Praxiteles' statue, the *Cnidian Venus* (Figure 2.2), created around the fourth century BCE, and

Figure 2.2 *Cnidus Venus*, Roman copy after a Greek original of the fourth century BCE, marble (Ludovisi Collection, Roman National Museums, Palazzo Altemps, Rome). Jastrow / Wikipedia / CC BY-SA 4.0

John Gibson's *The Tinted Venus* (c.1851–6) (Plate 2). The *Cnidian Venus*'s sexual allure is legendary; Nanette Salomon notes that Praxiteles' masterpiece was, as far as we know, 'the very first monumental cult statue of a goddess to be represented completely nude' (1996: 70).[15] It is also 'the first monumental female nude sculpture to be positioned with her hand over her pubis' which was at some point 'given the highly manipulative name "pudica" or so-called modest pose' thus suggesting that the goddess attracts our gaze to her private parts even as she conceals them (Salomon 1996: 70–1). Of special note is her scale which 'was only a little over life size' (Hersey 2009: 73). Praxiteles' Venus was therefore not only unusual in her nudity, but also in terms her human size and the voyeuristic scenario she invoked:[16]

> The goddess is shown suddenly reacting to an intrusive presence. She has been bathing, or was about to bathe, and someone – perhaps the sculptor – has startled her ... That is why she instinctively covers herself. Such a reading of the pose is backed up by a whole cluster of poems about this statue ... These emphasize the goddess's amazement and her instinctive physical reaction to the Peeping Tom who is, in fact, the viewer. And the poems often have the statue, or the goddess herself, speaking. (2009: 73–4)

The sexual frisson associated with this sculpture is reinforced both by its human dimensions and by the long-held belief that the model for Venus was Praxiteles' lover, the courtesan Phryne. Our knowledge of Praxiteles, gained from Pliny's *Natural History* (77 CE) and the sculptural ideal expounded by Winckelmann, suggests that he stands for both 'the introduction of "naturalism" or worldly pleasure to a formerly austere and ideal visual culture, and the "invention" of the female nude' (Arscott and Scott 2000: 5). These two aspects of his work are combined in the *Cnidian Venus*, enhanced by what Arscott and Scott describe as 'the fascination then and thereafter with the relationship between the sculptor and his model'; Pliny suggests that 'Praxiteles' capacity to transcend his materials, to capture nature *au vif* and to infuse it with thrilling sensuality' is directly attributable to the sculptor's love for Phryne, and that it is the sculptor's desire that 'elicits a corresponding response in the viewer' (Arscott and Scott 2000: 5).

The sexual allure of the sculptural body was a similarly intriguing concern when John Gibson exhibited *The Tinted Venus* at the International Exposition of 1862. The statue clearly caused 'a great stir', partly because it came hot on the heels of debates on polychromy prompted by Owen Jones's decision to colour a model of the Parthenon frieze for display in the Greek Court at the Great Exhibition of 1851.[17] While archaeological evidence suggested that Greek sculpture had been polychromed, the art world strongly resisted such indications, fearing that colour would 'debase the ideal body' and destroy 'the purity of the nude' (Hatt 2001: 39). As Michael Hatt notes, Gibson 'became famous – or infamous – for tinting his statues' and escaped the censure experienced by Jones only because critics 'did not wish to tarnish the name of the nation's greatest sculptor', and therefore pointed to 'the delicacy and restraint with which Gibson pursued this practice' (2001: 39). Gibson himself claimed that his decision to tint his statue was because 'he wanted to give his Venus "purity, sweetness, dignity, and grace"' (Arscott 2000: 122). Yet, some critics found his use of colour 'improper' and accused him of 'attempting to simulate the appearance of living flesh' (Smith 1996: 121). Moreover, the time it took for Gibson to part with his commissioned goddess implies an amorous attachment to his sculpted Venus. Caroline Arscott has suggested that the addition of colour brought her 'a little closer to life . . . making it possible for him to fantasise that she really is the goddess and that she has appeared to him' (2000: 122). In a biography of Gibson which the author describes as 'largely an autobiography, being entirely based on his own notes and letters and, as far as possible, in his own words', Gibson describes how he coloured his sculpture and the feelings the statue elicited in him when it was completed:

> When my Venus was finished, I then decorated her in a manner never seen before in these times. The flesh tinted like warm ivory (scarcely red), the eyes blue, the hair blonde, the net which contains the hair behind is of gold . . . The blue fillets winding round the head are edged with gold, and she has earrings; her armlet is also gold, likewise the apple in her hand, which has a Greek inscription on it: 'To the most beautiful' . . . When all my long labour was complete, I often sat down in quiet before my work, meditating upon it and consulting my own simple feelings. I endeavoured to keep myself free from self-delusion as to the effect of the colouring, which I put to the test of reason. (qtd in Matthews 1911: 182)

This 'test' consists of contemplating her and acknowledging her lifelike quality; 'Here', he observes, 'is a little nearer approach to the life, therefore more impressive . . . indeed she seems an ethereal being with her blue eyes looking upon me', and he confesses, 'I forgot that

I was gazing at my own production: there I sat before her, long and often. How was I ever to part from her?' (qtd in Matthews 1911: 182–3). This passage may be read on two levels: on the one hand this is a sculptor who admires his own craft, is aware of its potential impact on the art world and is reluctant to part with his handiwork. On the other hand, resonances with the Pygmalion myth are unignorable: like Pygmalion he appears to have fallen under the spell of his own statue; adorns her with jewels; wishes her alive and, as a Christian unable to pray for Aphrodite's pagan spark, he 'animates' her artificially by adding colour to the whiteness of her marble body. The rhetorical question, 'How was I ever to part with her?', suggests an enchantment, an 'enraptured contemplation' that extended 'to four years, during which Gibson kept the statue in his studio in Rome and failed to deliver it to the Prestons of Liverpool who had commissioned it' (Arscott 2000: 122).

The distinction between the sexual 'availability' of the *Cnidian Venus* modelled on Praxiteles' lover, Phryne, and the 'chastity' of *The Tinted Venus* is elided by Gibson's own confession and this tension between pagan eroticism and Christian purity is at the centre of O'Shaughnessy's 'Dialogue between Two Venuses'. The 'First Venus' is the Venus of antiquity who acknowledges that 'Praxiteles, with passionate Art/Sought me, and saw, and lifted me to strange/ Life, above life and death to stand apart', taking 'marble for a grave' (1881: 113, ll. 12–15), while the 'Second Venus' is 'The Venus of Gibson', 'the pure ideal' (1881: 114, l. 25). The dialogue is written in two distinct poetic forms: the First Venus speaks in lines of iambic pentameter organised in Sicilian quintains; the Second Venus speaks in lines of iambic pentameter arranged in heroic couplets. In the Parnassian tradition, in this dialogue form reflects content: the First Venus stresses the warm climes from which she hails, the 'midday sun' warming and 'caressing' her soul that lay, like the elusive marble lady in MacDonald's *Phantastes*, long 'in unchiselled marble slumbering', while the Second Venus, simply 'Repeating timidly a form sublime', comes from 'the cold quarries' of a 'northern clime', wrought 'beneath some ghost light of the pole', representing a rigidity and icy orderliness that is reflected in the traditional English form in which she speaks (1881: 113–14, ll. 20–5). The Second Venus is clearly associated with Christian chastity, and explains to the First Venus that since 'men put away/The ancient sin' she symbolises, 'A new and holier faith' has given man 'new strength' while 'Athens lies a ruin' (1881: 114, ll. 26–39). The First Venus counters the Second Venus's ascetic sense of life stating, 'I hear the language of some

Gothic lie,/That like a darkness bred of one blown cloud/Hath spread itself over man's azure sky', and goes on to explain the superior benefits of man's pagan past and the glories of love:

> For on the sure swift pinions of desire
>   The soul was wont to soar to every height
> Of heaven; and in Love's hand the only fire
>   Burnt upward, and in his hand the only light
> Shone for the soul to spring from and aspire.
>
> And I a little higher than the heart,
>   A little further than the outstretched hand,
> The very soul of man's soul, set apart
>   From all his shifting days, and toil by land
> And sea, dwelt with him never to depart.
>
> Sister of all his thoughts, nowise he read
>   The marble meaning in my eyes of fate;
> Made one with him, and mystically wed,
>   His bride, he left me still immaculate,
> Yet had content of me, and rests, being dead.
> (1881: 115–16, ll. 53–67)

Referring here to the practice of hierogamy, the First Venus highlights desire between mortals and statues, drawing attention to the 'purity' of the practice; though man may experience desire, she remains 'immaculate'. Yet these lines also suggest that this unattainable love inspires and makes man reach for higher goals, and her 'purity' is not the cold unresponsiveness of the Second Venus; she is the 'great love', the thing none 'may shun' (1881: 117, l. 76). Rejecting the First Venus's belief in the superiority of love and desire, the Second Venus then launches into a long tirade:

> A god of virtue walked upon the earth,
> And man repented him of love and mirth;
> He looked upon the image he had made,
> And, lo! 'twas naked; then he grew afraid,
> And, with a righteous zeal, he overthrew
> The marbles of Praxiteles: they strew
> The trampled land of Greece; the shameless stone
> Of Thespiæ fell, and grass of years has grown
> Over the broken Cnidian;
> ...
>   when the immortality
> Of marble, fashioned in the form of lust
> That once was Phryné, trodden into dust,

No longer stood between him and the sky,
Man put on sackcloth and rebuked the eye
Because of sight, and chid the hand for touch,
And chained the heart lest it should feel too much.
(1881: 117–18, ll. 81–109)

She goes on to rail against the 'lure of beauty ... sister of the serpent temptress' to whom man's sense is inescapably linked and for which he must pay penance till death releases him (1881: 19, l. 121). In response, the First Venus exclaims: 'Man raves', and declares that he should 'tear off the veil, and look once more/On woman, *white* divinity, of marble warm,/With all of life, the soul hath waited for' (1881: 120–1, ll. 134–48; original emphasis). She claims that only by looking once more at woman's beauty 'in glory sweet,/Unsullied by dull heresies or lust,/Or vile invented shames designed to cheat/The soul' can man find salvation (1881: 121, ll. 149–52). The poem ends with the First Venus's conviction that man can only be saved by beauty and art:

> If with surpassing revelation rare,
>   The mystery of the one ineffable line,
> Transcending time and space, changelessly fair,
>   Before and after all things, law divine
> Enter the soul and make religion there,
>
> Then man is saved; for in that soul's clear sight
>   No falsehood or impurity shall stand;
> That soul shall fashion darkness into light,
>   And moulding human clay with holy hand,
> Exalt man pure upon a marble height.
> (1881: 123, ll. 184–93)

The tensions between art, craft and desire are evident throughout O'Shaughnessy's 'Thoughts in Marble' series. In 'Paros', as Kistler notes, 'the sculptor doesn't wish for the stone to actually yield to his desiring touch' because he is shaping 'not his perfect woman, but the perfect art object' (2016: 106). With the advent of Christianity and the destruction of pagan statues of love, as the First Venus in the 'Dialogue' tells us, 'Man put on sackcloth and rebuked the eye/Because of sight, and chid the hand for touch,/And chained the heart lest it should feel too much' (O'Shaughnessy 1881: 117–18, ll. 107–9). Lust is kept at bay by art, but sight itself is censured for the part it plays in the mediation of desire. Though the touching of statues is forbidden, the eye that looks at sculpture becomes 'a hand, the ray of light becomes a finger and the imagination becomes a form of immediate touching' (Herder 2002: 19). In O'Shaughnessy's 'Thoughts in Marble' series, this imaginative 'touch' is continually demanded of the reader invited by the processes of sculpting depicted in the poems and the sculpted rigidity of the prosodic forms in which they are written. Despite his assertion that, in writing these poems, he has 'kept strictly within the lines assigned to the sculptor's art', and that they are to be read purely as 'thoughts in marble, or poems of form', we cannot but find 'a sense' in them, which is not inherent in the purest Parian (1881: viii). In employing the 'purity' of sculpture as a covert means to explore eroticism, O'Shaughnessy participates in the Victorian cult of statue love and its erotic implications while appearing to stay true to the Parnassian ideal of sculpted thought.

The Well-Beloved

Those conflicts between art, love and creativity that haunt O'Shaughnessy's 'Thoughts in Marble' are equally discernible in Thomas Hardy's own depiction of a sculptor in his 1897 novel, *The Well-Beloved*. Like O'Shaughnessy's, Hardy's interest in statuary emerges from a direct engagement with gallery sculptures. As Barry Bullen has observed, prior to Hardy's visit to Rome in 1887 as part of a tour of Italy, Hardy's love of the visual arts that had expressed itself primarily in a 'passionate interest in the art of painting' begins to focus on statuary (Bullen 1986: 15). In his discussion of Hardy's Italian tour, Bullen notes that 'classical sculpture seems to have featured more prominently in this part of their journey' (1986: 26). We learn that Hardy visited the Vatican 'to see the collection of marbles'; went to the Capitoline Museums; 'bought five photographs of sculptural subjects, including the Belvedere Apollo, a Faustina, and a Juno'; and 'may have also bought . . . two busts – one of Caesar, the other of the Venus de Milo – which stood for many years in his study at Max Gate' (Bullen 1986: 26).

Hardy's own responses to Rome and its sculptural bodies are recorded in poetic form in 'Rome: The Vatican: Sala delle Muse' written in 1887, and later published in *Poems of the Past and Present* (1902):

> I sat in the Muses' Hall at the mid of the day,
> And it seemed to grow still, and the people to pass away,
> And the chiselled shapes to combine in a haze of the sun,
> Till beside a Carrara column there gleamed forth One.

She looked not this nor that of those beings divine,
But each and the whole – an essence of all the Nine;
With tentative foot she neared to my halting-place,
A pensive smile on her sweet, small, marvellous face.

'Regarded so long, we render thee sad?' said she.
'Not you,' sighed I, 'but my own inconstancy!
I worship each and each; in the morning one,
And then, alas! another at sink of sun.

'To-day my soul clasps Form; but where is my troth
Of yesternight with Tune: can one cleave to both?'
– 'Be not perturbed,' said she. 'Though apart in fame,
As I and my sisters are one, those, too, are the same.'

–'But my love goes further – to Story, and Dance, and Hymn,
The lover of all in a sun-sweep is fool to whim –
Is swayed like a river-weed as the ripples run!'
– 'Nay, wooer, thou sway'st not. These are but phases of one;

'And that one is I; and I am projected from thee,
One that out of thy brain and heart thou causest to be –
Extern to thee nothing. Grieve not, nor thyself becall,
Woo where thou wilt; and rejoice thou canst love at all!'
(Hardy 1902: 50–2)

The poem introduces themes that are later developed both in the earlier, serialised version of this novel, *The Pursuit of the Well-Beloved* (first published in 1892), and in *The Well-Beloved*: sculpture, art and desire.[18] As Norman Page remarks, the argument posited in the poem functions as 'an aesthetic counterpart' to *The Well-Beloved* 'in which the hero's quest for an erotic or romantic ideal finds temporary fulfilment in a series of separate embodiments' (1999: 44). Indeed, Hardy's protagonist, Jocelyn Pierston,[19] like the speaker in his poem, visits Rome and spends an afternoon 'among the busts in the long gallery of the Vatican' (Hardy 1997: 284) and the speaker's claim: 'I worship each and each; in the morning one,/And then, alas! another at sink of sun' (Hardy 1902: 51, ll. 11–12) encapsulates Pierston's relationship with women in the novel. Discussing the complex nature of Pierston's encounters with the Well-Beloved, Hardy's narrator explains:

> To his Well-Beloved he had always been faithful; but she had had many embodiments. Each individuality known as Lucy, Jane, Flora, Evangeline, or what-not, had been merely a transient condition of her. He did

> not recognize this as an excuse or as a defence, but as a fact simply. Essentially she was perhaps of no tangible substance; a spirit, a dream, a frenzy, a conception, an aroma, an epitomized sex, a light of the eye, a parting of the lips. God only knew what she really was; Pierston did not. She was indescribable. (Hardy 1997: 184)

Noting that Pierston follows the Well-Beloved from the body of one woman to another, his friend Somers accuses him of fickleness, a charge Pierston denies, stating: 'I have always been faithful to the elusive creature whom I have never been able to get a firm hold of' (1997: 203). It is such fickleness but in the context of art which the speaker in Hardy's poem debates with the Vatican muse. Pondering his inability to choose between the arts, he is clearly perturbed by his own 'inconstancy' (Hardy 1902: 51, l. 10). Yet the muse reassures him that his supposed fickleness is not inconstancy at all, that his love of sculpture, music, 'Story, and Dance, and Hymn' are 'but phases of one', and that 'one' is the muse herself, a protector of the arts who is in turn a product of the artist: 'One that out of thy brain and heart thou causest to be' (1902: 52, ll. 17–22).

The speaker's fanciful encounter with the sculptural body of the muse in The Vatican subtly recalls the Pygmalion myth: the statue of a woman, made by man, comes to life and, similarly, the myth is implicit in *The Well-Beloved*. Hardy's novel is set on the isolated limestone peninsula of Portland, known by the Romans as 'Vindilia' and home, over the centuries, to Normans, Anglo-Saxons, Romans and the Balearic-British. The island retains a mythical quality imbued with Pagan history: a temple to Venus is said to have 'once stood at the top of the Roman road leading up into the isle' and 'one to the love-goddess of the Slingers' to have antedated this (Hardy 1997: 232).[20] On this ancient island, 'Pagan divinities' and 'Pagan customs' linger,[21] and it is in this haven of antiquity that Pierston, a sculptor, who lives and works in London, encounters versions of his Well-Beloved in women whom he later translates 'into plaster', and views most commonly as Aphrodite, yet, on occasion, as Juno or Minerva (1997: 186, 212). In *The Well-Beloved*, Pierston falls in love, at twenty-year intervals, with three generations of women from the Caro family: the original Avice whom he meets at the age of twenty; her daughter Ann Avice, whom he calls 'Avice' and encounters at the age of forty; and Avice the III, Ann Avice's daughter who is encouraged by her mother to marry him when he returns to the island at the age of sixty.

The path of true love does not run smooth for Pierston, however. Having expressed his desire to marry the first Avice, he finds that the

Well-Beloved migrates unexpectedly to the body of Marcia Bencomb with whom he has a brief liaison in London. The second Avice, to his surprise, shares his faithfulness – or faithlessness – having her own Well-Beloved who, like Pierston's, flits from body to body. Nevertheless, Pierston offers to marry her and, in the style of Pre-Raphaelite artists, plans to educate her in order to make her a fitting companion. But, finding that she is pregnant and married already, he insists that she return to her husband. Years later, now widowed, the second Avice contacts Pierston and introduces him to her daughter, guessing that his Well-Beloved will relocate to this younger version of herself. Her instincts are right, and the now elderly Pierston asks the young Avice to marry him. She initially accepts out of a sense of duty to her mother, but later elopes with a young lover, who is, in fact, Marcia Bencomb's stepson. Brought together in the final pages of the novel, Pierston and Marcia marry, but Pierston's Well-Beloved is no longer resident in her body, nor in any other woman's body, as she once was. Following an illness contracted at the funeral of Avice II, and his desertion by Avice III, Pierston finds that the 'artistic sense had left him, and he could no longer attach a definite sentiment to images of beauty recalled from the past' resulting in the 'strange death of the sensuous side of [his] nature' (1997: 330).[22]

The Platonic Idea

At one level, the novel clearly interrogates what J. Hillis Miller has called 'the relation between erotic fascination, creativity, and Platonic metaphysics' (1982: 148).[23] The Platonic nature of Pierston's engagement with the Well-Beloved has been charted; writing to Gosse on 31 March 1897 about *The Well-Beloved,* Hardy asks, 'I wonder if you know that the tale was sketched many years ago, when I was virtually a young man, & interested in the Platonic Idea' (1978a: 156), and in his original preface to the novel, published in 1897, he comments that the 'Well-Beloved' is a name given 'to a delicate dream which . . . is by no means new to Platonic philosophers' (Hardy 1997: 173). The 'Platonic Idea' is invoked by Hardy in the novel's intertextual play with Shelley's works. The text, as Hillis Miller points out, draws its epigraph, 'One shape of many names' from *The Revolt of Islam,* and 'also contains citations of *Prometheus Unbound* and *Epipsychidion*' as well as another quotation from *The Revolt of Islam* (1982: 148). Furthermore, as the reference to *Epipsychidion* suggests, the Well-Beloved shares features with the Romantic epipsyche, that 'soul within our soul,' that 'mirror whose surface reflects only the forms of purity and brightness', developed in Shelley's essay 'On Love', composed in 1818 (1977: 474). The influence of Romanticism is also evident in the resonances between Hardy's novel and Hazlitt's *Liber Amoris* noted by the writer Richard Le Gallienne soon after the novel appeared on the literary scene.[24] Following the publication of a malicious anonymous review, 'Thomas Hardy Humorist', in the London *World* on 24 March 1897, which accused Hardy of 'sex-mania' and, indirectly, of plagiarising Le Gallienne's *Quest of the Golden Girl* (1896), the younger author came to Hardy's defence and 'observed that Hardy's novel invited comparison with Hazlitt's *Liber Amoris* but was clearly superior to Hazlitt's work' (Pilgrim 1991: 135–6). One obvious link between the texts is that both works feature an older man's infatuation with a younger woman of lower status. Moreover, as seen in Chapter 1, Hazlitt's novel carries the full title: *Liber Amoris, or The New Pygmalion*, thus highlighting its mythical subtext. The beloved in Hazlitt's novella is referred to as a 'Greek statue' (1998a: 56) of 'unrivalled symmetry of form' (1998a: 43). Similarly, when Pierston, who is 'professionally sworn to form', first spots Marcia Bencomb, he describes her profile as classical, that of 'a very Juno'; she bears a 'Junonian quality' of 'form'; and, when unanimated by the spirit of the Well-Beloved, women become, like O'Shaughnessy's statues, creatures of 'lines and surfaces' (Hardy 1997: 190, 229).

That the novel's associations with late-Victorian aestheticism have received less attention is particularly surprising given that Pierston's interest in ideal sculpture resonates with the 'Classical training' evident in the art of the 'Olympian Dreamers' – works by artists such as Burne-Jones, Frederic Leighton, G. F. Watts, Albert Moore, Edward Poynter, and Lawrence Alma-Tadema – which dominated the Royal Academy in the second half of the nineteenth century (Marshall 1998: 9).[25] In addition to Burne-Jones's *Pygmalion* series, discussed in Chapter 1, examples of such paintings include Leighton's *Venus Disrobing*, exhibited at the Royal Academy in 1867; Watts's *Thetis* (1867–9); Albert Moore's *A Venus* (1869); Poynter's *Andromeda* (1869); and Alma Tadema's *The Sculptor's Model* (*Venus Esquilina*) (1877).[26] Although there is no open reference in Hardy's text to Walter Pater, whose writings were so influential on the development of late-Victorian aesthetics, Michael Ryan has observed that the novel's epigraph from Shelley – 'One shape of many names' – also 'recalls Pater's discussion of the relationship between the one and the many in *Plato and Platonism* (1894) as well as Plato's *Cratylus*, to which

Pater refers directly in his first lecture and which Hardy read shortly before writing the novel' (1979: 173). Ryan writes:

> Pater's lectures on Plato were originally delivered in 1891-92, a time when he was known to be a visitor at the Hardys' house in Kensington. It is conceivable, therefore, that Hardy was aware of Pater's work even at the time of the writing of the first version of the novel. Pater portrays Plato as an artist who sees the Ideal as 'vision' above all. He stresses Plato's aesthetic temper which compels him to worship Beauty as a lover. (1979: 174–5)

In his essay, which argues that *The Well-Beloved* constitutes a critique of Aestheticism, Ryan suggests that, in this novel, 'Hardy singles out Pater's version of Platonism as an object of mockery' (1979: 173), but it seems unlikely that Hardy, who had known and respected Pater since 1886; who admired Swinburne, read John Addington Symonds and knew Burne-Jones; who was a keen visitor to the Grosvenor Gallery; and who counted the sculptors Hamo Thornycroft and Thomas Woolner among his acquaintances would have engaged in such mockery. Indeed, the topic of Hardy's novel suggests that, far from critiquing aestheticism, Hardy may well have been inspired by the work of members of the aesthetic circles in which he moved in London: by Thornycroft's neoclassical sculptures or Woolner's *Pygmalion*, for example, or by Morris's 'Pygmalion and the Image' and Burne-Jones's *Pygmalion* series.[27]

Chasing Beauty

Given the London circles with which Hardy was acquainted, it is interesting to note that Ryan, Bullen and John Holmes (2004) all draw comparisons between Hardy's protagonist and the Pre-Raphaelite painter and poet, Dante Gabriel Rossetti. Certainly, Pierston's obsession with the Well-Beloved, which translates itself into repeated sculptural versions of mythical women (Aphrodite in particular) resonates with Christina Rossetti's reputed comment on her brother's paintings in her poem 'In an Artist's Studio': 'One face looks out from all his canvasses' (1994: 52, l. 1). As Bullen points out, like Rossetti, 'Pierston becomes "a one-part man" . . . he compulsively repeats an image in sculpture, and the titles of those pieces are strongly reminiscent of Rossetti's works' (1986: 231). Furthermore, 'like Rossetti himself, Pierston pursues relentlessly the image of his own soul or "Psyche'" (Bullen 1986: 231), recalling Shelley's own desire for an epipsychic other. In his discussion of *The Well-Beloved*, Bullen quotes from Hardy's diary entry dated 29 May 1888 in which the latter describes his experience of glimpsing a beautiful young girl:

> That girl in the omnibus had one of those faces of marvellous beauty which are seen casually in the streets but never among one's friends. It was perfect in its softened classicality – a Greek face translated into English. Moreover, she was fair, and her hair pale chestnut. Where do these women come from? Who marries them? Who knows them? (1986: 228–9)

Such 'professional beauty chases' clearly inform Pierston's 'pursuit of an intangible ineffable female ideal' in *The Well-Beloved* (1986: 228). The narrator explains:

> [the] study of beauty was his [Pierston's] only joy for years onward. In the streets he would observe a face, or a fraction of a face, which seemed to express to a hair's-breadth in mutable flesh what he was at that moment wishing to express in durable shape. (Hardy 1997: 211)

While Pierston's searches mirror those of Rossetti, the passage above also echoes Pater's description of Leonardo da Vinci's own 'beauty chases' in *The Renaissance*:

> He was smitten with a love of the impossible . . . Two ideas were especially confirmed in him, as reflexes that had touched his brain in childhood beyond the depth of other impressions – the smiling of women and the motion of great waters. And in such studies some interfusion of the extremes of beauty and terror shaped itself, as an image that might be seen and touched, in the mind of this gracious youth, so fixed that for the rest of his life it never left him. As if catching glimpses of it in the strange eyes or hair of chance people, he would follow such about the streets of Florence till the sun went down, of whom many sketches of his remain. Some of these are full of a curious beauty, that remote beauty which may be apprehended only by those who have sought it carefully; who, starting with acknowledged types of beauty, have refined as far upon these, as these refine upon the world of common forms. (2010: 59)

A similar love of the impossible, a similar desire to capture and still in art that 'curious beauty' seems to afflict Jocelyn Pierston and, by implication, Hardy himself, for there is an interesting slippage between the speaker's observation of the statue's 'sweet, small, marvellous face' in 'Rome: The Vatican: Sala delle Muse' (1978b: 207, l. 8), and Hardy's girl on the omnibus whose own 'marvellous beauty' represents a 'softened classicality' that mirrors that of those women whom Pierston longs to harden into 'durable shape' in *The Well-Beloved*.

I would suggest that it is this desire to harden beauty into 'durable shape', shared with O'Shaughnessy, that complicates Hardy's engagement with the Pygmalion myth. As discussed in Chapter 1, pygmalionism has been considered 'a form of erotomania founded on the sense of vision and closely related to the allurement of beauty' (Ellis 1936: 188), and the story of Pygmalion itself seems to stem from tales of what Scobie and Taylor would call 'agalmatophiliacs'. It is also important to remember that Pygmalion's love and physical engagement with the statue precedes its animation; as Kenneth Gross points out in *The Dream of the Moving Statue*, Ovid's text clouds the distinction between the animate and the inanimate object of desire. Although we are encouraged to understand that Pygmalion 'animates' his statue in his fantasies, we are nevertheless told that he takes it to bed with him before it has been brought to life by Aphrodite. As Gross explains:

> Ovid blurs his focus at this point, avoiding any explicit description of this contact of living and fictive nakedness, and hence modulating the impression of fetishism or necrophilia. But there is something no less disturbing in the way the text invites us simply to contemplate the weird, transgressive literalism of a statue's being taken down from its formalized repose on a pedestal and laid down stiffly, even painfully, on the softness of a bed; Ovid asks us also to consider the strangeness of inanimate, fictive flesh covered with real jewels and clothes, things that do their formal and symbolic work mainly insofar as they ornament, organize, and, as it were, make a statue of a living body.[28] (2006: 73)

Havelock Ellis's reading is more direct; he states: '[n]ecrophily [*sic*], or a sexual attraction for corpses, is sometimes regarded as related to pygmalionism' (1936: 188). Statues, then, animated or otherwise, can double for the dead and not simply in memorial terms. As Gross observes,

> [t]he dream of a statue's awakening can be an awakening into delusion and nightmare, a rebirth into what is not life, a kind of death-in-life ... The life of the statue often turns out to be that of a ghost or a galvanized corpse. (2006: 10)

Gross repeatedly associates the statue with the dead and the spectral: it is 'ghostly'; it 'feeds on threshold states between life and death'; it is a 'zombie', a 'revenant' (2006: 9–27) and, interestingly, such language also informs Pierston's engagement with the Well-Beloved.

Death-in-Life

While I do not mean to claim that Pierston is an agalmatophiliac or a necrophiliac,[29] Hardy's novel nevertheless resonates with oblique references to such paraphilia. In *The Well-Beloved*, Pierston is likened, not to Pygmalion whose statue comes to life, but to Praxiteles whose *Cnidian Venus* was the object of agalmatophiliac desire; a statue whose allure and potential for unresisting violation lies in its immobility.[30] Moreover, the name 'Pierston' while meaning 'Stone-stone', 'Fatherstone' (Ryan 1979: 180) and 'carrying a marine allusion' (Pilgrim 1991: 130), surely also suggests 'pierce-stone' which implies not only the process of sculpting, but also the fantasy of sexual penetration desired by the agalmatophiliac. Pierston's myriad statues of Aphrodite, those versions of the Well-Beloved in 'durable form', therefore function, like O'Shaughnessy's Venuses, simultaneously as objects of sculptural, creative and sexual desire.

In Hardy's novel, Pierston is both sculptor and lover: although he only responds to the Well-Beloved when she is animated, like Pygmalion's Galatea, by Aphrodite, his overriding desire is to still her 'into plaster' (Hardy 1997: 212). Like O'Shaughnessy's sculptor in 'Paros', what attracts him is not woman herself, but form. Pierston himself is aware that 'the artist in him had consumed the wooer' (Hardy 1997: 225) and declares himself 'professionally sworn to form' (Hardy 1997: 262). Like Pater's Plato, he sees the ideal as 'vision' and his 'aesthetic temper' compels him 'to worship Beauty', and not woman, as a lover (Ryan 1979: 174). In doing so, he comes close to Havelock Ellis's model of the pygmalionist whose erotomania is 'founded on a sense of vision and closely related to the allurement of beauty' (1936: 188). Furthermore, the animated Well-Beloved is often nothing more than a ghostly 'galvanized corpse' (Gross 2006: 10), a counterpart to the animated statue. When the Well-Beloved exits the body of a living woman, the substance she leaves behind is but 'a corpse', an 'empty carcase' (Hardy 1997: 203, 212). She is associated with ghosts (1997: 184, 305); phantoms (1997: 238, 251, 257); and spirits (1997: 184, 247, 252). When she re-enters the body of a live woman, that woman is described as 'resuscitated', 'revivified' or 'revitalized' (1997: 242, 245, 249).

The spectral metaphors employed in descriptions of the Well-Beloved imply a death-in-life existence and the images of reanimation suggest that the body entered by Well-Beloved is, in some sense, always already dead. The women Pierston desires in *The Well-Beloved* are therefore intrinsically associated with death. A telling moment in the novel is when Pierston finds that, following the death of the first Avice, '[h]e loved the woman dead and inaccessible as he had never loved her in life' (1997: 231), a sentiment which prefigures the tenor of Hardy's *Poems of 1912-13*, works produced following the death of his wife Emma. In his essay on Hardy and the poetics of melancholia, Jahan Ramazani argues that, in these poems, 'Hardy tries to sew up the ragged sleeve of their marriage with the thread of his earliest feelings toward her' (1991: 958). In his discussion of 'The Going', Ramazani notes that the elegy 'leaps from recrimination to intense nostalgia for the earliest stages of the relationship' (1991: 961). He goes on to say:

> Interpreting melancholia, the psychoanalyst Vamik D. Volkan cogently explains the relation between ambivalence and desire for reunion: 'This process of searching for the deceased is unconsciously intensified, and it is habitual and specific enough to be called a mechanism of defense – defense mainly against the tension of ambivalence and the eruption of derivatives of those aggressive and libidinal drives originally directed towards the deceased.' Having groped for his dead wife across the 'yawning blankness,' he finds her now, but only as she was more than forty years earlier during their courtship. Unlike the 'indifferent' and unpredictable wife, the younger beloved fastened her gaze on him . . . Throughout the sequence such regression to their premarital love enables Hardy to defend himself against the anger he feels toward both his wife and himself. (1991: 961)

Interestingly, like Hardy, O'Shaughnessy also wrote several poems in memory of his deceased wife, Eleanor, with whom he had a difficult relationship; these were published posthumously, along with the 'Thoughts in Marble' series, in *Songs of a Worker*. As Kistler notes, Eleanor O'Shaughnessy, whom he married in 1873, 'was a very intelligent woman, from a literary family, with literary aspirations of her own' and, in 1875, she and O'Shaughnessy co-authored a collection of children's stories entitled *Toyland* (Kistler 2016: 12).[31] Following the death of two children, her mother and sister, Eleanor took to drowning her sorrows in whiskey, and died of cirrhosis of the liver four years later in 1879. As Kistler observes:

> Her health [had] deteriorated with her drinking, and one can only guess the strain it placed upon the marriage. Eleanor's letters to O'Shaughnessy record that he left her behind with her father, incapacitated by 'illness', while he took several trips abroad, enjoying the literary life of Paris unencumbered by his sick wife. (2016: 14-15)

However, the poems written by O'Shaughnessy after her death do not express bitterness, but a profound sadness and sense of loss. In 'Elegy', which functions as a form of extended epigraph that precedes *Songs of a Worker*, the speaker states, 'I carry in my soul the loss of her,/A grief past words and tears' (1881: xiii, ll. 1–2). In 'At Her Grave', the speaker addresses his now dead love, saying 'I have stayed too long from your grave, it seems,/Now I come back again' and asks, 'And your flowers, how do they grow?/Your rose has a bud: is it meant for me?/Ah, little red gift put up/So silently, like a child's present, you see/Lying beside your cup!' (1881: 38, ll. 1–10). 'Silences' reads as a counterpart to 'At Her Grave' which was 'written literally at his wife's grave some few months after her death' (Chandler Moulton 1894: 44); while the latter suggests a romantic communion with the dead, the former speaks of the stony silence of the once beloved:

> I stood beside a grave. Years had passed by;
>   Sick with unanswered life I turned to death,
> And whispered all my question [*sic*] to the grave,
> And watched the flowers desolately wave,
>   And grass stir on it with a fitful breath,
> For all reply.
> (1881: 56, ll. 6–10)

Here, the budding flowers of 'At Her Grave' are grown desolate and no voice, albeit imaginary, answers the grieving speaker in 'Silences' who, though he prays to God, and fleetingly feels him near, finds the silence surrounding his lover's grave even deeper when He is gone:

> But you! If I can speak before I die,
>   I spoke to you with all my soul, and when
> I look at you 'tis still my soul you see.
> Oh, in your heat was there no word for me?
>   All would have answered had you answered then
> With even a sigh.
> (1881: 57, ll. 16–20)

Silence and remorse are also features of 'If She But Knew', where the speaker yearns for the voice of his lost beloved and for her absolution: 'If she but knew that it would save me/Her voice to hear,/Saying she pitied me, forgave me,/Must she forbear?' (1881: 78, ll. 5–6). These haunting poems of loss anticipate Hardy's poems in memory of Emma – poems such as 'The Voice', and 'The Shadow on the Stone' – while O'Shaughnessy's 'Lynmouth', where the sea, the green hills and the rocky ledges function as a 'charmèd space' to which a lover has brought his beloved to declare his love, resonates with Hardy's own memories of his courtship of Emma against the backdrop of a Cornish landscape (O'Shaughnessy 1881: 59, l. 3). Ramazani's analysis of Hardy's *Poems of 1912-13* might equally be applied to O'Shaughnessy's elegies; both necessarily prompt biographical readings of this kind. But it seems significant that a similar process of rejection and projection is at play in Hardy's *The Well-Beloved* written long before Emma's death. When Avice I dies, Pierston finds that the Well-Beloved, 'after flitting from Nichola Pine-Avon to the phantom of a dead woman whom he never adored in her lifetime, had taken up her abode in the living representative of the dead' (Hardy 1997: 251). Thus, *The Well-Beloved* rehearses those repetitions of younger and older versions of the same woman that characterise Hardy's elegies for Emma. The question is why? The critic Elisabeth Bronfen discusses the nature of such repetitions:

> The man's initial response to the loss of his beloved is a form of melancholia – he withdraws from the world, his desire is invested in the dead. The world of the living regains his interest only when he sees that he can retrieve his 'lost' love object by falling in love with a second woman who resembles the first. Because she is used as the object at which the lost woman is refound or resurrected, the second woman's body also functions as the site for a dialogue with the dead, for a preservation and calling forth of the first woman's ghost, and for the articulation of necrophiliac desire. The reciprocity of original and copy is such that while the copy may be the first presence of her model, she can disappear within the process of repetition, subsumed under the representation of the first wife, who in turn may be just a copy of an original absent female body. (1992: 326)

The language employed by Bronfen parallels those spectral metaphors and images of reanimation employed by Hardy in *The Well-Beloved*. More importantly, Bronfen's argument suggests that the dead woman's double offers the mourning lover a site for the 'articulation of necrophiliac desire' (1992: 326).

While necrophilia is associated with sexual congress with the dead, in her book, *Desiring the Dead: Necrophilia and Nineteenth-Century French Literature*, Lisa Downing offers a more fluid explanation of the term. Here, she provides other definitions such as that given by Erich Fromm in *The Anatomy of Human Destructiveness* (1973) who suggests that necrophilia is 'the passionate attraction to all that is dead ... the passion to transform that which is alive into something which is unalive' (Downing 2003: 4). For Downing, necrophilia is not limited 'to acts of sexual intercourse with a dead body', instead it is 'recast as a central feature of the human fantasy relationship with death' (2003: 5). Fromm's suggestion that the necrophiliac wishes to transform 'that which is alive into something which is unalive' (qtd in Downing 2003: 4) recalls Freud's discussion of the death drive in *Beyond the Pleasure Principle* (1920) in which it is identified as an urge to return to an inorganic state, a state identified with death in that it precedes existence. As Downing observes, the existence of the death drive is controversial and has been the topic of considerable discussion. For example, she notes that, according to the theorist and psychoanalyst Jean Laplanche, 'the unconscious is incapable of conceiving of its own death. This means that the death drive is only ever visible when directed outwards towards another person' (Downing 2003: 49).

In *The Well-Beloved*, Hardy seemingly plays with the connotations of necrophilia in its widest sense. According to Bronfen's formulation, in desiring those copies of the dead original represented by Avice II and Avice III, Pierston is in 'dialogue with the dead' and articulating a form of 'necrophiliac desire' (1992: 326). Moreover, in creating sculptures of the Well-Beloved, Pierston reverses the Pygmalion myth, and fulfils the necrophiliac impulse, identified by Fromm, to transform 'that which is alive into something which is unalive' (Downing 2003: 4). In doing so, he is perhaps projecting his own death drive, as Laplanche suggests, onto another. This proposition becomes increasingly valid when one examines the nature of the epi-psychic doubling between Pierston and his Well-Beloved. As Hillis Miller comments:

> The Avices are all closely related to him, since each native of the island is a near relation of all the others ... As his 'sisters,' they are also, in a manner of speaking, his female images in the mirror, his wraiths in a changed sex ... the merging of lover with beloved is the mating of a man with his image in the mirror. This is reinforced by the reduction of the beloved in the three successive love stories to a series of persons

with the same name, grandmother, mother, daughter, all cousins of the lover, representations of the single island face, which is Jocelyn's face too. (1982: 159-60)

This doubling also occurs on a narrative level. Pierston's discovery that, like himself, Avice II is 'engaged in the pursuit of an impossible ideal' that flits from man to man, marks a turning-point in the power relations between the doubles. As the narrator remarks, the search for the Well-Beloved is 'of the nature of a knife which could cut two ways. To be the seeker was one thing: to be one of the corpses from which the ideal inhabitant had departed was another' (Hardy 1997: 254). Shortly after, Pierston is described as being as 'cold as stone'; and later, in the final part of the novel, catching his reflection in a window he sees 'something ghostly', a 'spectre' and acknowledges his aging body to be a 'withering carcase' (1997: 260, 305). When Avice III sees him in daylight, she no longer sees a possible husband, but 'a strange fossilized relic in human form' (1997: 306); a human version of the 'cadaverous countenances' of his sculptural studies (1997: 309). Like the bodies abandoned by his Well-Beloved, Pierston becomes spectral and corpse-like, an image of the living dead. Yet, interestingly, this physical 'death' is once again displaced, this time onto his erotic desire and his creativity, for it is at this point in the novel that Pierston loses his 'artistic sense' and the 'sensuous side' of his nature (1997: 330).

According to Downing, necrophilia 'mobilizes psychical energy in order to make a lost object return at will, but equally to enable a glimpse of self-loss in the perception of the other's death' (2003: 58). Pierston's physical – and perhaps artistic – decline begins, as suggested above, when Avice II reverses the subject/object process of his engagement with the Well-Beloved. In making him (and other men) the object of her gaze, Avice II sets in motion the process of Pierston's ossification that continues during his encounter with Avice III and culminates in his artistic and psychic castration. While the Well-Beloved remains a fetishised and powerless ideal, an animated corpse or sculpture, Pierston can allay his own fears of death and/or castration. Avice II and Avice III implicitly challenge his idealisations and force a confrontation with his own mortality that he displaces onto his creativity, a creativity that is inextricably bound with his erotic desires. In a metaphorical sense, Pierston's Well-Beloved has consistently reversed the process and threatened castration. As Hillis Miller remarks:

> [I]t is not without significance that Jocelyn in his London studio, at the height of his artistic powers and artistic success, makes his statues of

blocks of stone cut out by his quarryman father from the rock of his native isle. That island is in fact a peninsula, a presqu'île. It is a single phallus-shaped block of limestone jutting out into the sea, a male member of stone four miles long. The monumental stones the father cuts out of this living rock are erected by Jocelyn in his studio and then made into images of his goddess. (1982: 164)

The transformation from phallic stone to feminine ideal suggested by this process leads Hillis Miller to argue that the island 'is already ambiguous in its sexuality, like Jocelyn himself, or like his name' (1982: 164). One might also contend that, made of the phallic rock itself, Pierston's Aphrodites function as disavowals of castration in which his libidinal energies are invested. Yet the fact that the rock must be chipped in order to create them, suggests that they are also the cause of castration. It is perhaps because of this that he names them his 'Venus failures', for they prefigure the eventual loss of his artistic prowess and his libidinal desires (Hardy 1997: 188).

Like O'Shaughnessy's 'Thoughts in Marble' series, Hardy employs the 'purity' of the sculptural ideal and the aesthetics of beauty to explore the complexities of sexual and artistic desire. However, whereas Morris, Woolner and MacDonald eschew the pleasure of Ovid's animating touch, and displace it onto the goddess Venus, O'Shaughnessy and Hardy's sculptors use touch – the moulding of clay, the chiselling of marble, the crafting of words – not to animate but, in acts of reverse pygmalionism, to turn living women to stone statues and seal desire in the sculptural bodies we meet in their works. The juxtaposition of O'Shaughnessy's elegies for Eleanor and the Venuses in his 'Thoughts in Marble' series, like the dead and living Avices in Hardy's *The Well-Beloved*, necessarily complicate the tensions between the dead beloved, the beauty of form, and ideal sculpture recalled in the First Venus's words in 'Dialogue between Two Venuses':

> A goddess when I stood upon the wave
>   Green haloed further than all arms could reach;
> A woman when I came to earth and clave
>   Unto men's lives, filling the heart of each—
> Then died, and took the marble for a grave.
> (O'Shaughnessy 1881: 113, ll. 10–14)

Similarly, Pierston's loss of Avice II leads him to see his sculptural studies, his 'Venus failures' as creatures from the grave: 'white and cadaverous' (Hardy 1997: 188, 280). Interestingly, after her brief sojourn with Pierston in his London studio, Avice II feels 'a refined kinship with sculptures', as if she herself becomes aware of her own statue status. Moreover, it is telling that it is as he sits by her now dead body that Pierston sees his own works in his mind's eye and equates them with her:

> As he sat darkling here, the ghostly outlines of former shapes taken by his Love came round their sister, the unconscious corpse, confronting him from the wall in sad array, like the pictured Trojan women beheld by Æneas on the walls of Carthage. Many of them he had idealized in bust and in figure from time to time, but it was not as such that he remembered and reanimated them now; rather was it in all their natural circumstances, weaknesses and stains. (1997: 312)

Jeremy Steele notes that, here, Pierston's imagination 'does not reanimate his women in idealized form (as he has portrayed many of them in sculpture), but rather "in all their natural circumstances, weaknesses and stains"' (2006: 215). To support his point, Steele quotes an entry from Hardy's diary dated 28 October 1891 which observes,

> It is the incompleteness that is loved, when love is sterling and true. This is what differentiates the real one from the imaginary, the practicable from the impossible, the Love who returns the kiss from the Vision that melts away. A man sees the Diana or the Venus in his beloved, but what he loves is the difference. (qtd in Steele 2006: 215)

But it seems significant that Pierston only appreciates his loves as 'natural' women once they are dead. Like Hardy's later elegies for Emma, it is the deceased woman who prompts a more realistic form of love, and it is the living woman who exists in the imaginary vision and 'melts away' while his Venus retains her durable form. Moreover, 'form' is as important in *The Well-Beloved* as it is in O'Shaughnessy's 'Thoughts in Marble'. In his essay on Hardy's novel, Bullen argues that 'Pierston's spontaneous renunciation of art seems to have some general correspondence with Hardy's own decision to abandon novel-writing' (1986: 232). Yet, *The Well-Beloved* might be read, not as Hardy's last novel, but as a novel-poem, blending novelistic and poetic attributes. Its tripartite structure suggests stanzaic division and its focus on form, repetition and refrain is poetic. The sculptural bodies that litter the text serve not only as displacements of death and decay, but also as doubles of the Vatican muse in Hardy's poem 'Rome: The Vatican: Sala delle Muse'. While O'Shaughnessy's

'Thoughts in Marble' become posthumous monuments in form to his poetic legacy, Hardy's statues simultaneously enable the coalescence of prose and poetry and sanction his infidelity to novelistic writing. In O'Shaughnessy's poems, as in Hardy's novel, statues function as focal points for meditations on love, loss and artistic legitimacy and similar concerns inform the novels I examine in Chapter 3: Hawthorne's *The Marble Faun* and James's *Roderick Hudson*. In these works, however, statuary facilitates complex negotiations of transgressive desire that are ultimately reinterred in the sculptural body.

Notes

1. To date, O'Shaughnessy's poetry has been unjustly neglected. Aside from Jordan Kistler's recent critical work on his poetry (2012, 2016), there is only a handful of articles written between 1939 and 2012; a mention in the 1985 edition *Dictionary of Literary Biography: Victorian Poets after 1850* and a 1954 dissertation by Sanford M. Goldstein from the University of Wisconsin. He is now best known as the writer of 'Ode' from *Music and Moonlight* (1874), the first two lines of which are famously quoted by Gene Wilder in the 1971 version of *Willy Wonka and the Chocolate Factory*: 'We are the music makers,/And we are the dreamers of dreams'. Edward Elgar set the ode to music in *The Music Makers* (Op. 69: 1912) and Aphex Twin sampled the poem on 'We are the music makers' from his album, *Selected Ambient Works 85–92*.
2. Kistler considers his roles as naturalist and poet and demonstrates how these inform a symbiotic relationship between science and art in his work.
3. Leonee Ormond (1970) has argued that O'Shaughnessy is the true model for the poet 'Cosmo Chough', usually identified as Swinburne, in Vernon Lee's *roman-à-clef*, *Miss Brown* (1884). See also Kistler (2016: 15).
4. The Parnassians laid the foundations for later Symbolist and Decadent traditions. Their work was informed by Gautier's poetry and criticism and associated with the work of Baudelaire, Leconte de Lisle, Théodore de Banville and Paul Verlaine. The twelve poems in the 'Thoughts in Marble' sequence are: 'Her Beauty', 'A Priest of Beauty', 'Living Marble', 'Black Marble', 'The Line of Beauty', 'Pentelicos', 'Paros', 'Carrara', 'Dialogue between Two Venuses', 'A Venus', 'The Last Look' and 'Fragment'.
5. Victor Hugo (1802–86), French writer and dramatist of the Romantic movement, is best known for *Notre-Dame de Paris* (1831) and *Les Misérables* (1862); Charles Marie René Leconte de Lisle (1818–94) and Catulle Mendés (1841–1909) were both poets of the Parnassian movement.

6. Théodore de Banville's 'Á Venus de Milo' was first published *Les Cariatides* (1839–42); Leconte de Lisle's 'Vénus de Milo' was first published in 1846 in the March issue of the Fourierist magazine *La Phalange* and later collected in *Poèmes antiques* (1852); Baudelaire's 'La Beauté' appeared in *Les Fleurs du Mal* (1857).
7. 'L'art' was first published in *L'Artiste* in 1857, and added to subsequent editions of *Émaux et camées*. The lines quoted here are from Johnson's own translation of Gautier's poem.
8. The original text in French reads: 'En soutenant que le langage, ou le vers est, en quelque sorte, comme le marbre, une *matière* qu'il faut travailler comme le sculpteur la pierre, Gautier érige en principe théorique ce que pratiquaient certains poètes français . . . à savoir, l'importance de l'aspect *plastique* de la langue ou du vers. Cet aspect plastique se manifeste dans la poésie sous forme de structures prosodiques – mesure, rime, stance – qui, autant que des thèmes ou idées explorés dans le texte, inspirent le poète'.
9. A. C. Swinburne's 'Hermaphroditus' appeared in his controversial collection, *Poems and Ballads I* (1866), and Dante Gabriel Rossetti's sonnet was first produced in 1880 as an illuminated text for his mother's birthday. It later introduced 'The House of Life' sequence published in *Ballads and Sonnets* (1881).
10. For a detailed discussion of the acquisition and history of the display of the Elgin Marbles in the British Museum, see Ian Jenkins (1992) and for the discovery and subsequent history and reception of the *Venus de Milo*, see Gregory Curtis (2003).
11. This four-volume collection was published serially and contained engravings of paintings, sculptures and gems. The engravings of sculptures and gems are of mythological subjects; the paintings are of Christian and mythological subjects, as well as portraits, landscapes and 'genre' scenes; *Les collectionneurs de l'ancienne Rome. Notes d'un amateur* refers to a book on collectors of Roman antiquities by the French art historian Edmond Bonaffé (1825–1903), who was himself a collector.
12. See Lewis et al. (1992: 215–16) for the use of pentelic marble in the building of the Parthenon.
13. The *Amores*, also known as *Affairs of the Heart* (Gk. *Erōtes* or 'The two kinds of love'), is a dialogue purportedly written by the Roman satirist, Lucian. As the authorship is in doubt, but the style resembles Lucian's, the work is often referred to as being by 'Pseudo-Lucian'. It is a form of 'contest' literature that compares the love of women and the love of boys. It decides that the love of boys is preferable.
14. The epithets 'Aphrodite Urania' (spiritual Venus) and 'Aphrodite Pandemos' (the more earthly 'people's Venus') were used in classical literature to distinguish between chaste, or celestial love and lustful desire.
15. See also Pollock (1996: 70).

16. The original statue no longer exists and is now known to us via Roman copies such as the Colonna Venus in the Museo Pio-Clementino, Vatican Museums collection, and the Ludovisi Venus (second century CE) in the Roman National Museum, Palazzo Altemps, Rome.
17. Jones was one of the architects responsible for the Fine Arts Courts at the Exhibition. Due to the critical furore that ensued, he felt obliged to mount a defence, which he published under the title *An Apology for the Colouring of the Greek Court* (1854).
18. *The Pursuit of the Well-Beloved. A Sketch of a Temperament* was serialised in the *Illustrated News* from 1 October to 17 December 1892; *The Well-Beloved. A Sketch of a Temperament* was published in volume form in March 1897.
19. In *The Pursuit of the Well-Beloved*, Jocelyn's surname is spelt 'Pearston'.
20. Reference to the native islanders who protected themselves by slinging stones (Hardy 1997: 354, n. 4).
21. Among them, the custom of pre-marital sex to prove a woman's fertility.
22. The serialised version of the novel shares a tripartite structure with the later text, but the plot differs in some aspects. In *The Pursuit* Pearston, engaged to the first Avice, elopes with Marcia Bencomb whom he marries. The marriage is unhappy and they agree to separate. Later, believing Marcia dead, Pearston falls in love with the succeeding Avices. He marries Avice III, but plans to release her by committing suicide when he discovers that she has a prior attachment to a younger man. Almost drowned, he is rescued and nursed by his first wife Marcia, now old and withered, who has returned to the island.
23. For a further discussion of the Platonic ideal in *The Well-Beloved*, see Steele (2006).
24. Richard Thomas Gallienne (1866–1947) was a poet, journalist and aesthete who in the 1890s was a contributor to *The Yellow Book*.
25. It is worth noting that this 'Classical training' would have consisted of drawing and painting sculptures. The period in which these artists were producing works influenced by antique statues corresponds with the rise in the number of art students admitted to the sculpture galleries of the British Museum for the purpose of copying sculptures. As a Royal Academician of the late-Victorian period who sculpted classical subjects, Pierston may also be considered an 'Olympian Dreamer'.
26. See also Hatt (2001).
27. Jane Thomas notes that Hardy was introduced to both Thornycroft and Woolner in 1883 and that when 'Hardy and Thornycroft were introduced . . . Hamo was probably the most talked about sculptor of the day'; Edmund Gosse, Thornycroft's close friend and supporter, who had known Hardy since the 1870s, was instrumental in developing the writer's knowledge of classical and neoclassical sculpture (2018: 8–9).

28. The awkwardness of taking a statue down from its pedestal and laying it on a bed is reimagined by Morris in 'Pygmalion and the Image' discussed in Chapter 1.
29. Two nouns: 'necrophiliac' and 'necrophile' describe people who engage in such practices, and 'necrophiliac' is also used as an adjective. Throughout this book, unless quoting directly, I use the term 'necrophiliac' as both adjective and noun.
30. Scobie and Taylor write: '[m]ost tales of agalmatophilia were associated with Praxiteles' naked statue of Aphrodite that was exhibited at an open shrine on the island of Knidos and it apparently deranged many visitors' (1975: 50–1). They cite works by Pliny, Valerius Maximus, Pseudo-Lucian and Lucian as sources.
31. Eleanor O'Shaughnessy (née Marston) was the daughter of the dramatist and critic John Westland Marston (1819–90). Marston wrote several plays including *The Patrician's Daughter* (1841), *The Wife's Portrait* (1862), *Life for Life* (1869) and *Under Fire* (1885). He became editor of the *National Magazine* in 1837 and from around 1863 wrote critical pieces for the *Athenaeum*.

Chapter 3

'Of marble men and maidens': Sculptural Transformations

In Nathaniel Hawthorne's *The Marble Faun* (1860), another important sculpture by Praxiteles becomes the focus of desire. In their discussion of Hawthorne's use of the visual arts in his works, Rita Gollin and John Idol trace his engagement with painting and sculpture in the exhibitions and galleries he encountered during his sojourn in Europe in 1853–60, which he detailed in his English, French and Italian Notebooks.[1] From their observations, it is clear that, faced in these spaces with antique sculpture, Hawthorne, like George Eliot's Dorothea and Thomas Hardy, felt overwhelmed by the burden of history. Following a second visit to the British Museum he finds himself crushed by the 'dead weight' of the past that had struck him on the first and wishes 'that the Elgin marbles and the frieze of the Parthenon were all burnt to lime' (qtd in Gollin and Idol 1991: 72). Yet, once he becomes more familiar with the collections and discovers that he is no longer 'weighed down by the multitude of things to be seen', he is able 'to discern "grace and nobility" even in the "battered and shattered" remains of Greek sculpture' (Gollin and Idol 1991: 73).[2] Gollin and Idol observe that, in time, Hawthorne came to prefer sculpture to painting, in part due to its realism, and that his appreciation of statuary improved with greater exposure to it, especially in Rome and Florence where he begins to engage in Pygmalionesque fantasies of animation. In Rome he admires 'Michelangelo's Lorenzo de Medici ... because "after looking at it a little while, the spectator ceases to think of it as a marble statue; it comes to life"':

> on one visit to the Vatican's sculpture gallery, the Apollo Belvedere suddenly [seems] 'ethereal and godlike; only for a flitting moment, however, and as if he had alighted from heaven, or shone suddenly out of sunlight, and then had withdrawn himself again'. (Gollin and Idol 1991: 90)

Figure 3.1 The *Medici Venus*, Hellenistic copy after original by Praxiteles c.370–330 BCE, Roman, first century, marble (Galleria degli Uffizi, Florence). Bridgeman Images

His experiences with sculpture in Rome evidently affected his perception and recognition of statuary. In a diary entry dated 8 June 1858 in *The French and Italian Notebooks*, Hawthorne logs a visit to the Uffizi, during which he pays special attention to the gallery's statues. As he retraces his steps for his readers, he notes that its labyrinthine rooms are filled with 'many beautiful specimens of antique, ideal sculpture ... Apollos, Bacchuses, Venuses, Mercurys, Fauns' all of which are now so familiar to him that he can recognise them 'at a glance' (Hawthorne 1980: 296). But the *Venus de' Medici* (Figure 3.1), the 'mystery and wonder of the gallery' appears to elude him and he seems unsettled at the thought of seeing her:

> I could not quite believe that I was not to find the *Venus de' Medici*; and still, as I passed from one room to another, my breath rose and fell a little, with the half-hope, half-fear, that she might stand before me. Really, I did not know that I cared so much about Venus, or any possible woman of marble. (1980: 297)

Of his eventual encounter with the statue in the Tribune, he writes:

> She is very beautiful ... and has a fresh and new charm about her, unreached by any cast or copy that I have seen. The hue of the marble is just so much mellowed by time as to do for her all that Gibson tries, or ought, to try, to do for his statues by color; softening her, warming her almost imperceptibly, making her an inmate of the heart as well as a spiritual existence. I felt a kind of tenderness for her; an affection, not as if she were one woman, but all womankind in one. Her modest attitude – which, before I saw her I had not liked, deeming that it might be an artificial shame – is partly what unmakes her as the heathen goddess, and softens her into woman. (1980: 297–8)

In this description, time seems to have warmed the statue to life, effecting a transformation that in Ovid occurs at Pygmalion's touch as the ivory seemingly softens, like the wax of Hymettus, and becomes flesh (2008: X, ll. 288–93). In this passage, a similar transmutation occurs: the goddess melds into a universal symbol of womanhood and Hawthorne's doubts concerning her modesty dissolve. But Hawthorne's passage also refers to another sculptural figure, John Gibson's *Tinted Venus*, which he had seen while on a visit to Harriet Hosmer's studio and to which he appears to have been attracted, though unsettled by the impropriety of the statue's life-like colouring. Of Gibson's Venus, Hawthorne writes:

> The tint of the Venus seemed to be a very delicate, almost imperceptible shade of yellow, I think, or buff ... I must say that there was something fascinating and delectable in the warm, yet delicate tint of the beautiful nude Venus, although, I should have preferred to dispense with the colouring of the eyes and hair; nor am I at all certain that I should not, in the end, like the snowy whiteness better for the whole statue. Indeed, I am almost sure I should; for this lascivious warmth of hue quite demoralizes the chastity of the marble, and makes one feel ashamed to look at the naked limbs in the company of women. (1980: 157)

Following a further visit to the Uffizi, Hawthorne juxtaposes the two statues once more in his thoughts; he finds that the *Venus de' Medici*'s charm 'does not diminish on better acquaintance' and wonders how, given that the Venus is 'incapable of decay and death' and will be 'as young and fair as long as a beautiful thought shall require physical embodiment', any sculptor 'has had the impertinence to aim at any other presentation of female beauty' (1980: 308). He goes on to declaim that, while he 'means no disrespect to Gibson or Powers, or a hundred other men who people the world with nudities', the world 'would be all the richer if their Venuses, their Greek Slaves . . . were burnt into quicklime' leaving only the *Venus de' Medici* 'as our image of the beautiful' (1980: 308).

Hawthorne's privileging of the antique Venus at the expense of her contemporary counterpart anticipates Arthur O'Shaughnessy's 'Dialogue between Two Venuses' where Praxiteles' Venus is considered the superior sculpture. However, Hawthorne's preference for the *Venus de' Medici* may have less to do with the glories of ancient sculpture than with an aversion to neoclassical statues such as those of Gibson and Powers whose nudity may have seemed gratuitous to him, and unsanctioned by pagan religion.[3] Writing of Hawthorne's disapproval of nude statuary, Henry James observes:

> The plastic sense was not strong in Hawthorne; there can be no better proof of it than his curious aversion to the representation of the nude in sculpture. This aversion was deep-seated; he constantly returns to it, exclaiming upon the incongruity of modern artists making naked figures. He apparently quite failed to see that nudity is not an incident, or accident, of sculpture, but its very essence and principle; and his jealousy of undressed images strikes the reader as a strange, vague, long-dormant heritage of his straight-laced Puritan ancestry. (1883: 161)

For James, then, Hawthorne's distaste for contemporary 'nudities' is based on his puritanism, yet his concerted engagement with the sculptural body – both antique and modern – in *The Marble Faun* (1860) suggests complex negotiations of desire that eschew this simple explanation, and the novel's Roman setting, replete with galleries, public sculpture and sculptors' studios, offers an interesting location in which to explore the clash between pagan and contemporary culture that causes Hawthorne such unease.

Hawthorne's Roman Romance

Notably, Rome – and Italy more broadly – also features in James's own exploration of creative and sexual desire in his early novel, *Roderick Hudson* (1875).[4] Italy has often featured significantly in the nineteenth-century American imagination and the list of American authors who have written about Italy, in either journals or literary works, is long enough to merit a comprehensive study; indeed, the critic Nathalia Wright has argued that 'no other foreign country has figured so provocatively in American fiction' (1965: 29). For nineteenth-century American tourists, Italy held a special fascination and, in particular, Rome's architectural layers, and plethora of antiquities offered a close encounter with the European cultural heritage that had nourished their ancestors, and that their own country could not match. The number of American visits to Rome rose considerably in the nineteenth century, increasing from approximately 200 in 1835, and 1,000 in 1840, to 30,000 by 1900 (Brodhead 1990: xiii). For one of these tourists, Henry Leland, Rome is the 'antithesis' of America; it is 'all of the past' and 'full of lessons' (1863: 3). For others, the historical materiality of Rome challenged both notions of identity and sexuality, undermining American ideas of civilization and morality (Martin and Person 2002: 1-2).

While in Italy in 1858–9, engaging in his own touristic encounter with the city, Hawthorne moved in Roman circles of expatriate artists that included the American sculptors Paul Akers, William Wetmore Story, Randolph Rogers and Harriet Hosmer.[5] *The Marble Faun: Or, The Romance of Monte Beni*, to give its full title, features romanticised versions of such artists, and unwittingly contributed to American tourism, providing an unofficial guide to Rome (Brodhead 1990: xii). However, as Deanna Fernie has argued, 'sculpture in Hawthorne is never simply about sculpture' (2011: 8). The novel's plot centres on four protagonists: Miriam, an artist with a secret past that torments her; Hilda, a copyist; Kenyon, a sculptor who is in love with Hilda; and Donatello, their Italian friend who is in love with Miriam.[6] The novel plays with the multi-layered history of Rome, and its pagan, medieval and renaissance pasts infiltrate the present in unexpected ways: the friends note that Donatello is the double of Praxiteles' marble faun, displayed in the Capitoline Museums, a doubling that 'might be tested by absolute touch and measurement' (Hawthorne 1990a: 7); Hilda becomes increasingly identified with the Virgin Mary; and Miriam and Hilda are implicitly associated with the renaissance parricide, Beatrice Cenci.[7]

As the novel progresses, the foursome's friendships are seriously tested. Miriam is pursued through the streets of Rome by a man they name 'The Model', a sinister figure from her past, and Donatello, wishing to free her from his power, murders him and loses his faun-like innocence in the process. While bringing Miriam and Donatello closer together, this act alienates Hilda from them both but especially from Miriam with whom she has a close friendship. Kenyon, ignorant of the crime, cannot understand the change in Donatello, nor Hilda's change of heart regarding Miriam. Donatello and Miriam, now criminal and accomplice, sully their friends' purity but, arguably, this 'purity' is already in question and the foursome's relationships complicate any simple notion of heterosexual couplings. As a symbol of pagan licence and sexual ambiguity, the sculptural body of Hawthorne's faun, which is at the heart of the novel and binds the protagonists, channels the erotic instability of the friends' desires, and calls attention to other statues in the text that have significant implications for my reading of Hawthorne's text. Prior to the publication of the American edition of *The Marble Faun* in March 1860, Hawthorne's final novel appeared in Britain, in February of the same year, as *Transformation: Or, The Romance of Monte Beni*, a title which, it seems, he subsequently 'resisted using' (MacKay 1984: 102). This resistance posits a tension between the two titles: 'Transformation' suggests slippage, change and ambiguity, while the 'marble' body of the faun focuses the mind on stasis, ossification and fossilisation. This movement from animation to stasis is also charted through the explicit and implicit erotic relationships of the novel's main characters – Miriam, Hilda, Kenyon and Donatello – a movement that is played out via the sculptural bodies that appear in the text and the tactile responses they elicit.[8]

The novel opens with a chapter dedicated to the four protagonists in which they visit a sculpture gallery at the Capitoline Museums in Rome. Here, they encounter the eponymous 'marble faun', the Faun of Praxiteles, which they identify as Donatello's double. However, before the faun appears, we are greeted by other statues which are of equal if unacknowledged importance. Hawthorne writes:

> FOUR INDIVIDUALS, in whose fortunes we should be glad to interest the reader, happened to be standing in one of the saloons of the sculpture-gallery, in the Capitol, at Rome. It was in that room . . . in the centre of which reclines the noble and most pathetic figure of the Dying Gladiator, just sinking into his death-swoon. Around the walls stand the Antinous, the Amazon, the Lycian Apollo, the Juno, all famous productions of antique sculpture. (1990a: 5)

The sculptural figures depicted here point to significant events and themes in Hawthorne's novel. At the core of the story lies a sin, ostensibly a murder: Donatello kills 'The Model'. This act is prompted by Miriam's gaze, which is interpreted by Donatello as a look of assent. It is a deed that proceeds to bind them 'closer than a marriage-bond' (1990a: 174). The *Dying Gladiator* (Figure 3.2) is mentioned briefly prior to the incident. As the group take a moonlit walk, they stop

110 The Sculptural Body in Victorian Literature

Figure 3.2 The *Dying Gladiator*, also known as the *Dying Gaul*, Roman copy of a Greek original of the late third century BCE, marble (Capitoline Museums, Rome). © Look and Learn / Bridgeman Images

at the Colosseum, where, we learn, a black cross 'marks one of the especial blood-spots of the earth, where, thousands of times over, the Dying Gladiator fell, and more human agony has been endured, for the mere pastime of the multitude, than on the breadth of many battle-fields'; the 'crime and the suffering' symbolised by the black cross, prefiguring the crime and suffering to come following the murder of The Model (1990a: 154). The Capitoline Antinous and the Lycian Apollo also have interesting connotations. The Antinous, representing the emperor Hadrian's lover signals the novel's homoerotic subtext as indeed does the Lycian Apollo, given that Apollo is a god who, in Greek myth, loves the beautiful boy, Hyacinthus, a name that functions as a homosexual pseudonym.[9] Sharing the faun's ephebic masculinity, the Antinous and Apollo, by association, draw attention to Donatello's own sexual ambiguity and, arguably, the Apollo also stands for Kenyon who, as a sculptor, indulges in what Nietzsche defined as an Apollonian art (2003: 14).[10] Similarly, the Amazon and the Juno have their counterparts in Hilda and Miriam. The Amazon mirrors Hilda's asexuality and the latter's name, meaning 'battle-maiden' (Baym 1971: 359), recalls the Amazon's military prowess, while the Juno, whose name can mean 'vital force' (Eliade 1982: 125), captures Miriam's sexual energy and, connoting maternal worship, hints at Miriam's implicit role as the object of Hilda's homoerotic desire.[11]

These sculptural doubles point to other aesthetic doublings that occur in the text. Jonathan Auerbach notes that throughout *The Marble Faun* 'the Actual' and 'the Imaginary' are constantly in flux (1980: 104). As Auerbach explains, 'people gain identity through works of art, and works of art are transformed into human beings'; moreover, Miriam and Donatello become 'living models' who are 'repeatedly defined in terms of art objects': Kenyon refers to the Faun of Praxiteles as Donatello's 'identity' and we only know what Miriam looks like from the narrator's description of her self-portrait (1980: 104). Similarly, Kenyon's *Cleopatra* (Figure 3.3), based on William Wetmore Story's statue of the same name, functions as a sculptural double for Miriam (Hawthorne 1990a: 126).[12] As Miriam views the sculpture in Kenyon's studio, she proposes that the Cleopatra looks as if she 'had sunk down out of the fever and turmoil of her life', had 'for one instant . . . relinquished all activity', and is now resting

Figure 3.3 William Wetmore Story, *Cleopatra*, 1858, marble (Metropolitan Museum of Art, New York). Bridgeman Images

'throughout every vein and muscle' (1990a: 126). Yet this statue of Cleopatra at rest has a hidden energy: in its repressed passion and desolation, figured in a repose 'held between two pulse-throbs', Miriam recognises her own (1990a: 126). For Miriam it is 'the repose of despair', but she knows that 'deep down in the woman's heart' is 'a great, smouldering furnace' (1990a: 126). While the repose seems to her 'as complete as if she were never to stir hand or foot again', such is 'the creature's latent energy and fierceness, she might spring up on you like a tigress, and stop the very breath that you were now drawing, midway in your throat' (1990a: 126). Prompted by what she perceives to be Kenyon's understanding of such a woman, Miriam considers revealing her secret past to him but, sensing his reluctance to know, exclaims, 'You can do nothing for me, unless you petrify me into a marble companion for your Cleopatra there' (1990a: 129).[13]

This combination of dangerous energy and 'repose' recurs in the image of Beatrice Cenci in which Miriam and Hilda are twinned.[14] Spencer Hall argues that the painting functions as 'a kind of nexus' between the two women, a '"symbolic mirror" in which each recognizes both self and other, thus reflecting the inexorable bond of common humanity' that binds them together (1970: 86). Hall points to two key moments in the text when this 'mirroring' occurs in chapters entitled respectively 'Beatrice' and 'Miriam and Hilda' (1970: 86–7). He notes that in these chapters the women's images appear at times to merge in interesting ways and these moments of identification merit closer examination. In 'Beatrice', while looking at her copy of Guido Reni's painting of the parricide, Hilda declares her 'a fallen angel, and yet sinless', a phrase which foreshadows both women's negotiations of guilt and innocence following their witnessing of Donatello's crime (Hawthorne 1990a: 66). Later, in 'Miriam and Hilda' which occurs after the murder and charts an encounter between the former friends, the painting once again takes centre stage:

> The chair, in which Hilda sat, was near the portrait of Beatrice Cenci, which had not yet been taken from the easel. It is a peculiarity of this picture, that its profoundest expression eludes a straightforward glance, and can only be caught by side glimpses . . . Now, opposite the easel, hung a looking-glass, in which Beatrice's face and Hilda's were both reflected. In one of her weary, nerveless changes of position, Hilda happened to throw her eyes on the glass, and took in both these images at one unpremeditated glance. She fancied – nor was it without horrour [sic] – that Beatrice's expression, seen aside and vanishing in a moment, had been depicted in her own face, likewise, and flitted from it timorously. (1990a: 205)

The play of reflections depicted in this passage merges Beatrice, Miriam and Hilda, for the doubled expression of innocent fallenness in Beatrice and Hilda is predicated on a doubling between Miriam and Beatrice's father; of Beatrice's expression, the narrator states, 'It was the consciousness of her father's sin that threw its shadow over her', and that, similarly, 'It was the knowledge of Miriam's guilt that lent the same expression to Hilda's face' (1990a: 205). Hall's argument that these moments underscore the women's 'sisterhood' is complicated and eroticised by the fact that Miriam is posited as Francesco Cenci's double, a man accused of incest by his own daughter (Hall 1970: 88). Furthermore, the centrality of Guido Reni's painting in a book primarily concerned with sculpture, hints at displacement and points us towards another image of Beatrice Cenci: Harriet Hosmer's sculptural representation of the same figure (Figure 3.4).

In an essay which considers the impact of Hawthorne's work on that of Henry James, John Carlos Rowe argues that 'Hawthorne's frequent references to Beatrice Cenci, albeit made primarily to Guido Reni's portrait, also include Hosmer's sculpture' and he notes that James referred to Hosmer and her fellow female artists working in Rome in the midnineteenth century disparagingly as a 'strange sisterhood of American

Figure 3.4 Harriet Hosmer, *Beatrice Cenci*, 1857, marble (Art Gallery of New South Wales, Sydney). Bridgeman Images

"lady sculptors"' (2002: 76).¹⁵ James's 'strange sisterhood' no doubt also alludes to the romantic friendships or Boston marriages that were common in Hosmer's circle.¹⁶ Among the same-sex relationships Lillian Faderman identifies in *Surpassing the Love of Men: Romantic Friendship and Love between Women from the Renaissance to the Present* are those between members of 'the Roman colony of artists who gathered around the sculptor Harriet Hosmer' (1981: 219); she observes that 'Hosmer's letters as well as biographies of friends' imply that she probably had romantic friendships with a number of women including the writer Matilda Hays and the American actress Charlotte Cushman (1981: 449, n. 3).¹⁷ Interestingly, in her analysis of Hosmer's sculpture, *Beatrice Cenci*, Vivien Green Fryd, using Terry Castle's concept of the apparitional lesbian, suggests that, via the incest taboo, Hosmer's statue 'ghosts' her own complex homoerotic desires.¹⁸ Fryd contends that Hosmer 'was drawn to the contradictions, conflicts, and silences manifested in the Cenci narrative' because 'her own sexuality had to be hidden', her desire buried in the reclining statue of Beatrice Cenci which, lying on its rectangular base, 'evokes entombment' (2006: 306, 300). In *The Marble Faun*, in which Hosmer's statue 'ghosts' the portrait of Beatrice Cenci, sculpture is similarly suggestive of homoerotic desire between Miriam and Hilda, a matter to which I will return later in this chapter.

Fauns of Flesh and Marble

While Hosmer's relationships with women have received critical scrutiny, the erotic charge underlying the relationship between the two women in *The Marble Faun* has been overlooked even though, as Martha Vicinus points out, Hilda is partly modelled on Hosmer (2004: 37). Instead, it is the homoerotic relationship between the men in the novel that has received greater attention. Drawing on Hawthorne's description of the faun in Rome's Capitoline gallery, Robert Martin demonstrates how his fascination with Praxiteles' sculpture is expressed in language resonant of homoerotic desire (Figure 3.5). In an entry dated 30 April 1858, Hawthorne writes:

> The faun is an image of a young man, leaning with one arm upon the trunk or stump of a tree; he has a pipe, or some such instrument of music, in the hand which rests upon the tree, and the other, I think, hangs carelessly by his side. His only garment falls half way down his back, but leaves his whole front, and all the rest of his person, exposed, displaying

Figure 3.5 *Faun*, Roman copy of a Greek original by Praxiteles, fourth century BCE, marble (Capitoline Museums, Rome). © Look and Learn / Bridgeman Images

a very beautiful form, but clad in more flesh, with more full and rounded outlines, and less development of muscle, than the old sculptors were wont to assign to masculine beauty. The figure is not fat, but neither has it the attribute of slender grace. The face has a character corresponding with that of the form; beautiful and most agreeable features, but rounded, especially about the throat and chin; a nose almost straight, yet very slightly curving inward, a voluptuous mouth, that seems (not quite) to smile outright; – in short, the whole person conveys the idea of an amiable and sensual nature, easy, mirthful, apt for jollity, yet not incapable of being touched by pathos. (1980: 191–2)

Martin notes that Hawthorne lovingly records how the faun's front is exposed, 'displaying a very beautiful form' and argues that, in the figure of the faun, he appears to celebrate the male body and, in particular, the faun's 'voluptuous mouth' and 'sensual nature' (2002: 34). In Hawthorne's novel, the narrative draws on this impression, but the language oscillates between images of innocent playfulness and sculptural beauty. Instead of the word 'exposed' which suggests a human figure, the narrator refers to the entire front of the figure being 'nude', thus using a term applied to nakedness in sculptural art

(Hawthorne 1990a: 8). Instead of referring to the faun's 'beautiful form', in the novel the statue is 'marvellously graceful'; the voluptuousness of the mouth characterises the face as a whole and the description of the mouth itself, 'with its full, yet delicate lips' is not equated with the same alluring sensuality, but instead segues seamlessly into the narrator's identification of the faun's 'mirthful[ness]' and 'jollity' (1990a: 8–9). However, here, the statue shares that potential for animation which Hawthorne had formerly identified in the statue of the *Apollo Belvedere* in Rome. Of the faun he writes:

> It is impossible to gaze long at this stone image without conceiving a kindly sentiment towards it, as if its substance were warm to the touch, and imbued with actual life. It comes very close to some of our pleasantest sympathies. (Hawthorne 1990: 9)

In both the original ekphrasis and its fictional revision, Hawthorne's eyes double as tactile fingers that trace the sculpture's line of beauty: the serpentine curves of its 'rounded outline', the similarly 'rounded' and 'voluptuously developed' shape of the faun's face, and the fullness and delicate contours of its lips. Desire is still present in the temptation to 'touch' and in the fantasy of animation, yet it is prompted – ostensibly at least – not by an erotic engagement with the statue, but by a 'kindly sentiment' which recalls that one might feel towards a charming child with whom one is not closely acquainted.

This passage anticipates Walter Pater's discussion of Greek sculpture in 'Winckelmann' where he claims that the 'beauty of the Greek statues was a sexless beauty' (2010: 111), despite the erotic undercurrent of Winckelmann's descriptions of sculpture, most notably of the *Apollo Belvedere* (Figure 3.6). In a famous passage from *History of the Art of Antiquity*, Winckelmann extols the statue's beauty which, he claims, surpasses all other images of Apollo:

> His build is elevated above the human, and his stance bears witness to the fullness of his grandeur. An eternal springtime, like that of the blissful Elysian fields, clothes the alluring virility of mature years with a pleasing youth and plays with soft tenderness upon the lofty structure of his limbs ... No veins or sinews heat and move this body, but rather a heavenly spirit that, flowing like a gentle stream, has saturated, as it were, every contour of this figure ... and his eyes are full of sweetness, as if he were among the muses as they seek to embrace him. ... His soft hair plays about this divine head like the tender, waving tendrils of the noble grapevine stirred ... it seems anointed with the oil of the gods and bound at the crown of his head with lovely splendour by the Graces. (2006: 333–4)

Figure 3.6 Statue known as the *Apollo Belvedere*, copy after Greek bronze original of the fourth century BCE, marble (Vatican Museums and Galleries, Vatican City). De Agostini Picture Library / G. Nimatallah / Bridgeman Images

Additionally, Winckelmann's gaze, like Hawthorne's, invokes an imaginary animation. As Winckelmann writes, 'In gazing upon this masterpiece, I forget all else . . . and I feel myself transported to Delos and the Lycian groves, places Apollo honored with his presence – for my figure seems to take on life and movement, like Pygmalion's beauty' (2006: 334). Stefano Evangelista observes that Winckelmann's 'homoerotic approach to ancient Greek art' engages in a 'complex play of removals and displacements' noting that just as 'the ancient Apollos are always on the point of resuming human shapes, the living Winckelmann is forever trying to fade away into the ancient past' (2009: 31). He argues that in this text 'of suspended atmospheres the ancient and the modern subjects engage in a fantastic "love story"', a Pygmalionesque fantasy in which 'Winckelmann's romance with Apollo is a myth of just reward of sexual desire' (2009: 31). In Winckelmann's ekphrasis, as in Hawthorne's description of Praxiteles' faun, there is a focus on the youthful, virile body, on the flowing contours of the sculptural line, and on the figure's gracefulness. Like Pater's Winckelmann,

Hawthorne 'fingers those pagan marbles with unsinged hands' (Pater 2010: 112) and in both cases the androgynous sculptural body encodes male homoeroticism.

In *The Marble Faun*, the statue's androgyny is transposed onto the living body of Donatello who, in a moment of narrative fantasy that resembles Winckelmann's reverie, imbues the statues in the Capitoline gallery with life:

> [T]he realization of the antique Faun, in the person of Donatello, gave a more vivid character to all these marble ghosts. Why should not each statue grow warm with life! Antinous might lift his brow, and tell us why he is forever sad. The Lycian Apollo might strike his lyre; and, at the first vibration, that other Faun in red marble ... should frisk gaily forth, leading yonder Satyrs ... to clatter their little hoofs upon the floor, and all join hands with Donatello! Bacchus, too, a rosy flush diffusing itself over his time-stained surface, would come down from his pedestal, and offer a cluster of purple grapes to Donatello's lips, because the god recognizes him as the woodland elf who so often shared his revels![19] (Hawthorne 1990a: 18)

Hawthorne extends this animation to 'the exquisitely carved figures' on a sarcophagus,

> who might assume life, and chase one another round its verge with that wild merriment which is so strangely represented on those old burial coffers, though still with some subtle allusion to Death, carefully veiled, but forever peeping forth amid emblems of mirth and riot. (1990a: 18)

This sarcophagus signals what Sheldon Liebman has identified as a recurring motif in *The Marble Faun* to which I will return in my conclusion to this book, but for the moment I wish to focus on the statues of fauns and satyrs, Antinous, Apollo and Bacchus that people Hawthorne's own Winckelmannian daydream (1967: 74). Notably, in this Capitoline fantasy, the narrator makes no mention of the female statues of the Amazon and Juno that are also present in the room,[20] thus suggesting a preference for and delight in the youthful male body of antique Greek sculpture. The image of Bacchus offering 'a cluster of purple grapes to Donatello's lips' and the faun's affinity with the god imply an acknowledgement of Dionysian licence and sexual ambiguity which figure together in the carnivalesque scenes that litter Hawthorne's novel and play a part in the eventual restoration of order. However, it is primarily the slippage between Donatello and the figure of the faun that reinforces the presence of homoerotic attraction, albeit negotiated via the heterosexual couplings of Miriam and Donatello, Kenyon and Hilda. Moreover, this homoerotic desire manifests itself through three key triangular relationships: Miriam, Donatello and Kenyon; Kenyon, Miriam and Hilda; Hilda, Miriam and Donatello.

While acknowledging the problematic nature of René Girard's theory of mimetic desire which is predicated, as Robert Casillo points out, on the primacy of 'normative heterosexuality', the triangular models of desire posited in *The Marble Faun* have interesting implications (1997: 409).[21] In the penultimate chapter of Hawthorne's novel which sets Miriam, Donatello and Kenyon in a Roman carnival, the protagonists hold hands and are referred to by the narrator as 'a linked circle of three' (Hawthorne 1990a: 448) recalling the reverie in the Capitoline Museums where Praxiteles' faun and the marble satyrs also joined hands with Donatello. The word 'circle' points to the implicit 'circulation' of desire that characterises their relationships within the story. Girard's 'mimetic desire' is opposed to 'desire *selon soi*, desire that is a spontaneous and autonomous manifestation of an individual's inherent wants or preferences' (Livingston 1992: 1). As Paisley Livingston explains, instead of having 'an "immediate" relation to his or her object of desire, the person who desires mimetically has a "mediated" relation to them, one that takes a detour through a model' (1992: 1). Desire, then, is considered 'triangular', involving 'the agent who desires, the object of this agent's desire, and the agent who serves as the "model" or "mediator" of the desire' (1992: 1). Although Hilda is ostensibly Kenyon's love object, the doubling of Hilda and Miriam through the figure of Beatrice Cenci complicates the simplicity of that heterosexual coupling. Moreover, his statue of Cleopatra, bearing Miriam's sexual and spiritual energy in its 'hot life', is inspired in a moment of creative passion that is at odds with the tepid nature of his relationship with Hilda (Hawthorne 1990a: 127). When Miriam tells the sculptor, 'My dear friend, it is a great work!' and asks 'How have you learned to do it?' Kenyon replies:

> It is the concretion of a good deal of thought, emotion, and toil of brain and hand ... I kindled a great fire within my mind, and threw in the material ... and, in the midmost heat, uprose Cleopatra, as you see her. (1990a: 127)

Miriam continues:

> What I most marvel at . . . is the womanhood that you have so thoroughly mixed up with all those seemingly discordant elements. Where did you get that secret: You never found it in your gentle Hilda. Yet I recognize its truth. (1990a: 127)

In comparison to the magnificent Cleopatra, clearly modelled on Miriam, Hilda inspires only a fetishistic marble hand, 'delicately sculptured in marble' (1990a: 120).

The contrast between these two works of art suggests a passion for Miriam that is mediated through sculpture. Yet Kenyon also attempts to sculpt a bust of Donatello, an act which consolidates him as the object of Kenyon's homoerotic gaze. Miriam's consciousness of Kenyon's unexpressed attraction to their mutual friend surfaces in a discussion that takes place in the marble saloon of Donatello's Tuscan home. Told that Kenyon plans to ramble among the hills and valleys of the region with Donatello in order to lift his spirits, Miriam 'not without jealousy' comments, 'You are taking him from me, and putting yourself, and all manner of living interests into the place which I ought to fill' (1990a: 285). In reply, Kenyon states:

> I do not pretend to be the guide or counsellor whom Donatello needs; for, to mention no other obstacle, I am a man, and, between man and man, there is always an insuperable gulf. They can never quite grasp each other's hands; and therefore man never derives any intimate help, any heart-substance, from his brother man, but from woman – his mother, his sister, or his wife. (1990a: 285)

Miriam's 'jealousy', or consciousness of Kenyon's latent desire resurfaces towards the end of the novel. '[W]atching the sculptor's eye as it dwelt admiringly on Donatello', Miriam asks 'Is he not beautiful?' (1990a: 434). The first exchange suggests Kenyon's disavowal of his desire for Donatello even as it reinforces it. In recognising that what Donatello needs is a 'mother', a 'sister' or a 'wife', he simultaneously tacitly acknowledges that he is playing at least one, or more, of these parts. In addition, by referring to the emotional and physical gulf between men, he also implicitly suggests his desire to overcome that chasm; to offer that 'intimate help' and 'heart-substance' that it is woman's prerogative to provide, and to grasp Donatello's hand, an intimate touch that is substituted by the 'tactility' of the artist's eye as he contemplates Donatello's beauty. As John Carlos Rowe remarks, such instances represent 'a threatening homoeroticism that conventional modes of homosociality cannot control' (2002: 86). He argues that the 'incomplete friendship' between Kenyon and Donatello, 'qualified as it is by their at times conflicting sexual desires for Miriam and even at times for each other' is a good example of Hawthorne's homoerotic anxieties (2002: 86). In Girardian terms, Kenyon's mimetic desire for Miriam (the object of Donatello's love) is displaced and becomes a homoerotically charged love for Donatello.

This slippage between homoerotic and heterosexual desire is represented in sculptural terms in the modelling of Donatello's bust. Requesting to sculpt him, Kenyon tells Donatello, 'Your head in marble would be a treasure to me. Shall I have it?' (Hawthorne 1990a: 228). Donatello expresses his reluctance finding it troubling to 'be looked at steadfastly' (1990a: 228). In response, Kenyon states that this will be no hindrance, and that he will 'catch the likeness and expression by side-glimpses' recalling those 'side-glimpses' required to obtain a true view of Reni's image of Beatrice Cenci, thus linking Donatello to the doubled images of Miriam and Hilda. However, the process presents Kenyon with unexpected difficulties. He finds that, despite his best efforts, he has trouble 'hitting the likeness' and capturing the inner thought on the outer surface of the countenance:

> Wielding that wonderful power which sculptors possess over moist clay, . . . he compressed, elongated, widened, and otherwise altered the features of the bust, in mere recklessness, and, at every change, inquired of the Count whether the expression became anywise more satisfactory.
>
> 'Stop!' cried Donatello, at last, catching the sculptor's hand. 'Let it remain so!'
>
> By some accidental handling of the clay, entirely independent of his own will, Kenyon had given the countenance a distorted and violent look . . . Had Hilda, or had Miriam, seen the bust, with the expression it had now assumed, they might have recognized Donatello's face as they beheld it at that terrible moment, when he held his victim over the edge of the precipice. (1990a: 270–3)

Ignoring Donatello's protestations, Kenyon continues to mould the clay with his 'artful fingers' thus compelling the bust 'to dismiss the expression that had so startled them both' (1990a: 273). Leland Person claims that this incident and its dramatic climax are revealing. For Person, 'Donatello's bust operates like a prosthesis, a second, replicated head', and he reads Donatello's staying of Kenyon's hand as a 'homo-aesthetic orgasm', a 'laying on of hands in a play of passion that massages another man's body until he cries out in pleasure and self-recognition' (2002: 121–2). Here, the act of sculpting is itself eroticised. However, he acknowledges that the process is given 'a perverse twist' and argues that 'What Kenyon brings forth . . . is an erotically charged Donatello, but constructed heterosexually through Miriam's desiring gaze into a homosocial and jealous lover' (2002: 122), one whose deed binds them 'closer than a marriage-bond' (Hawthorne 1990a: 174). It is unsurprising, then, that Kenyon ignores Donatello's desire to still the bust's expression, and proceeds to remodel the head to his own satisfaction.

Sister-Wives: Hilda and Miriam

Intriguingly, Miriam also shares a 'marriage-bond' with Hilda. This suggests a triangular Girardian relationship between Kenyon, Hilda and Miriam in which Hilda's heterosexual coupling with Kenyon displaces her homoerotic desire for Miriam. This is implied in the text by the language used to describe the women's relationship. Considering the nature of Miriam's sin and her own rejection of her former friend, Hilda asks herself 'whether there were not other questions to be considered, aside from the single one of Miriam's guilt or innocence; as, for example, whether a close bond of friendship . . . ought to be severed on account of any unworthiness' which is subsequently detected in one's friend (1990a: 385). 'For', Hilda considers, 'in these unions of hearts, (call them marriage, or whatever else) we take each other for better, for worse' (1990a: 385). Earlier in the novel, when Miriam visits Hilda following the murder of The Model, she tells her, 'I loved you dearly! I love you still! You were to me as a younger sister; yes, dearer than sisters of the same blood' (1990a: 207). The relationship between Miriam and Hilda is posited as a form of romantic friendship that recalls those of their real-life 'sisters', Henry James's 'strange sisterhood' of American artists, and hints at homoerotic desire between the two women.

Moreover, it seems significant that Hilda's 'marriage-bond' with Miriam mimics Donatello's own, a bond that is forged at the very moment The Model is murdered. Interestingly, this moment also has important repercussions for Hilda's sense of self. According to Person, the crime marks Donatello's fall 'into heterosexuality', transforming him into 'a man who instantaneously enjoys a "union" born in passion, [that is] "cemented with blood"' (2002: 121). Crucially, Hilda witnesses this crime, and feels herself 'stained with guilt' and 'spotted' with sin, resulting in her confession to a Catholic priest (Hawthorne 1990: 205, 329). In her essay on Harriet Hosmer's implicit presence in *The Marble Faun*, Nancy Proctor argues that Donatello's crime hides another crime which is also 'a crime of passion, a crime of desire' (2002: 62). This crime centres on Hosmer, the absent woman sculptor who, in Hawthorne's novel is, like Edgar Allan Poe's 'purloined letter', hidden in full view (2002: 62–3). But equally, Donatello's crime hides another 'sin', one that, like the crime, is founded on desire and again, like Poe's purloined letter, is there for us to find if we would only look in the right place or pose the right questions. One might ask, for example, what is the sin by which Hilda feels stained? Is it truly her ambiguous position as bystander at the time of the murder, or is it something else? Does the murder, while triggering an eroticised moment of heterosexual desire between Miriam and Donatello, similarly provoke Hilda's tacit recognition of her own love for Miriam? Her actions, following the murder, could certainly be construed as those of a spurned lover. Miriam's role in the murder is interpreted, by Hilda, as an act of 'faithlessness' and she decides that they must thenceforth 'be forever strangers' (Hawthorne 1990a: 206).

The imagery used to describe Hilda following the murder of The Model, her obsession with the Virgin Mary, despite being a 'daughter of the Puritans' (1990a: 362), and the doubling between Miriam and herself, all point towards a homoerotic subtext that requires attention. The slippage between Hilda's innocence and guilt is figured graphically in the image of her painted by an Italian artist who frequents the same galleries. The painting and its subsequent purchase by a 'picture-dealer' are described to the reader in detail:

> It represented Hilda as gazing, with sad and earnest horrour [sic], at a blood-spot which she seemed just then to have discovered on her white robe. ... By many connoisseurs, the idea of the face was supposed to have been suggested by the portrait of Beatrice Cenci ... But the modern artist strenuously upheld the originality of his own picture, as well as the stainless purity of its subject, and chose to call it, (and was laughed at for his pains,) 'Innocence, dying of a Blood-stain!' (1990a: 330)

When the artist takes the picture to the dealer, the latter tells him it would fetch a better price if he gave it 'a more intelligible title', and argues:

> 'Looking at the face and expression of this fair Signorina, we seem to comprehend ... that she is undergoing one or another of those troubles of the heart, to which young ladies are but too liable. But what is this

Blood-stain? And what has Innocence to do with it? ... The picture being now my property, I shall call it "The Signorina's Vengeance." She has stabbed her lover, over night, and is repenting it betimes, the next morning. So interpreted, the picture becomes an intelligible and very natural representation of a not uncommon fact.' (1990a: 331)

This debate between artist and buyer symbolises the tacit struggle between author and reader and the vagaries of interpretation, while also drawing attention to transformation and thus the ambiguous titling of Hawthorne's novel. However, on another level, it also problematises Hilda's sorrow, and casts doubt on whether the stain that mars her innocence is caused by her own or another's actions or guilt. Furthermore, the picture-dealer's interpretation of the painting as that of a vengeful lover, eroticises the cause of Hilda's grief and the reasons behind it. The focus on the staining and spotting of Hilda's whiteness also hints at homoeroticism; 'Krafft-Ebing cited a hereditary *taint* [my emphasis]' as the cause of homosexuality, and the sexological 'stigma' attached to lesbianism (Jeffreys 1985: 112) associates it 'with both stain and disease' (Pulham 2008a: 83). This suggests that the stains and spots that colour Hilda's conscience imply more than simply her guilty knowledge of the murder.

Similarly, Hilda's increasing obsession with the Virgin Mary, as the novel progresses, has important implications. Hilda is keeper of the Virgin's shrine that crowns the tower in which she lives; she lights the Virgin's lamp and tends the doves that flutter round it. In her grief, she turns to the Virgin's image again and again. While she trims the lamp, she gazes 'at the sacred image', fancies 'a woman's tenderness responding to her gaze' and prays, seeking 'the sympathy of Divine Womanhood' (Hawthorne 1990a: 332). Later, during her aimless wanderings around Rome she lingers 'before the shrines and chapels of the Virgin' and departs from them 'with reluctant steps' (1990a: 347), anticipating Freud's Dora who spends '*two hours* in front of the Sistine Madonna, rapt in silent admiration' and who was herself in love with another woman (1977: 135–6; original emphasis). Yet, we learn that Hilda 'never found just the Virgin Mother whom she needed', that she 'looked for ... a face of celestial beauty, but human as well as heavenly, and with the shadow of past grief upon it; bright with immortal youth, yet matronly and motherly, and endowed with a queenly dignity, but infinitely tender' (Hawthorne 1990a: 348). Hilda's quest is doomed to fail because, whether she knows it or not, it is Miriam she seeks.[22] Miriam, a beautiful woman, shares the Virgin's 'celestial beauty' that is both 'human' and 'heavenly'; she carries a past sorrow; her own 'queenly dignity' is enough to inspire Kenyon to sculpt the Cleopatra;[23] and, prior to the murder, she is tender and loving towards Hilda. Moreover, her affinity with the statue of Juno, mentioned above, endows her with maternal attributes.

In her discussion of the importance of the Virgin Mary for homosexual couples, and same-sex communities such as the Anglican sisterhoods established under the influence of Edward Pusey, Ruth Vanita writes:

> Mary, flying in the face of biology and heterosexual normativity, is the exemplary figure for the odd lives of male and female saints who choose same-sex community over marriage ... It does not seem to me accidental that a liturgy to the Virgin is part of every ceremony of same-sex union unearthed by John Boswell; she is called upon to bless these unions along with Christ and other saints but is not invoked in the same way in heterosexual marriage services.[24] (1996: 8–9)

The link between Hilda and same-sex sisterhoods has been established, but it is additionally worth noting that she is also referred to as a 'Saint', both prior to her acknowledgement of Kenyon's love, and after, when we are told that, following her marriage, she herself will become a form of religious statue, 'enshrined and worshipped as a household Saint' (Hawthorne 1990a: 53, 461). It seems that, even as a bride, Hilda will mirror the Virgin Mary. Yet, paradoxically, towards the end of *The Marble Faun*, Hilda the Virgin seemingly 'transforms' into a pagan statue of Venus.[25]

Seeking Venus

In a sense, this is unsurprising given that Hilda is described in sculptural terms throughout the novel. She dresses in 'white' and is 'white-souled', displaying a whiteness that permeates to her core (1990a: 202). The 'small, beautifully shaped hand ... delicately sculpted in marble' by Kenyon functions synecdochically for the beautiful, delicate, yet rigid Hilda whose white soul permits no sympathetic or empathetic understanding; Kenyon's devotion to his 'cold art' and sculptural objects that he perceives as 'Being of so cold and pure a substance' similarly mirror his devotion to the 'cold', 'white' and 'pure' Hilda (1990a: 390). Moreover, her affinity with Venus is prefigured by her doves which are traditionally recognised as Venus Aphrodite's birds (Lee 2006: 81, n. 2). This 'transformation' from Christian Virgin to pagan goddess is reinforced by the description of the marble Venus unearthed during Kenyon's walk on the Campagna. The sculpture is 'either the prototype or a better repetition of the Venus of the Tribune' and 'one of the few works of antique sculpture in which we recognize womanhood . . . without prejudice to its divinity' (Hawthorne 1990a: 423).[26] The moment of discovery is related in detail:

> Protruding from the loose earth . . . Kenyon beheld the fingers of a marble hand; it was still appended to its arm, and a little further search enabled him to find the other. Placing these limbs in what the nice adjustment of the fractures proved to be their true position, the poor, fragmentary woman forthwith showed that she retained her modest instincts to the last. . . . For these long–buried hands immediately disposed themselves in the manner that nature prompts, as the antique artist knew, and as all the world has seen, in the Venus de' Medici. (1990a: 423)

Kenyon's eyes land, in the first instance, on 'the fingers of a marble hand' recalling the sculpted image of Hilda's own hand. The focus on the Venus's 'womanhood' accompanied by 'modesty' and divinity also lead us back to the saintly Hilda. But we do not have to rely simply on our conjectures: Kenyon makes the connection explicit when he exclaims, 'What a discovery is here! . . . I seek for Hilda, and find a marble woman!' (1990a: 423). The statue's 'snowy lustre', mirroring Hilda's whiteness, only serves to strengthen the similarity between these two objects of desire (1990a: 424).

Nina Baym points out that it is, in fact, Miriam and Donatello, whom she refers to as 'Venus and Eros in the flesh', who are the original discoverers of the statue, and claims that the encounter marks the renewal of their love (1971: 373).[27] Nevertheless, it is significant that Hilda, represented by the Venus – a marble double of Miriam's rather more earthy version of the goddess – is at the heart of this rediscovery of their desire for each other. As at the precise moment of Donatello's crime, the union between Donatello and Miriam is mirrored by the figurative union of Miriam and Hilda. However, what is it in the unearthing, reburial and re-excavation of sculpture that signals – at least in the context of the novel itself – the reestablishment of heterosexual couplings? To consider this, we need to return to the scenes that take place in Kenyon's studio between Miriam and the sculptor. The finding of 'true womanhood' suggested in this scene by the unearthing of the Venus, whose counterpart is Hilda, is complicated by the discussion that accompanies Miriam's discovery of Hilda's sculpted hand in Kenyon's studio kept by him in 'a little old-fashioned ivory coffer, yellow with age' (Hawthorne 1990a: 120). Lifting its lid, Miriam finds 'lapped in fleecy cotton, a small, beautifully shaped hand, most delicately sculptured in marble' (1990a: 120). On this hand, 'Such loving care and nicest art had been lavished . . . that the palm really seemed to have a tenderness in its very substance' and 'Touching those lovely fingers, – had the jealous sculptor allowed you to touch, – you could hardly believe that a virgin warmth would not steal from them into your heart' (1990a: 120).

Here, mediating Miriam's response, the narrator engages in a pygmalionesque fantasy of animation. Yet the hand – inert, buried in its coffer, covered in its 'fleecy cotton' shroud – also suggests an agalmatophiliac, or perhaps necrophilic, pleasure. Viewing it, Miriam asks: 'How have you persuaded that shy maiden to let you take her hand in marble?' thus equating the process of sculpting Hilda's hand to taking her hand in marriage (1990a: 121). To which Kenyon replies: 'Never! She never knew it! . . . I stole it from her' (1990a: 121). While the narrator implies that Kenyon is 'anxious to vindicate his mistress's maidenly reserve', the nuptial allusions mentioned above, suggest that the process of sculpting Hilda's hand without her consent equates to a non-consensual erotic experience (1990a: 121). Moreover, Miriam's observation that Kenyon 'must have wrought it passionately, in spite of its maiden palm and dainty fingertips' only reinforces this perception. Hilda's unattainability is further marked by her self-sufficiency. When Miriam expresses her hope that he will win Hilda's hand one day, Kenyon replies: 'I have little ground to hope it . . . gentle and soft as she appears, it will be . . . difficult to win her heart'; he observes that despite her 'delicacy and fragility' she gives the impression of 'being utterly sufficient to herself' and exclaims, 'No; I shall never win her . . . she has no need of love' (1990a: 121). In response, Miriam observes, 'It is a mistaken idea, which men generally entertain, that nature has made women especially prone to throw their whole being into what is technically called love' and notes,

> When women have other objects in life, they are not apt to fall in love. I can think of many women distinguished in art, literature, and science . . . who lead high, lonely lives, and are conscious of no sacrifice so far as your sex is concerned. (1990a: 121)

In doing so, she draws attention to Hilda as a double for Harriet Hosmer and representative of the 'strange sisterhood' of women artists by whom Hawthorne was inspired.

In contrast to Hilda's cold, marble hand, Kenyon's Cleopatra, inspired by Miriam, is equated with heat and tactile warmth: 'Were you not afraid to touch her, as she grew more and more towards hot life beneath your hand?' asks Miriam of Kenyon, invoking the eroticism of Pygmalion's touch as he caresses his statue to life (1990a: 120). In a novel that focuses on sculpture, the language of tactility becomes the code through which desire is expressed. Kenyon's modelling of Donatello's head substitutes for his lament that men 'can never quite grasp each other's hands' in intimate friendship (1990a: 285). Conversely, the rupture in Hilda's friendship with Miriam, expressed in the language of sisterhood, is marked by her refusal to hold Miriam's hand. As Hilda rejects her, Miriam states,

> You were to me as a younger sister; yes, dearer than sisters of the same blood ... will you not touch my hand? Am I not the same as yesterday? ... Were you to touch my hand, you would find it as warm to your grasp as ever. (1990a: 207)

While this exchange occurs following the murder of The Model witnessed by Hilda and is therefore rationalised by Hilda's consciousness of Miriam's guilt by association, the references to sisterhood and physical touch also suggest a romantic friendship between women of the kind Miriam alludes to in the discussion that takes place in Kenyon's studio.

The intensity of the relationship between Hilda and Miriam is reinforced when, later in the novel, Hilda visits Kenyon's studio and comments on his Cleopatra. At this point, Kenyon's artisans have almost completed the chiselling of the statue in marble and the Cleopatra 'had now struggled almost out of the imprisoning stone; or, rather, the workmen had found her within the mass of marble, imprisoned there by magic, but still fervid to the touch with fiery life' (1990a: 377).[28] As Hilda views the statue, she tells Kenyon: 'I am ashamed to tell you how much I admire this statue ... No other sculptor could have done it' (1990a: 378). While her reasons for being 'ashamed' are never explained, the oddity of the expression recalls her sense of sinfulness, a sense of guilt that one might argue is here provoked by Hilda's homoerotic desire for Miriam on whom the statue of Cleopatra is reputedly modelled. Such a reading is invited by Hilda's own comment: 'Nobody, I think, ought to read poetry, or look at pictures or statues, who cannot find a great deal more in them than the poet or artist has actually expressed. Their highest merit is suggestiveness' (1990a: 379).

Writing Sculptors: *Roderick Hudson*

Such slippages in sexual identity are similarly expressed through the medium of statuary in *Roderick Hudson* (1875), which follows the fortunes of a young American sculptor, and James's novel has much in common with Hawthorne's *The Marble Faun*. During his own stay in Rome during the winter of 1873–4 James met members of the American artists' circle immortalised in Hawthorne's novel, including the sculptor William Wetmore Story about whom he later wrote *William Wetmore Story and His Friends* (1903), and Harriet Hosmer, whom he compared unkindly to a 'remarkably ugly little grey-haired boy, adorned with a diamond necklace' (James 1974: 339). As David Alworth asserts, *The Marble Faun* is clearly 'a novel that James had in mind as he wrote *Roderick Hudson*' (2015: 221), and as Robert Emmet Long observes, when James began to work on the novel in the winter of 1873–4, 'he must necessarily have been conscious of Hawthorne' as '*The Marble Faun* was by then firmly established as a "classic" work about Americans in Rome' (1976: 312). Moreover, the 'dominance of Hawthorne's influence' on his early writings more generally has also been noted (Long 1976: 312). Both works are set in Rome and James's experiences in the city, Anna de Biasio argues, mark 'a crucial stage' in his early development (de Biasio et al. 2013: 3). For Leland Person, *Roderick Hudson* signifies James's 'coming to terms with Rome and his imaginative relationship with it' which 'alternate[d] maniacally between positive and negative poles' and ends up 'reflected in the novel, ultimately producing a manic plot that ends melodramatically with Roderick Hudson's death' (2013: 40–1). The novels also share a subtext of lost innocence and a focus on four key characters. James's players are the eponymous sculptor Roderick; Rowland Mallet, the rich dilettante who becomes his patron; Mary Garland, Hudson's American fiancée, with whom Mallet ostensibly falls in love; and Christina Light, a European beauty, with whom Hudson becomes fatally infatuated.

In both works the male protagonists are embroiled in complex emotional exchanges that are overtly heterosexual, but which may also be read as covertly homoerotic. According to Naomi Sofer, *Roderick Hudson* exhibits 'a profound pessimism about heterosexual relationships' which are 'destructive to all concerned'; but she notes that 'particular emphasis is placed on homosexuality's deleterious effect on the male characters' in the novel (1999: 186). Nevertheless, the central relationship is one between men that hovers uneasily between the homosocial and the homoerotic. As Sofer observes, in

Roderick Hudson the 'intersection of the homosocial and the heterosexual takes the shape of triangular relationships between two men and a woman' (1999: 186). Her understanding of the way in which such relationships function

> is loosely based on Eve Kosofsky Sedgwick's model of homosocial triangles . . . structural relationships in which a woman is exchanged (not necessarily literally) between men in a transaction that serves to solidify the bonds of homosocial desire and power between men and over women, on which patriarchal society is based. (1999: 186)

As Sedgwick acknowledges, this model of homosociality recasts Girard's 'triangular schematization of the existing European canon in *Deceit, Desire, and the Novel*' which becomes a foundational text for the concept of mimetic theory that is predicated on the imitation of another's desire; this phenomenon may result in rivalry, but allows same-sex desire to be mediated by the figure who is ostensibly the object of heterosexual desire (2016: 17). In *Roderick Hudson* as in *The Marble Faun*, homoerotic attraction, then, is facilitated through triangular relationships that exploit Girard's model of mimetic desire and permit expressions of homoeroticism through homosociality.

In her analysis of James's novel, Michèle Mendelssohn concurs that 'the relationship between Roderick, Mary, and Rowland' may be read as an instance of mimetic desire, and argues that Mary is the 'mediator' whose role is to 'create a diversion from the novel's same-sex relationship' (2003: 537). While Mary Garland may be the flesh-and-blood conduit of such passions, I suggest that, as in *The Marble Faun*, the sculptures that feature in the text are far more fascinating mediators of homoerotic love, a desire expressed through visual imagery that doubles as tactile excess. In James's novel, imaginary touch is implicit in visual experience and the mediation between them is present in both aesthetic and erotic processes. In my introduction, I quote Hagi Kenaan who explains that our visual and tactile senses do not function independently of one another, that when sculpture is viewed, we must 'explore an intersection, a double proximity, a tactility whose resonance is visual, and a visuality whose inner pulse is the desire to touch' (2014: 46). Drawing on Merleau-Ponty, Kenaan argues that vision is grounded in the body that sees, and that when that body finds itself in the same space as sculpture, touch is always a possibility if not a certainty (2014: 53–4). It is this play between touch and vision in James's novel that permits the negotiation of same-sex desire primarily through sculpture but additionally, at times, through painting.

Like Hawthorne, on arriving in Rome in 1869 James visited the Capitoline Museums. Writing to his sister Alice, he tells her that he has seen the *Dying Gladiator*, the *Lydian Apollo* and the *Amazon* (James 1974: 167) but, as Person notes, 'James omits any mention of Praxiteles' faun in this letter, even though that sculpture was in the same room at the Capitoline as the sculptures he does mention' (2002: 123). Yet, in *Roderick Hudson* the first statue we encounter is *Thirst*, sculpted by Hudson and given to Mallet's cousin, Cecilia, a figure that is clearly informed by the ephebic figure of the faun:

> The statuette, in bronze, something more than two feet high, represented a naked youth drinking from a gourd. The attitude was perfectly simple. The lad was squarely planted on his feet, with his legs a little apart; his back was slightly hollowed, his head thrown back; his hands were raised to support the rustic cup. There was a loosened fillet of wild flowers about his head, and his eyes, under their dropped lids, looked straight into the cup ... The figure might have been some beautiful youth of ancient fable – Hylas or Narcissus, Paris or Endymion. (James 1986: 59)

The youths mentioned in this passage suggest both homoerotic and heterosexual love. In Greek myth, Hylas is Heracles's lover; in falling in love with his own image, Narcissus implies same-sex desire; Paris seduces Helen of Troy; and Endymion, in one version of the myth is doomed to eternal sleep for falling in love with Hera. As 'cup-bearer', the figure of *Thirst* also connotes Ganymede, the cup-bearer of the gods, and Zeus's beloved.[29] Moreover, despite the heterosexual couplings of Paris and Helen, and Endymion and Hera, Paris and Endymion are also versions of the 'beautiful boy'. The parallels between *Thirst* and Roderick Hudson's own beauty are implied in Mallet's conversation with his cousin. As Sofer observes, 'Roderick Hudson is first introduced by the statue he has made for Cecilia, which she dubs "a pretty boy" ... an epithet that may be applied with equal accuracy to the artist himself' (1999: 188). Moreover, as Gregory Woods points out:

> The eponymous Roderick is susceptible to the physical attractions of other men – as an artist at least – and himself attracts other men ... Roderick first appears, not in person, but in the shape of a naked youth over whom he has attentively passed his eyes and hands: a statuette of 'Thirst'. This item of his handiwork, his art, is Greek in spirit: the title

is inscribed in Greek on its base . . . Being beautiful, young and male, he conventionally fits a number of classical roles. The attributes of a generalised classicism are what save him from seeming to be a pornographic representation of a Victorian boy. (1999: 69)

The statue's name, 'Thirst', is also, as Woods argues, significant. Although his thirst 'is literal – he is drinking from a bowl' it is also 'figurative' as it is 'not just his throat that thirsts, but the whole of his physique. Nor is it he alone who thirsts: for he, or his beauty, is offered as a legitimate focus for the parched eye. He quenches what his name evokes' (1999: 69). When Mallet finally sees Hudson, following this encounter by proxy, his 'impressions build toward a climactic image of "extraordinary beauty"' (Sofer 1999: 188), and clearly attracted to him, alludes to 'his personal charm and his probable genius', while also noting that he possesses 'the something tender and divine of unspotted, exuberant, confident youth' (James 1986: 68). Hudson not only sculpts beautiful boys, but is himself a thing of Hellenic beauty that resembles the ephebic loveliness of the *Apollo Belvedere* described by Winckelmann above; it is therefore fitting that in the novel he is likened to a 'Phoebus Apollo' and has the look of a 'nervous nineteenth-century Apollo' (1986: 122, 238). As Sofer notes, in these first encounters with Hudson, 'the older man's attraction to Roderick's "tender" youth and beauty is foregrounded' and 'the relationship between the two men rapidly grows quite intimate'; in fact they soon engage in what she calls 'a typical nineteenth-century courtship ritual' taking a long walk together, flinging themselves on the grass, and conversing like close friends (1999: 188–9). During one of these intimate talks, Mallet introduces the possibility of taking Hudson to Italy for educational purposes: 'if you are to be a sculptor', he tells Hudson, 'you ought to go to Rome and study the antique' (James 1986: 71). Aware that Hudson cannot fund the journey himself, he explains,

> To go to Rome you need money. I am fond of fine statues, but unfortunately I can't make them myself. I have to order them. I order a dozen from you, to be executed at your convenience. To help you I pay you in advance. (James 1986: 71)

Thus offering his friendship as a form of business arrangement. The success of this transaction is dependent on 'having a friend with a good deal more than he wants and not being too proud to accept a part of it' (1986: 71).

Plate 1 Edward Coley Burne-Jones, *The Godhead Fires*, from the 'Pygmalion and the Image' series, 1868–70, oil on canvas (private collection). By courtesy of Julian Hartnoll / Bridgeman Images

Plate 2   John Gibson, *The Tinted Venus*, c.1851–6, marble (Walker Art Gallery, National Museums, Liverpool). Bridgeman Images

Plate 3 Warrington Wood, *Keats Memorial*, 1875 (Protestant and non-Catholic Cemetery, Rome). Photo by Dan Kitwood / Getty Images

Plate 4 Edward Onslow Ford, *Shelley Memorial*, 1892, marble with bronze base (University College, Oxford). Andrew Shiva / Wikipedia / CC BY-SA 4.0

Hellenism and Jamesian Homoeroticism

The figure of the beautiful boy befriended by an older man is a recurrent trope in late-Victorian expressions of homoeroticism, based on the model of 'ideal education' associated with 'the Platonic or Socratic doctrine of eros' (Dowling 1994: 81). As Linda Dowling explains in her study of Oxford Hellenism and homosexuality:

> This model of love – by which an older man, moved to love by the visible beauty of a younger man, and desirous of winning immortality through that love, undertakes the younger man's education in virtue and wisdom – could be recaptured within the existing structures of Oxford homosociality: the intense friendship, the tutorial, the essay society. (1994: 81)

Such 'intense friendships' feature in Pater's essay, 'Winckelmann', first published in the *Westminster Review* (January 1867) and reprinted in *Studies in the History of the Renaissance* (1873), in which appreciation of the male body is a prerequisite for the appreciation of the Hellenist aesthetic and is posited as intrinsic to Winckelmann's study of Greek sculpture during his time in Rome. Pater writes that 'Winckelmann's Roman life was simple, primeval, Greek', and that in Rome, he found himself free to embrace his 'native affinity to the Hellenic spirit' (2010: 93). He proceeds to acknowledge that, for Winckelmann, this 'affinity to Hellenism' was not 'merely intellectual', but had its physical correlation in 'his romantic, fervid friendships with young men', many of whom he found 'more beautiful than Guido's archangel' (Pater 2010: 93–4).[30] Winckelmann's homoerotic desire for the body of such youths is soon translated by Pater into a study of sculptural form: 'These friendships', he writes, 'bringing him in contact with the pride of human form, and staining his thoughts with its bloom, perfected his reconciliation with the spirit of Greek sculpture' (Pater 2010: 94). Here, Pater simultaneously acknowledges and obscures Winckelmann's sexual proclivities; as Dowling notes:

> Pater's mode is never that of outright statement or even suggestion. It is one, rather, of a constantly beckoning and receding suggestiveness, as homoerotic themes – most often Platonic ones – are constantly either raised to visibility or veiled in their explicitness within the richly various materials of Pater's prose. (1994: 94)

The same might be said of James's prose which positions Mallet in the roles of educator and benefactor, consistent with Platonic models of love, and places Hudson, his beautiful protégé, in the role of pupil while relying on allusion and omission to maintain the tension between friendship and courtship. As Robert K. Martin states, *Roderick Hudson* 'is the story of a man who fell in love with a handsome young artist, adopted him as his protégé and took him to Italy' (1978: 101). Given that this is the case, Mallet's suggestion that Hudson visit Rome to 'study the antique' (James 1986: 71) is a covert, yet unmistakable reference to Winckelmann's penchant for male sculpture and beautiful youths. Unsurprisingly, then, Wendy Graham reads the transactional relationship between Mallet and Hudson as 'a variation on what Sedgwick has called "queer tutelage"' (1999: 105).[31]

Interestingly, in his article 'Henry James among the Aesthetes' Richard Ellmann argues that Pater's *Renaissance*, published during James's residence in Italy, 'played a large part in the composition of *Roderick Hudson*' (1984: 210).[32] Recording James's reaction on seeing Pater's book, expressed in a letter to William James, Ellmann writes:

> He was living in Florence, and that day happened to see in a bookseller's window a copy of Walter Pater's new book, *Studies in the History of the Renaissance*. For a moment James was 'inflamed', as he wrote to his brother, to buy it and to compose a notice of it. But then he recognized, he said, that it treated of several things he knew nothing about, and gave up the idea. (1984: 210)

As Ellmann observes, James 'gives the impression that he never looked at the book, except in the window. But he must have gone inside the shop and thumbed it, for otherwise he could not have known that some of its contents were on unfamiliar subjects' (1984: 210). Despite his disavowals, it is clear that James did read Pater's book, and that his reading of it coincides with 'the very time when he was writing *Roderick Hudson*' (Ellmann 1984: 210).[33] For Ellmann, James's reluctance to openly associate himself with Pater's work was likely due to his recognition of its contents. Given 'his homosexual propensity', Ellmann argues, 'he could not fail to observe how Pater's book covertly celebrated such a propensity by dwelling on Leonardo, Michelangelo, and Winckelmann'; in his view, hearing 'the incriminating footfalls', James 'took alarm' wishing to 'inscribe himself as neither aesthetic nor homosexual' (1984: 211). Nevertheless, it is evident that, despite these attempts to disengage his text from Pater's, the influence of *The Renaissance* remains indelible; in his essay, Pater 'repeatedly stress[es] Winckelmann's "exercise of sight and touch" in his study of the art of Antiquity' (Østermark-Johansen 2011: 72), an exercise that is repeated in *Roderick Hudson* where James, like Winckelmann 'fingers those pagan marbles with unsinged hands' (Pater 2010: 112). Like Winckelmann, Rowland Mallet finds ideal beauty in antique sculpture, and pleasure in the friendship of a young man who resembles the 'beautiful youth' figured in *Thirst* (James 1986: 59). Moreover, Mallet, like Winckelmann, appreciates rather than creates sculpture, while Hudson takes on the role of a Michelangelesque sculptor. He asserts that he 'could rush in a rage at a block of unshaped marble, like Michael A.' (1986: 135); his *Lazzarone*, 'an image of serene, irresponsible, sensuous life' is inspired by Michelangelo's *Bacchus* (James 1986: 240);[34] and he plans to sculpt a monumental statue like Michelangelo's *David*. In Rome, Hudson declares himself a Hellenist and, despite the Hebraic origins of the biblical David, he intends to depict him as 'a young Greek' who will look 'like a beautiful runner at the Olympic games' (James 1986: 122–3).

Hudson's attempts to emulate Michelangelo result in a statue inspired by the sculptural beauty of a Venetian gondolier who rows Mallet and Hudson out to one of the city's islands. Afloat on a gondola, the friends observe his physical perfection and he later becomes a model for *Adam*, the first sculpture Roderick produces in Rome:

> [O]ne morning the two men had themselves rowed out to Torcello, and Roderick lay back for a couple of hours watching a brown-breasted gondolier making superb muscular movements, in high relief, against the sky of the Adriatic, and at the end, jerked himself up with a violence that nearly swamped the gondola, and declared that the only thing worth living for was to make a colossal bronze and set it aloft in the light of a public square.[35] (1986: 69)

As Person points out, this 'triangulated scene in which two men gaze at another man's semi-naked body serves James as a means of mediating a relationship he would find it difficult to name' (2002: 129). Here, vision functions as a form of phantom touch, one that Roderick will later translate into sculpture, moulding the terracotta model with his fingers, caressing the clay with his hands before transforming it into marble. Once in Rome, Hudson sets to work on the statue whose success is 'miraculous' and is described as 'the finest piece of sculpture of our modern time' (James 1986: 114). While 'all the world' comes to see it, we learn that this early glory is not a springboard to greater things as he 'never surpassed it afterwards' (1986: 114–15).[36] Once completed, it passes 'formally into Rowland's possession', paid for 'as if an illustrious name had been chiselled on the pedestal' (1986: 115). Ostensibly, Rowland's acquisition of the statue symbolises the fulfilment of his contractual agreement with Hudson whose works Mallet has purchased in advance through his financial support of Roderick's journey to Rome and his subsistence. Yet, given the statue's origins in their admiration of the 'brown-breasted gondolier' (1986: 69) who drew their mutual gaze, this exchange vibrates with homoerotic tension. Moulded initially by Hudson's hands and bearing his touch, the statue mediates desire: by possessing the statue, Mallet not only 'possesses' Hudson, but is also free to touch a sculptural body that doubles the handsome gondolier, and merges Hudson's touch and his own in the process.

Touching Friendships

The homoeroticism of tactile exchange expressed in *Roderick Hudson* has also been explored by Daniel J. Murtaugh. Tracing significant differences between the 1875 and 1907 editions of *Roderick Hudson*, Murtaugh considers James's growing awareness of his own sexuality which, he claims convincingly, is realised through metaphors of touch that appear in 'his letters to, or concerning, male companions during the 1870s and the 1900s'. According to Murtaugh:

> The original version of the novel . . . and the revised New York Edition . . . trace the developing sexual awareness of the novelist from the nontactile, idealized concept of male companionship held by him during the initial composition period (1874–75) to that of physical intimacy and possessive sexual yearning evident during the revision period (1905–06). These progressive aspects of James's homoerotic awareness are reflected in the alternately idealized or tactile language of his letters to, or concerning, male companions during the 1870s and the 1900s, a language which in turn finds its way into the contemporaneous versions of the Rowland Mallet-Roderick Hudson relationship. (1996: 182–3)

By the time James revised *Roderick Hudson* for the *New York Edition* of 1907, he had cultivated 'friendship[s] of the legendary sort' with younger men such as William Morton Fullerton, Jonathan Sturges and most notably, perhaps, with the Norwegian sculptor Hendrik Andersen who was himself a beautiful boy (Murtaugh 1996: 186).[37] In his biography of James, Fred Kaplan sheds light on changes that occurred in the author's life at this time that, Murtaugh argues, affected his revision of *Roderick Hudson* (1996: 194). According to Kaplan, in the mid-1890s, James 'fell in love a number of times' and 'established intimate relationships, beyond his usual friendships, that for the first time provided him with the feeling of being in love'; 'He had a need for intimacy. He wanted to be flexible, to be open to emotional interaction, to "only live" in the sense of being true to his own desires and needs, difficult as they were to identify' (1999: 401).

James's friendship with Andersen lasted sixteen years; yet the friends rarely met. Their first meeting in Rome in 1899 was followed by another in the city eight years later, and by sporadic visits by Andersen to James's home in Rye (Bell 2004: x). However, their relationship is charted in the seventy-eight letters written by James during the sixteen-year period of their acquaintance. James's first letter to Andersen, dated 19 July 1899, resonates with the transactional relationship between patron and protégé in *Roderick Hudson*. In it James acknowledges receipt of a 'terracotta bust of Alberto Bevilacqua Lazise, a friend of Hendrik Andersen' that he had seen in Andersen's studio in Rome and purchased 'to help the sculptor' (James 2004: 2, n. 3). James writes:

> It is, the beautiful bust, I rejoice to tell you, in perfect condition . . . without a flaw or a nick – & is more charming & delightful to [see] even than it was in Rome. I heartily rejoice to possess it – & I am by this post writing to my bankers in London for a draft on Rome for the amount of $250 – that is Fifty Pounds – which will immediately reach me & which I will instantly, on its arrival, transmit to you. I find the sum modest for the admirable & exquisite work. I have perched the latter on the chimney-piece of my dining room . . . where he commands the scene . . . & where, moreover, as I sit at meat, I shall have him constantly before me as a loved companion & friend. (2004: 1)

As in *Roderick Hudson*, the sculpted object mediates between the untouchable beloved and the desiring admirer; here, the art object stands for the 'charming & delightful' Andersen, James's 'loved companion & friend' whom he would truly like to have constantly before him. As their correspondence continues, James's desire for intimacy becomes increasingly evident. In a letter dated 9 February 1902, replying to Andersen's news of his brother Andreas's death, James writes:

> Your news fills me with horror & pity, & how can I express the tenderness with wh[ich] it makes me think of you & the aching wish to be near you & put my arms round you? . . . The sense that I can't *help* you, see

you, talk to you, touch you, hold you close & long, or do anything to make you rest on me, & feel my deep participation – this torments me, dearest boy, makes me ache for you, & for myself . . . I wish I could go to Rome & put my hands on you (oh, how lovingly I should lay them!) but that, alas, is odiously impossible. (2004: 26; original emphasis)

While the sentiments expressed are due, no doubt, to James's genuine sympathy for a friend in distress, the language used might be considered unsuitably passionate given the circumstances: the need to 'touch', 'hold', and lay his hands 'lovingly' on Andersen suggests an eroticised response to the image of the grieving sculptor, and the desire to touch remains a feature of James's letters to Andersen throughout their correspondence. James frequently ends his letters with a variety of allusions to tactile contact: 'I put, my dear boy, my arm around you, & feel the pulsation, thereby, as it were, of our excellent future & your admirable endowment'; 'Always grasping you hard and holding you close, I am yours, dearest Hendrik immensely'; 'I pat you on the back, tenderly, tenderly'; 'I take you, my dear old Boy, to my heart, & beg you to feel my arms around you' (qtd in Bell 2004: xiv). Interestingly, Person highlights how references to hands and fingers also arise in James's epistolary discussions of sculpture with Hendrik Andersen, and argues that this permits a triangulation of tactile 'relationships between men through the medium of sculpted bodies' (2002: 109).

Having met in 1899, while James was in Rome to engage in research for his biography of William Wetmore Story, Andersen may well have triggered memories of James's own visit to the city as a young man, and recalled the artistic circles in which he moved at that time. But as Millicent Bell notes, his relationship with Andersen uncannily echoes that between Roderick and Rowland in *Roderick Hudson*: 'His Roderick – like Story, like Andersen – was a sculptor. It was as though – eerily – he had predicted this man whose very name resembled that of his fictional character' (2004: xv).[38] Murtaugh argues that this resonance between fact and fiction informs the New York Edition of *Roderick Hudson*; he points out that the expressions of desire for erotic proximity that we find in James's letters to Andersen – communicated by the need to touch, clasp, squeeze, caress, hold (1996: 186) – find themselves reflected in the deeper sense of communion expressed in the revised edition of the novel. He claims that 'the New York Edition revisions make the Mallet-Hudson relationship more explicitly homoerotic' (1996: 195). To give an example: Murtaugh points to the episode in the novel where Rowland and

Roderick spend their first afternoon alone together: in the 1875 edition, we merely learn that 'they talked like old friends' (James 1986: 69); by contrast, in the 1907 edition they 'fall into intimacy, like old friends' and 'the far-spreading view' suggestive of their future relationship 'affects [Rowland] as melting for them both into such vast continuities and possibilities of possession' that it touches his heart and elicits 'a strange feeling of prospective regret' (James 1907: 32). For Murtaugh, James's revisions signpost a stronger homoeroticism: for 'the innocuous "it [the far-spreading view] seemed to him beautiful" of the original . . . James has substituted tactile imagery suggestive of sexual union' (1996: 196). The 'language of physical possession' used here by James is, as Murtaugh remarks, 'analogous to that used by James in his letters to Hendrik Andersen' and other young men 'in which he imaginatively "embraces," "clutches," or "enfolds" these companions in his arms' (1996: 196).

Over His Dead Body

While much of the critical focus on homoeroticism in the novel has fallen on the relationship between Rowland Mallet and Roderick Hudson, a more explicit expression of homoerotic desire remains underexplored. The lover in this case is Sam Singleton, a landscape artist who mingles with Rowland and Roderick in Rome. Singleton's name in itself suggests a commitment to bachelorhood, and he is feminised by James's description of both his person and his work. He paints 'small landscapes, chiefly in water-colours'; he is 'a diminutive attenuated personage'; he looks 'like a precocious child'; and his face bears an expression of extraordinary 'modesty and patience' (1986: 118–19). He listens 'much more willingly' than he talks, blushes when he speaks, and offers 'his ideas in a sidelong fashion, as if the presumption were against him' (1986: 119). Tellingly, from the outset he expresses 'a fervent admiration for Roderick's productions', recalling Winckelmann's 'fervid friendships with young men' (Pater 2010: 93–4) mentioned above, and when he meets the sculptor for the first time, looks up at him 'as if Roderick had been himself a statue on a pedestal' (James 1986: 119). Later in the novel, mesmerised as Roderick speaks, Sam Singleton gazes and listens to him 'open-mouthed, as if Phoebus Apollo had been talking' (1986: 122) and voices his wish that Roderick should 'not grow any older' (1986: 124). He declares Roderick 'the handsomest fellow in Rome' (1986: 171) who, in his memories of his 'Roman artist life' will be the 'central figure' standing 'there in radiant relief as beautiful and unspotted as one of his own statues' (1986: 317). In the final pages of the novel, it is Singleton who discovers Roderick's body after his fatal fall into a ravine. In death, as in life, Hudson remains a figure of outstanding beauty:

> He had fallen from a great height, but he was singularly little disfigured. The rain had spent its torrents upon him, and his clothes and hair were as wet as if the billows of the ocean had flung him upon the strand ... The eyes were those of a dead man, but in a short time when Rowland had closed them, the whole face seemed to awake. The rain had washed away all blood; it was as if Violence, having done her work, had stolen away in shame. Roderick's face might have shamed her; it looked admirably handsome. (1986: 386)

Contemplating Roderick's corpse, Singleton echoes Mallet's unspoken attraction to Hudson's dead body, exclaiming: 'He was a beautiful fellow' (1986: 386). Lying in an Alpine ravine, Hudson's aestheticised cadaver is represented by 'a vague white mass' reminiscent of unchiselled marble, and the description of him 'wet as if the billows of the ocean had flung him upon the strand' anticipates Onslow Ford's *Shelley Memorial*, which features a reclining statue of the poet's drowned corpse washed up on the beach at Viareggio.[39] This is perhaps fitting given that Roderick in his moments of despondency had engaged in 'Romantic talk of a desire for death' (Cutting 2005: 20), imagining himself dead to the world and crying, 'Dead, dead; dead and buried! Buried in an open grave, where you lie staring up at the sailing clouds, smelling the waving flowers and hearing all nature live and grow above you!' (James 1986: 348). What is striking about the reactions of Mallet and Singleton to Hudson's death is the focus on his beauty; in each his aestheticised corpse elicits not immediate expressions of sorrow, but exclamations of scopophilic pleasure – 'it looked admirably handsome'; 'He was a beautiful fellow' (James 1986: 386) – that connote, in light of Lisa Downing's broader understanding of necrophilia in the nineteenth century as 'both an aesthetic and a sexological category', necrophiliac desire (Cutting 2005: 54). In his book, *Death in Henry James*, Andrew Cutting suggests that, in the novel, Mallet's necrophiliac impulse is discernible in the text's omission of any detailed description of his vigil, during which he 'has the opportunity to examine his friend's body directly, to be physically intimate with it in a way that he could never enjoy while Roderick was alive' (2005: 54). 'Any such examination or intimacy', he argues, 'is carefully excluded from the narrative' (2005: 54). Indeed, the narrator tells us only that:

> He [Mallet] watched for seven long hours, and his vigil was for ever memorable. The most rational of men was for an hour the most passionate. He reviled himself with transcendent bitterness, he accused himself of cruelty and injustice, he would have lain down there in Roderick's place to unsay the words that had yesterday driven him forth on his lonely ramble. (James 1986: 387)

As Cutting observes, this statement 'falls short of revealing full-blown necrophilic desire for the physical corpse, either in gothic mode or as art of a realist study of sexual perversion'; however, he contends that, here, James 'flirts with necrophilia rather than exploring it for its own sake' (2005: 55). While Cutting focuses on the deathbed scene, I would argue that this 'flirtation' with necrophilia is far clearer, if similarly silenced, in the narrator's use of free indirect discourse to describe Mallet's initial response to the beauty of Roderick's corpse, while his thoughts are vocalised directly by Singleton's exclamation: 'He was a beautiful fellow' (James 1986: 386). The question is: why is Mallet's desire ventriloquised through Singleton?

Clearly James chose to feminise Singleton and to imply throughout the novel that his passionate interest in Hudson was more than purely professional. Singleton focuses on Roderick's personal charms, and his admiration is evidently informed by his visual pleasure in Hudson's face and form. Indeed, his imagination transforms Roderick into a sculptural body, an action that is effectively realised towards the end of the novel when Singleton spots Roderick's white corpse whose rigidity suggests a sculptural materiality. I would also add that this final scene shared by Singleton and Mallet points to the conflation of their desire for Hudson. Moreover, as Michèle Mendelssohn has suggested, though not literally an artist, Mallet in some sense wishes to be one and fulfils this wish by 'creating' Hudson; 'Rowland is not only buying Roderick's artwork but also "buying the picture," in the sense that patronage becomes a means for him to paint himself into the *tableau vivant* of the Roman art world' (2003: 526). In doing so, she argues that Mallet becomes a Pygmalionesque figure, whose name 'is indicative of his role as creator, as a human incarnation of a sculptural tool', and posits 'the patron-artist relationship as an instance of the creator-creature relationship' (2003: 528–30). However, she argues that while in *Roderick Hudson* this 'patron-artist relationship represents a socially sanctioned homosocial bond', for Rowland

Mallet 'it moves further along the sexual continuum and becomes eroticized' (2003: 529).

Mendelssohn's view of Mallet as a version of Pygmalion is convincing, yet in a book that centres on the sculptural arts, why should James choose to shift the focus onto Sam Singleton, a painter? The answer may lie in Ellmann's suggestion that, at the time the novel first appeared, James did not wish to be associated with either aestheticism or homosexuality. It is worth noting that, in the novel, Mary Garland exclaims: 'I am so glad . . . that Roderick is a sculptor and not a painter . . . It's not that painting is not fine . . . but sculpture is finer. It is more manly!' (James 1986: 271). It is intriguing, then, to find that in his preface to the *New York Edition* of *Roderick Hudson*, whose alterations, according to Murtaugh, indicate a coming-to-terms with his own sexuality, the metaphor James employs to discuss his revision of the text is not sculptural, but painterly:

> I speak of the painter in general and of his relation to the old picture, the work of his hand, that has been lost to sight and that, when found again, is put back on the easel for measure of what time and weather may, in the interval, have done to it . . . The anxious artist has to wipe it over, in the first place to see; he has to 'clean it up,' say, or to varnish it anew, or at the least to place it in a light, for any right judgement of its aspect or its worth. But the very uncertainties themselves yield a thrill, and if subject and treatment, working together, have had their felicity, the artist, the prime creator, may find a strange charm in this stage of the connexion. It helps him to live back into a forgotten state, into convictions, credulities too early spent perhaps, it breathes life upon the dead reasons for things, buried as they are in the texture of the work, and makes them revive, so that the actual appearances and old motives fall together once more, and a lesson and a moral and a consecrating final light are somehow disengaged. (James 1907: 41)

In this passage, the sculptor and the painter coalesce. The preface, like the novel, points implicitly to the significance of both arts and to their dual investment in the coordination of hand and eye, touch and vision, but it also merges James and Singleton, a shift that implies an acceptance of his own nature. In addition, the revival of dead and buried matter suggests not only the Pygmalion myth, but also the archaeological artefact. While Mallet's homoerotic desire may remain 'buried . . . in the texture of the work', James's preface invites us to unearth the novel's tangled networks of sensory responses, to wipe away the layers of critical varnish, and to shed new light on the complexities of the novel's sculptural bodies.

Notes

1. Hawthorne took up the position of United States Consul in Liverpool in 1853, and toured France and Italy with his family, returning to the family home in Concord, Massachusetts in 1860. The English notebooks were kept by Hawthorne between 1853 and 1857. The French and Italian notebooks are an extension of these, begun on his arrival in Paris on 6 January 1858, and concluded on the day he left Le Havre for England on 22 June 1859 (Hawthorne 1980: 903).
2. This reference to the 'grace and nobility' of the statues he encounters suggests Winckelmann's allusion to the 'noble simplicity' and 'still grandeur' of the Laocoön group in Rome (Potts 2006: 8).
3. Ironically, many nineteenth-century sculptors who produced neoclassical sculptures justified their statues' nudity by suggesting that their own art was not one of heathen worship, but 'imbued with Christian virtues and morality' (Rowe 2002: 86).
4. *Roderick Hudson*, Henry James's first acknowledged novel, was initially serialised in *The Atlantic* magazine in 1875 and then revised in 1907 for the *New York Edition*, a twenty-four-volume collection of his works. James practically disowned his first novel, *Watch and Ward*, also serialised in *The Atlantic Monthly* in 1871, and published in book form in 1878.
5. (Benjamin) Paul Akers (1825–61) was a sculptor who worked in Rome from 1855 till his death; William Wetmore Story (1819–95) was a sculptor, writer and art critic who lived in Rome briefly in 1848, and again from 1850; Randolph Rogers (1825–92) was a sculptor who owned a studio in Rome from 1854 till his death; Harriet Hosmer studied in Rome under the Welsh sculptor, John Gibson, from 1853 to 1860.
6. The subtitle is reminiscent of Ann Radcliffe's novels *A Sicilian Romance* (1790) and *The Romance of the Forest* (1791), while its Italian setting also resonates with that which features in *The Mysteries of Udolpho* (1794) and *The Italian* (1797).
7. Satyr, or faun of Praxiteles (second century BCE); Beatrice Cenci (1577–99) was a notorious Italian noblewoman tried and executed for the murder of her father, Francesco Cenci, who had abused her.
8. John Carlos Rowe acknowledges that Donatello and Miriam's gender roles are unstable, and 'part of the supernatural aura of *The Marble Faun*' and argues that the atmosphere of the novel 'reflects nineteenth-century anxieties about sexuality prompted in part by destabilizations of conventional gender hierarchies' (2002: 85).
9. For a discussion of 'Hyacinthus' as a homosexual pseudonym, see Pulham (2007: 173).
10. The term 'ephebic masculinity' is used to describe the ambiguity of the adolescent male body; see Solomon-Godeau (1997: 202).

11. Baym notes that Hilda is 'separated from her sexuality' and that her name means 'battle-maiden'. The etymology of 'Juno' is disputed; its Latin root comes from 'iuvenis' meaning 'young man' while its Indo-European root suggests 'yeu-' meaning 'vital force'. See *American Heritage Dictionary* (2001).
12. In his preface to *The Marble Faun*, Hawthorne confesses to having 'stolen' 'a magnificent statue of Cleopatra, the production of Mr. William W. Story' for his novel (1990b: 4).
13. Miriam's secret is never revealed.
14. Originally attributed to Guido Reni, the portrait of Beatrice Cenci is now thought to have been painted by a woman artist of his circle: Elisabetta Sirani.
15. For an interesting discussion of the women sculptors living in Rome, see Melissa Dabakis (2014).
16. In her respected discussion of same-sex love, Faderman found that in the nineteenth century 'there were common terms to describe love relationships between women, such as "the love of kindred spirits," "Boston marriage," and "sentimental friends"', and adds that although she had at first assumed that this kind of romantic attachment was a Victorian phenomenon, she soon found such friendships not only in the seventeenth and eighteenth centuries, but also in the Renaissance (1981: 16).
17. Matilda Hays (1820–97) was a writer, editor and translator of Georges Sand; Charlotte Cushman (1816–76) was one of the well-known American actresses of the mid nineteenth century. Hays and Cushman were involved for a time before Hays left Cushman for Hosmer in 1854.
18. Castle (1993) identifies 'spectrality' as a trope for cultural representations of lesbianism in literature and film.
19. The 'Antinous' is a nude marble statue originally unearthed in the eighteenth century at the emperor Hadrian's villa, Tivoli, then purchased by Pope Clement XII in 1733, whose collection formed the basis of the Capitoline Museums; the Capitoline Antinous is now thought to be a Roman copy of a Greek statue of Hermes *c*. fourth century BCE. The faun in red marble is the *Fauno Rosso*, a satyr, also taken from Hadrian's villa; the satyr is depicted holding a cluster of grapes, signalling that he is a follower of Dionysus.
20. The Amazon is a copy of the wounded Amazon sculpted by Phidias and the Juno is an original of the Pergamene School, which was initially part of the Cesi collection, then of the Albani collection before becoming part of the Capitoline collection in 1733; she is also sometimes referred to as the 'Juno Cesi'.
21. René Girard's theory is introduced in *Deceit, Desire, and the Novel* first published in French in 1961 and in English in 1965. Girard suggests that all canonical novels are concerned with triangular desire which centres on the importance of a mediator between the desiring subject and the object of desire.

22. Nina Baym argues that Hilda's search for a mother fails because 'the mother is not a virgin' (1971: 368).
23. In chapter 31, Kenyon, waiting for Miriam, imagines her 'arrayed in queenly robes' (Hawthorne 1990a: 279).
24. Edward Pusey (1800–82) was associated with the Oxford Movement and High Anglicanism.
25. Theodore Ziolkowski notes that as a result of Christianity's general demonisation of the pagan, the Virgin Mary often replaces Venus in Christian versions of pagan myths. Interestingly, here, a reversal from Christian to pagan takes place thus complicating Hilda's 'virginity' (1977: 27).
26. In this description we find echoes of Hawthorne's response to the *Venus de' Medici* when he first sees her in the Uffizi gallery: 'I felt a kind of tenderness for her; an affection, not as if she were one woman, but all womanhood in one' (1980: 298). This incident also seems based on another experience, a trip he took to the campagna with William Wetmore Story in order to visit a newly excavated statue that was considered the model for the *Medici Venus*. Brodhead notes that the statue 'was still so freshly uncovered that Story, like Kenyon, had to brush the earth out of its marble lips' (Hawthorne 1990a: 483, n. 1).
27. Miriam and Donatello reinter the statue so that Kenyon may discover it.
28. The word 'fervid' used here recalls Winckelmann's 'fervid' friendships with young men, discussed in Pater's essay on the art historian in *Studies in the History of the Renaissance* (2010: 93–4), that inform his appreciation of Hellenic sculpture. The reference to 'the imprisoning stone' suggests Michelangelo's 'prisoners' in the Accademia in Florence, consisting of four statues that appear to be in the process of emerging from their marble blocks, thus suggesting their pre-existence within them.
29. For a discussion of visual and textual representations of Zeus and Ganymede, *paiderastia* more generally, and the erotic relationship between *erastes* (adult male) and *eromenos* (adolescent boy beloved) in Ancient Greece, see Lear and Cantarella (2008).
30. Guido's archangel is a reference to an altarpiece by Guido Reni (1575–1642) featuring *The Archangel Michael* (*c.*1635) at Santa Maria della Concezione dei Cappuccini in Rome.
31. See Sedgwick (1993) for a full discussion of this term and other examples of this 'tutelage' in texts such as Diderot's *La Religieuse* (*The Nun*; 1796) and Oscar Wilde's *The Importance of Being Earnest* (1895).
32. This article by Ellmann was initially given as a lecture, part of the Sarah Tryphena Phillips Lecture on American Literature and History on 19 May 1983. It was later published in 1984 as part of the proceedings of the British Academy.
33. Ellmann notes that in 'Florentine Notes', which James contributed to the *Independent* (a New York weekly), he refers to a chapter on Sandro

Botticelli that appears in Pater's *Renaissance* and refers specifically to Pater in the article as 'an ingenious critic' (1984: 210).
34. Michelangelo's *Bacchus* (1496–7) depicts the Roman god of wine in an unsteady pose that suggests inebriation. It can be seen at the Museo Nazionale del Bargello in Florence. His *David* (1501–4), considered his masterpiece, is in the Galleria dell'Accademia, Florence.
35. This quotation is taken from the 1878 edition; the 1907 edition changes 'making superb muscular movements' to 'making superb muscular movements . . . of a breadth and grace he had never seen equalled'.
36. Hudson's sudden but quickly fading fame stands in contrast to 'Gloriani', the other American sculptor, reputedly of French and/or Italian extraction (his nationality varies across James's works), who appears not only in *Roderick Hudson*, but also in *The Ambassadors* (1903) and 'The Velvet Glove' (1909) who sustains a lucrative trade. For a discussion of Gloriani in James's work, see Alworth (2015).
37. William Morton Fullerton (1865–1952) was an American journalist and author, and is now known best for his affair with Edith Wharton; Jonathan Sturges (1864–1911) was an American author and travel writer; Hendrik Andersen (1872–1940) was a Norwegian-born sculptor and painter whose family emigrated to America when he was a child. Andersen studied sculpture in Newport, Rhode Island, where the family lived and, in 1893, went to Rome to study art where he finally settled, and where he met James in 1899.
38. This coalescence of life and art resembles the prefiguration of Wilde's destructive relationship with Lord Alfred Douglas in *The Picture of Dorian Gray* (1890–1).
39. Edward Onslow Ford (1852–1901) was an English sculptor and Royal Academician associated with the New Sculpture movement (which will be discussed in greater detail in Chapter 4). The *Shelley Memorial* is housed at University College, Oxford.

Chapter 4

Statuephilia and the Love of the Impossible

The relationship between Rowland Mallet and Roderick Hudson discussed in Chapter 3 – that of benefactor and artist – is repeated in a different context in the romantic friendship between Edmund Gosse and the sculptor Hamo Thornycroft who became an important figure in the New Sculpture movement.[1] The term 'New Sculpture' was coined by Gosse in a series of articles published in *The Art Journal* in 1894, and its parameters, formulated in 1880 and 1881, emerged from his 'deep engagement' with Thornycroft's thought and work (Getsy 2004: 3).[2] Like Mallet, Gosse could not sculpt, but he supported Thornycroft's art and, also like Mallet, Gosse's desire to promote his friend was energised by his homoerotic attraction to the sculptor which informed his 'new-found interest in sculpture criticism' and permitted a 'persistent advocacy in the press that catapulted Thornycroft to fame and helped to codify the New Sculpture' (Getsy 2004: 43).[3]

Charting the rise of the New Sculpture in the first article of *The Art Journal* series, Gosse explains that the 'central principle of the movement had been a close and obedient following of nature' (1894: 139). Indeed, the naturalistic qualities of Thornycroft's sculpture are reminiscent of what Hazlitt described as the 'master-excellence' of the Elgin Marbles, referred to in Chapter 1, visible in sculptures that seem 'to be actuated by an internal machinery and composed of the same soft and flexible materials as the human body' (1998b: 82–3). Thornycroft's own admiration for Ancient Greek statuary is documented by David Getsy who observes that he considered the Elgin Marbles and the *Venus de Milo* 'sculptural exemplars' and notes how, as a student, Thornycroft 'became increasingly dissatisfied with the cold abstractions of neoclassical sculptors' who seemed unable to reproduce the 'vitality of Greek sculpture' (2004: 45). Unlike his predecessors Thornycroft set out 'to rejuvenate and recreate the Classical ideal, rather than merely replicate it' (2004: 25).

Figure 4.1 Sir Hamo Thornycroft, *The Mower*, 1888–90, bronze (Tate Gallery, London). © Tate, London 2014

This reimagination of the 'vitality' of the Classical ideal is evident in Thornycroft's *Artemis* (1880), *The Stone Thrower* (1880)[4] and *Teucer* (1881), but it is Thornycroft's *The Mower* (1884), arguably his best-known work, that encapsulates the naturalistic detail which characterises the New Sculpture. Prompted by the socialist writings of Ruskin and William Morris, and reacting to direct and indirect critiques of the vacuity of contemporary statuary, *The Mower* (Figure 4.1) represents 'Thornycroft's answer to charges of sculpture's irrelevance as well as to his own questioning of the political stakes of his work' (Getsy 2004: 77). Writing retrospectively of *The Mower*'s impact on the art world, Gosse recalls:

> It was in 1884 that Mr. Thornycroft made an entirely new departure with his virile modern statue of 'The Mower.' Here was a figure of the life of to-day, seized in a position of perfectly natural grace, treated in the costume of his class. Something of the sentiment of Fred Walker, and something, too, of the ideal realism of such young French sculptors as Coutan and Albert Lefeuvre, inspired this very noble statue, in which the beauty of the every-day life of to-day was heroically captured for the art which had seemed most definitely to decline to touch it. . . . [I]t

is indisputable that it was the pioneer of a whole class of statuary of a modern and 'actual' kind.[5] (1894: 280)

Gosse's description of Thornycroft's *Mower* as 'the pioneer of a whole class of statuary of a modern and "actual" kind' posits the statue as a response to critics who argued that 'sculpture had failed to incorporate accessible subject matter' (Getsy 2004: 75). Among these was Oscar Wilde who, during his American tour of 1882, issued a challenge to contemporary sculptors:

> If a modern sculptor were to come and say, 'Very well, but where can one find subjects for sculpture out of men who wear frock-coats and chimney-pot hats?' I would tell him to go to the docks of a great city and watch the men loading or unloading the stately ships, working at wheel or windlass, hauling at rope or gangway. . . . I would ask the sculptor to go with me to any of your schools or universities, to the running ground and gymnasium, to watch the young men start for a race, hurling quoit or club, kneeling to tie their shoes before leaping, stepping from the boat or bending to the oar, and to carve them; and when he was weary of cities I would ask him to come to your fields and meadows to watch the reaper with his sickle and the cattle-driver with lifted lasso. For if a man cannot find the noblest motives for his art in such simple daily things as a woman drawing water from the well or a man leaning with his scythe, he will not find them anywhere at all. (1913: 185)

While in this lecture Wilde stakes a claim in the value of the natural, rather than idealised, body in art, and mentions 'a woman drawing water from the well' as an apt subject for sculpture, read in the context of the later Wilde trials and his own enjoyment of working-class youths; the privileging of beautiful young athletes in Pater's 'Winckelmann'; and John Addington Symonds's own delight in 'sailors of the marine', 'blue vested & trowsered fishermen' and 'swaggering gondoliers' (1969: 516), one might detect a homoerotic subtext to this investment in the sculpted body of the male worker. Here the labourer is not the artist's counterpart, as in O'Shaughnessy's 'Song of a Fellow-Worker', but an object of creative desire.

Wilde's investment in the working body recalls Rowland Mallet's and Roderick Hudson's admiration of the muscular gondolier who becomes the model for Hudson's *Adam*, but it also resonates with Gosse's description, in a letter to John Addington Symonds, of Thornycroft's own body at work:

> He is very fine looking, extremely powerful in frame . . . he was dressed in his white embroidered blouse, hard at work with the chisel on a mass of marble, the top-light in his studio isolating his red and gold

head among all the white things, marble, plaster, blouse, and so on. You would have thought him very picturesque, and his face, with all its unusual bright colour, has an extraordinary elevation that generally goes only with pallor . . . He had both your *Greek Poets* there in the studio. (Thwaite 2007: 202)

While Ann Thwaite suggests that this letter to Symonds demonstrates how, as a result of his close friendship with Thornycroft, Gosse was now 'seeing everything through a sculptor's eyes', and becoming 'more aware of his own physical being and that of his friend' (2007: 202), his allusion to Symonds's '*Greek Poets*' in this brief sketch points to his homoerotic attraction to Thornycroft and his willingness to share it, albeit coded in this instance, with Symonds. In order to do so he alludes to *Studies of the Greek Poets* (1873, 1876), in the first volume of which Symonds alludes to Hellenic sculptural ideals to draw attention to male statues' 'shapely limbs, crisp curls, and flowerlike mouths', a strategy noted and attacked by John Tyrwhitt in his essay on 'The Greek Spirit in Modern Literature', published in the *Contemporary Review* in March 1877 (Dowling 1994: 90). Here, Tyrwhitt objects to Symonds's discussion of 'a phallic ecstasy perfectly free from pruriency', his 'talk about the frank sensuality of Priapus', and his 'concluding exhortation to follow Walt Whitman as far as our Hebraistic training and imperfect nature will enable us' (1877: 557).[6]

Amatory Comradeship

As Martin Goodman observes, like Symonds, Gosse found solace in Whitman's poetry; at the age of twenty-three he wrote to Whitman for permission to send him a copy of his own volume of poetry, *On Viol and Flute* (1873), expressing his delight in *Leaves of Grass* (1855), referring to him as 'the poet of comrades', and confessing himself 'drawn' toward him (qtd in Goodman 2014: 88). The potential nature of Whitman's friendship is implied in the poem 'Whoever you are holding me now in hand' from the 'Calamus' section in *Leaves of Grass* in which the speaker suggests a secret tryst:

But just possibly with you on a high hill, first watching lest
  any person for miles around approach unawares,
. . .
Here to put your lips upon mine I permit you,
With the comrade's long-dwelling kiss or the new

husband's kiss,
For I am the new husband and I am the comrade.
(Whitman 2004: 148, ll. 17–21)

According to Goodman, taking place high on a hill away from prying eyes, this 'comradeship' functions as 'a fair expression of . . . a gay sensibility in strong arousal' (2014: 89), and recalls the nature of what Naomi Sofer refers to as Roland Mallet and Roderick Hudson's early 'courtship ritual'; in James's novel the newly acquainted men take 'a long walk together', fling themselves on the grass, and converse 'like close friends' (1999: 188-89). Whitman's 'Calamus' is also referenced in the early correspondence between Symonds and Gosse; as Goodman explains, having been approached by the older man:

> Gosse wrote back and spoke of friendship. Symonds flashed back with two privately printed poems, which explicitly touched on 'Greek Love'. They came with a caveat: 'Of course this Greek love is different in quality from what can be expected to flourish in the modern world, & to attempt to replant it would be anachronistic. Yet I do not see, having the root of Calamus within our souls why we should not make the Hellenic passion of friendship a motive in art.' (2014: 90)

Although when asked whether Gosse was homosexual, Lytton Strachey quipped: 'No, but he's Hamo-sexual' (qtd in Thwaite 2007: 204), it is clear that Gosse's desire for 'comradeship' was not exclusive and that he sought it in those who championed manly love and homoeroticism in their works. It is clearly no accident that, on the fateful vacation that cemented his romantic investment in Thornycroft, he writes to his wife: 'We [he and Thornycroft] are lying now in a delicious quiet creek full of the scented rush – the calamus' (qtd in Thwaite 2007: 196). By mentioning 'the calamus' – a wetland reed – Gosse alludes not only to Whitman's *Leaves of Grass* but also to the myth of Kalamos in Nonnus's *Dionysiaca* which refers to love between men.[7] Gosse's letter, written on 19 June 1879 while cruising the Thames with Thornycroft and others, a date 'he was to remember all his life', is marked by his intensifying friendship with the sculptor (Thwaite 2007: 196). According to Thwaite, 'when it was all over, the feelings of longing turned into a poem' sent to Thornycroft with an accompanying letter in which he apologised for its 'exaggerated key' (2007: 196). The poem itself was later published as 'Desiderium' in Gosse's *New Poems* (1879), a collection that carries the dedication: 'To my friend Hamo Thornycroft sculptor'.[8] The poem is suffused with yearning and amorous regret and, here, Gosse 'sculpts' the sculptor, begging him to 'Sit there for ever, dear and lean/In marble as in fleeting flesh . . ./ For ever let the morning light/Stream down that forehead broad and white,/And round that cheek for my delight' (1879: 70, ll. 1–7). The memory of the calamus re-emerges as Gosse's speaker states:

> Already that flushed moment grows
>   So dark, so distant; through the ranks
> Of scented reed the river flows
>   Still murmuring to its willowy banks;
> But we can never hope to share
> Again the rapture fond and rare,
> Unless you turn immortal there.
> (1879: 70, ll. 8–14)

Desperate to capture this enchanted moment of male communion, the speaker draws on sculptural metaphor to still his beloved, beseeching him to 'sit for ever, dear, in stone,/As when you turned with half a smile', while he haunts the spot and suspends the flow of time (1879: 72, ll. 42–9). In this poem, the speaker becomes sculptor; the 'statue' of his lover functioning both as a memorial to lost love, and a silent receptacle of forbidden desire.

Yet, as Getsy has shown, Gosse was often more apt to identify with Thornycroft's statues than with Thornycroft himself. He points out that Gosse was particularly fond of *Artemis* on which Thornycroft had been working as their friendship developed, and in which the sculptor himself had an 'emotional investment' (Getsy 2004: 68).[9] Thornycroft gave a cast of *Artemis*'s head to Gosse which the latter kept in his study, and, according to Getsy, 'Gosse identified himself with the statue to an extent and . . .with Thornycroft's sculpture in general'; his critical interest in the processes of sculpting becoming one of the means by which he mediated his desire. As Getsy explains:

> With *Artemis*, Gosse attached his fantasies onto the act of sculpting itself – the formation of the statue through the slow and deliberate contact between sculptor and matter. Gosse's language for praising sculpture continued to draw upon this fantasy, and it became a central means of understanding the New Sculpture. The ideas of tangibility and physical contact were crucial to Gosse's language . . . For Gosse, imagined tactility became emphasized and eroticized in his sculpture criticism as he drew upon a fantasmatic identification of himself with Thornycroft's clay models. Through his influential writings, Gosse's

own erotic investments contributed to the New Sculpture's explorations of corporeal fusions between bodily image and the physical, material, sculptural object. (2004: 68)

Gosse's literary investment in the craft and its processes therefore facilitates a fantasy of tactile congress. As in *Roderick Hudson* where Mallet possesses the statue of *Adam* moulded initially by Hudson's hands and bearing his touch, Thornycroft's *Artemis* channels Gosse's libidinal longing: in possessing the cast, Gosse 'possesses' Thornycroft and is free to let his fingers linger where the sculptor's own have been, reliving the impress of their warmth in the sculpture's curves and lines. Yet, in 'Desiderium', Gosse features a speaker who operates as a 'reverse Pygmalion', one who wishes to enshrine his beloved in cold marble. This desire to express 'comradeship' through the tactility of sculpture and preserve the intensity of attraction across time is equally evident in Oscar Wilde's 'Charmides' (1881a) which, I argue, employs the haptic sense to attain a form of virtual access to the long-dead Romantic poet, John Keats, and in Olive Custance's statue poems which engage in complex and 'hermaphroditic' expressions of desire that negotiate between her investment in Oscar Wilde and his lovers, John Gray and Lord Alfred Douglas, and her own lesbian and artistic identity.[10]

Wildean Statuephilia

Given that, as mentioned in Chapter 1, 'Victorian scholars' considered touch 'a crude uncivilized form of perception' (Classen 2012: xii), it is conceivably odd that Wilde should have employed tactile metaphor to commune with Keats, a poet whom he held in the highest esteem. However, as Classen points out, 'touch makes the past come alive. It clothes the dry bones of historical fact with the flesh of physical sensation' (2012: xii), and it is perhaps Keats's own dry bones, clothed with tactile 'flesh' that Wilde sought to resurrect in 'Charmides'. Here, he appears to draw on what James Najarian calls 'the sensory optimism of the early Keats, the Keats in whom sensory pleasure "can lead to union with the beloved object" as in Keats's *Endymion*', the latter's prescient poem about another boy whose beauty is maintained by his everlasting sleep (2002: 3). Wilde's passion for Keats – both man and work – is well known. John Stokes has argued that Keats was always 'a subject close to Wilde's heart' (1997: 75), and critics have noted how often Keats features both explicitly and implicitly in Wilde's poetry, fiction and prose. Wilde mentions Keats in letters to a variety of correspondents; writes two versions of a sonnet inspired by Keats's grave in the Protestant cemetery in Rome: 'Heu Miserande Puer' (1877) and 'The Grave of Keats' (1881); refers to Keats by name in 'The Garden of Eros' (1881) and in 'Flower of Love' (1881); and in 1885 wrote 'On the sale by auction of Keats' Love Letters', a poem which inadvertently anticipates the sale of his own effects in the aftermath of the 1895 trials (Skelton 1990: 7). Furthermore, Keats's spirit and physical beauty are present in the beautiful boys that appear in Wilde's 'The Burden of Itys' and 'Endymion', both of which appeared alongside 'Charmides' in *Poems* (1881). Indeed, Keats, the author of 'La Belle Dame Sans Merci' (1819), might himself be considered an unwitting prototype for the male counterparts of the Decadents' fatal women, those *hommes fatals* we find in Wilde's fictional and non-fictional writings. Throughout his life and works Wilde debated the inevitable transience and destructive property of youthful beauty (Skelton 1990: 7), a topic realised indelibly and prophetically in *The Picture of Dorian Gray* (1890–1). While in such poems as 'The Tomb of Keats' and 'On the sale by auction of Keats' Love Letters', Keats is presented as the beautiful martyr, in other works by Wilde his avatars – Hylas, Narcissus, Adonis – all seemingly anticipate the beautiful destroyer we find in Dorian Gray; they share his loveliness and are similarly desirable and inaccessible.[11] For Wilde, 'the real Keats' is a figure of 'passionate wilfulness', 'fantastic moods' and 'fine inconsistence' (Wilde 1919: 202), a description that might apply equally to Dorian – the Decadents' *homme fatal* par excellence – and to Lord Alfred Douglas (later to become Olive Custance's husband) who drove Wilde to his own destruction.[12]

The homoeroticism implicit in Wilde's reaction to Keats is discussed by Najarian who observes, 'When Wilde visited Keats's grave in 1877, he saw in the dead poet a beautiful precursor of himself, and he metaphorically associated Keats, the doomed poet, with the man attracted to his own sex' (2002: 19). For Robin Skelton 'The Grave of Keats' draws similar attention to the sensuality, homoeroticism and sexual ambiguity of Wilde's response to his Romantic predecessor:

> If we look at the poem again we can see that Keats's death is presented in the context of, firstly, the murder of the 'lovely brown boy' St. Sebastian ... secondly, the weeping violets of fidelity which are laid so often on the grave of a loved one; thirdly, the comparable beauty of the poetess Sappho ... and lastly the grief of Isabella over the murdered Lorenzo whose only fault was his desire for a forbidden love. (1990: 6–7)

Alluding to St Sebastian, a figure of homoerotic admiration; to Sappho, a poet known for same-sex desire; and to Lorenzo, a character in Keats's 'Isabella; or, The Pot of Basil' (1820) whose buried severed head keeps Isabella's love unnaturally alive, Wilde's poem becomes implicitly an ode to homosexual and 'perverse' love, but the object of that desire – the dead Keats – also determines the impossibility of that love. In *The Decadent Image: The Poetry of Wilde, Symons, and Dowson*, Kostas Boyiopoulos argues that Wilde's 'erotic partaking – almost invasion – of the self in the sensuous and sensual artifice of inanimate *objets d'art*' is predicated on an 'erotic impulse' that 'thrives on its impossibility and is foredoomed because of it' (2015: 30). In a letter to the Pre-Raphaelite scholar, H. C. Marillier, written in December 1885, Wilde acknowledges how 'the love of things impossible' makes experience seem illusory, as '[o]ur most fiery moments of ecstasy are merely shadows of what somewhere else we have felt, or of what we long some day to feel' (qtd in Boyiopoulos 2015: 30).[13] Such unattainable love manifests itself most prominently in 'Charmides' in two key ways: in the poem's treatment of statuephilia and in an implied desire for the dead.

In Wilde's poem, Charmides sees and is enthralled by an imposing statue of Athena and feels compelled to violate the effigy with kisses and caresses. In revenge, the goddess Athena has him drowned, and when his body is washed ashore, a dryad, thinking Charmides asleep rather than dead, falls in love with him.[14] Killed by Artemis, who is affronted by her lust, the virgin dryad's love remains unrequited until Aphrodite, with Proserpine's help, grants that her desire may be fulfilled in the afterlife. To its homoerotic implications, then, the poem seemingly adds 'a touch of necrophilia' and both aspects attracted comment from Wilde's critics (Skelton 1990: 13). 'Charmides', the name Wilde chose for his protagonist, provides a significant clue to the homoeroticism that underlies this poem. Charmides' namesake features as the object of male desire in *Charmides, or Temperance* (380 BCE), a Hellenic text in the form of a dialogue between the philosopher Socrates and others, set in an ancient Greek version of the gym, 'The Palaestra of Taureas'. For John Addington Symonds, the palaestra 'was the place at Athens where lovers enjoyed the greatest freedom' (1901: 37) and, according to Walter Pater, in Greek culture gymnastics originated as part of a religious ritual. Worshippers tried to please by modelling themselves on the gods' bodies (as represented in sculpture), and the artists in turn used such worshippers as models for their gods: a youth would try to rival the athletic beauty of his gods, and 'his increased beauty passed back into them' (Pater 2010: 104). In *Charmides, or Temperance*, this idea is evident in the discussion that takes place between Socrates and his friend, Critas, as the latter's cousin, Charmides, 'considered the most beautiful' arrives at the palaestra with his admirers. Describing his impressions, Socrates states:

> Just about everyone that age is a beauty in my eyes. This one, however, struck me as wondrously tall and beautiful, and it seemed that everyone else was in love with him, seeing how dazzled and thrown into confusion they were by his entrance – and there were even more admirers following behind. It's no surprise that we older men reacted this way, but I was paying attention to the boys, too, and I noticed that not one of them – not even the littlest – was looking anywhere else: they were all gazing at him as if he were a statue. Then Chaerephon called to me and said, 'How does the young man strike you, Socrates? Isn't he good-looking?'
> 'Extraordinarily,' I said.
> 'Well, if he were willing to undress,' he said, 'you wouldn't even notice his face, he's so perfectly formed.' (Plato 2019: 4)

This response to Charmides' beauty requires contextualisation in terms of the Platonic model of love that operated in ancient Greece.[15] While, here, Charmides is clearly a beautiful object of desire, the Socratic dialogue in which Charmides is discussed also identifies him with temperance and goodness. As Symonds observes:

> The whole tenor of the dialogue makes it clear that, in spite of the admiration he excited, the honour paid him by a public character like Socrates, and the troops of lovers and of friends surrounding him, yet Charmides was unspoiled. His docility, modesty, simplicity, and healthiness of soul are at least as remarkable as the beauty for which he was famous. (1901: 39)

Such slippages between love and philosophy clearly gave Wilde ways in which to simultaneously veil and express his desire for men. As Stefano Evangelista points out, Wilde used Platonic models of love to forge 'a solid link between physical desire and philosophical thought' thus arguing for 'a natural progression from "the love of the beautiful object" to "the ideal"' and, 'in explicitly homoerotic terms', from Charmides to the 'idea of the good' (2009: 150). However, by the time Wilde's poem was published, the acceptability of such a model, recaptured in the nineteenth century in the conventional structures of the Oxford tutorial experienced by Wilde, had already come under scrutiny as testified by Tyrwhitt's review of Symonds's *Studies of the Greek Poets*.

The critical responses to Wilde's 'Charmides' reflect and share Tyrwhitt's concerns. In the *Saturday Review* on 23 July 1881, an anonymous reviewer commented on the 'sensual and ignoble tone' of Wilde's poetry, finding the poem's references to 'grand cool flanks' and 'crescent thighs' decidedly offensive (qtd in Beckson 1974: 29). Similarly, in the *Academy* on 30 July 1881, Oscar Browning writes of 'Charmides' that 'the story, as far as there is one, is most repulsive'; Wilde, he adds, 'has no magic to veil the hideousness of a sensuality which feeds on statues and dead bodies' (qtd in Beckson 1974: 32). Such implicit necrophiliac tendencies also manifest in Wilde's thank you letter, dated 21 March 1882, to Emma Speed, Keats's niece, who sent him the manuscript of Keats's 'Sonnet on Blue'. To Speed he writes:

> I am half-enamoured of the paper that touched his hand, and the ink that did his bidding . . . for since my boyhood I have loved none better than your marvellous kinsman, that godlike boy, the real Adonis of our age . . . In my heaven he walks eternally with Shakespeare and the Greeks . . . I thank you for this dear memory of the man I love. (Wilde 1962: 108)

In this letter, '[e]rotic metaphor shades into erotic fantasy ("the man I love")' (Ross 2013: 75), but it is worth noting that the nature of that fantasy suggests tactile congress with Keats through the means of the paper that has 'touched his hand'. Subverting the sentiment expressed in Keats's poem 'This living hand, now warm and capable' in which the speaker threatens his lover with the grasp of his dead hand from the 'icy silence of the tomb' (Keats 1988: 459), Wilde welcomes Keats's touch from beyond the grave and the uncanny contact it signifies between death and life, past and present.[16]

As Mark Paterson argues, any study of touch requires more than 'a series of physiological explanations' (2007: 2). For Aristotle, touch is vision's poor relation; due to its intrinsic connection with the body and purported distance from the 'higher' cognitive functions, touch has been considered 'a sense incapable of affording aesthetic experience' (Zuchert 2009: 285). But for Diderot, it is 'the most profound and philosophical of the senses' (Paterson 2007: 1–2). While, physiologically, touch may be 'a modality resulting from the combined information of innumerable receptors and nerve endings concerned with pressure, temperature, pain and movement', it is also much more than that:

> It is a sense of communication. It is receptive, expressive, can communicate empathy. It can bring distant objects into close proximity . . . It is a carnal world, with its pleasures of feeling and being felt, of tasting and

touching the textures of flesh and of food. And equally it is a profound world of philosophical verification, of the communication of presence and empathy with others, of the co-implication of body, flesh and world. (Paterson 2007: 2)

In Wilde's 'Charmides', touch becomes the principal sense through which his protagonist engages with the statue of Athena, and touch is also the sense through which Wilde communes with a sculptural monument to Keats.

In its engagement with statue love, 'Charmides' reworks the ancient tale of a young man's sexual violation of the *Cnidian Venus* told in *Amores* (fourth century BCE) to which I referred in Chapter 2. While Isobel Murray suggests that in 'Charmides' Wilde substitutes Athena for Aphrodite in order to make the sexual assault on the statue seem more shocking (Wilde 1997: 185–6, n. 53), it is worth remembering that Lucian's *Amores* is a dialogue that compares the love of women to the love of boys, and decides that the latter is preferable. Furthermore, Wilde's choice of the name 'Charmides' for his protagonist signals that boy-love is at the heart of the poem. Pater's 'Winckelmann' is clearly an additional influence as is Wilde's own encounter with Greek antiquity, during his then recent trip to Greece in 1877 with his former Classics tutor at Trinity College, Dublin, John Pentland Mahaffy (Ellmann 1988: 134). In this context, Wilde's choice of the androgynous Athena seems less a plan to shock, than a reluctance to engage imaginatively with Aphrodite, the epitome of womanly eroticism. Whatever the reasons behind his choice, reading between the lines of Wilde's poem, it is evident that boy-love, or at least the love of one particular boy, Keats, features implicitly in 'Charmides', not least because of the name's allusion to a boyish goodness that has become so intertwined with common perceptions of Keats as a poet wronged by his critics.

Oddly, given that, as Michèle Mendelssohn notes, it is 'Wilde's favourite' and the 'beating heart of *Poems*' (2018: 86), 'Charmides' has received comparatively little detailed critical attention, notable exceptions being Boyiopoulos's chapter on the poem in *The Decadent Image* and Iain Ross's article, '*Charmides* and *The Sphinx*: Wilde's Engagement with Keats', which appeared in the Winter 2008 issue of *Victorian Poetry* and was later revised for inclusion in his book, *Oscar Wilde and Ancient Greece* (2013).[17] Ross's article examines the ways in which the poem confuses 'the old mythical Greece and the new archaeologically determined Greece' (2008: 451), due to Wilde's use of Keats's *Endymion* (1818) and 'Lamia' (1820) as poetic models. He rightly locates the opening action of the poem in the Athenian Parthenon, a space denoted by Wilde's allusion to the 'frieze' on which the 'prancing horses neighed' (Wilde 1881a: 108). Athens is represented synecdochally by 'a burnished spear/ Like a thin thread of gold against the sky' (1881a: 103), Charmides' first sight of the city being the spear of the monumental bronze statue of Athena Promachos on the Acropolis (Ross 2008: 455). The violation scene set within the Parthenon also refers to the statue's 'breasts of polished ivory' (Wilde 1881a: 109) which suggests that it is the fifty-foot high chryselephantine statue of Athena Parthenos that is the object of Charmides' lust, a strange choice it seems, for if this were the case then, as Ross remarks, 'Charmides would have had to be content with embracing her shin' (Ross 2008: 455–7). I propose that, here, Wilde is less interested in historical or archaeological specificity, than in communing with Keats, and in establishing an imaginative tactile connection with both Keats's sculptural body and his body of poetry.

Ross's suggestion that Charmides is the 'child' of *Endymion* and 'Lamia' would position Keats in the role of 'grandparent' who gave birth to both. Yet, Wilde's mentions of Keats in his letters and works sound more like allusions to a young dead lover than references to a literary forefather. In a letter to Lord Houghton, written in 1877,[18] Wilde writes,

> I don't know if you have visited Keats's grave since a marble tablet in his memory was put up on the wall close to the tomb . . . what is really objectionable in it is the bas-relief of Keats's head – or rather a *medallion profile* [Plate 3], which is *extremely ugly*. (Wilde 1962: 41; original emphasis)

With evident indignation, he writes:

> [I]nstead of the finely cut nostril, and Greek sensuous delicate lips that he had, [the medallion] gives him thick almost negro lips and nose. Keats, we know, was as lovely as Hyakinthos, or Apollo, to look at, and this medallion is a very terrible lie and misrepresentation. I wish it could be removed and a tinted bust of Keats put in its place, like the beautiful coloured bust of the Rajah of Koolapoor at Florence. Keats's delicate features and rich colour could not be conveyed I think in plain white marble.[19] (Wilde 1962: 41–2)

Later, in his essay 'The Tomb of Keats' published in the *Irish Monthly*, in July 1877, Wilde includes a footnote that once again mentions the Keats medallion:

> [S]ome well-meaning persons have placed a marble slab on the wall of the cemetery with a medallion-profile of Keats on it, and some mediocre lines of poetry. The face is ugly, and rather hatchet-shaped, with thick, sensual lips, and is utterly unlike the poet himself, who was very beautiful to look upon . . . I think the best representation of the poet would be a coloured bust, like that of the young Rajah of Koolapoor at Florence, which is a lovely and life-like work of art.[20] (Wilde 1970: 4, n.1)

Wilde's comments highlight the conflict between idealised and realistic depictions of Keats. The traditional image of the beautiful, sensitive poet owes much to Keats's close friend Joseph Severn who emphasised Keats's beauty and his physical weakness both in his writings and his art, sentimentalising, and by implication, feminising him, thus 'calling his masculinity into question' (Najarian 2002: 43). In contrast, the medallion, by Warrington Wood, is based on a medallion plaque by Guiseppe Girometti made in 1822 which used Severn's sketches and Keats's death mask as sources (Najarian 2002: 45). According to Najarian, Keats's friends, Charles Armitage Brown and John Reynolds, thought it was the best likeness of him;[21] the medallion 'with its strong features, prominent nose, and heavy lips, has more in common with the masks and the drawing by Brown than with any of Severn's portraits' (2002: 45). But Wilde clearly prefers Severn's images of Keats in which he is beautified and idealised.

Eroticising Keats

Wilde's 1877 essay on Keats's tomb also includes 'Heu Miserande Puer', which in its later revised form is now more commonly known as 'The Grave of Keats'. Here, the poet is referred to as 'The youngest of the martyrs . . . /Fair as Sebastian and as foully slain' (Wilde 1970: 5) and elsewhere, as we have seen, Wilde refers to Keats as 'that godlike boy, the real Adonis of our age' who 'walks eternally with Shakespeare and the Greeks' (Wilde 1962: 108). For Najarian, Wilde's comparison of Keats to Sebastian and Adonis makes Keats a kind of saint 'pierced by the arrows of his critics, implicitly taking the tale of *Adonais* at face value'; but, as he argues, this image has other connotations:

Wilde adds a distinctly homoerotic element. Wilde's picture of the poet is erotically charged, as is Guido's portrait of the naked, swooning, penetrated Sebastian . . . Keats's physical beauty transposes Keats's worship of beauty. For Wilde 'A thing of beauty is a joy for ever,' but Wilde reads that beauty into Keats's person as much as his work. (2002: 19)

Given Wilde's avowed love of Keats, both boy and poetry, it is worth dwelling for a moment on the implications of Wilde's suggestion that Keats's beauty merits a 'coloured bust', a 'life-like' work of art, and on his comparison of Keats to St Sebastian in this poem, as well as in the revised version 'The Grave of Keats'. The first suggests a desire to bring the poet back to life, albeit via the death-like quality of an 'animated' statue; the second homoeroticises Keats's beauty. As Richard Kaye has observed, in the late-Victorian period, St Sebastian became 'a powerful visual metaphor for . . . a male who could induce – if not exactly represent – otherwise unsanctioned, homoerotic yearning' (1999: 272). Moreover, to call Keats 'Adonis' is on the one hand to allude to *Adonais* (1821), Shelley's elegy to Keats, as Najarian remarks, and on the other to position Keats as an object of erotic love.[22] Given Wilde's predilection for male beauty and Greek love, I would argue that 'Charmides' plays out Wilde's fantasy of physical and poetic unison with Keats established through allusions to touch and vision. Being one of many beautiful boys in Wilde's *oeuvre*, Charmides 'a Grecian lad' with 'crisp brown curls' (Wilde 1881a: 103), might easily 'have been named Hyakinthos or Hylas or Adonis' or, indeed, Keats (Ross 2008: 458). In this context, the violated statue of Athena functions as a witty comment on Keats's troubled embrace of classical culture (Aske 1985: 35), while Charmides himself is the Keatsian martyr and object of necrophiliac desire.

In Wilde's poem, Athena is portrayed as unassailable and forbidding. Her own 'awful image' is accompanied by a second, that of Medusa's head whose impotent passion and cold 'bloodless lips' appear on Athena's shield, foreshadowing Charmides' death (1881a: 107).[23] With nonchalant audacity, Charmides touches Athena's throat, and 'with hands violate' bares her 'breasts of polished ivory', to reveal 'the secret mystery/Which to no lover will Athena show/ The grand cool flanks, the crescent thighs, the bossy hills of snow' (1881a: 109). Vision fuels touch: half-swooning from the 'sight' of 'such luxuries', his lips feed 'on her lips' and kiss 'Her pale and argent body undisturbed', while he presses his 'hot and beating heart upon her chill and icy breast' (1881a: 109–10). This early scene of unrequited – and impossible – love is mirrored later in the poem when the dryads encounter Charmides' drowned body which has been washed ashore. Thinking the dead Charmides to be the sea-god Poseidon pretending sleep in order to entrap them, most of the dryads run away, except for one, 'who deemed it would not be/So dread a thing to feel a sea-god's arms/Crushing her breasts in amorous tyranny' (1881a: 124). Unaware that Charmides has been dead for three days, the dryad finds Charmides 'very beautiful' (1881a: 128); his lips are 'made to kiss' (1881a: 128) and she makes 'havoc of his mouth' (1881a: 124).[24] However, finding him unresponsive, she fears that 'his lips upon her lips would never care to feed' (1881a: 126), and attempts to draw him out by speaking of other erotic couplings: Apollo and Daphne, Venus and Adonis, yet he remains unyielding. While, here, the beautiful boys 'Apollo' and 'Adonis' are matched with female paramours, the poem as a whole contains allusions to other figures such as 'Hylas', 'Narcissus', 'Dionysus' and 'Hyacinthus', all of which point to the subtext of homoerotic love that underlies Wilde's choice of 'Charmides' as the name for his protagonist. In addition, situating the androgynous Athena in the Parthenon by focusing our vision on the 'prancing horses' of the Parthenon frieze, Wilde draws implicit attention to the ideal beauty of the male youths who ride them and thus to objects of desire. But this allusion also points the reader towards Keats's poem, 'On seeing the Elgin marbles' (1817), in which the speaker exclaims: 'mortality/Weighs heavily on me like unwilling sleep' (Keats 1988: 99, ll. 1–2), thus auguring Charmides' and – perhaps one might say, Keats's – liminal position between sleep and death.[25]

For the Greeks, 'vision was not a neutral contemplation of the world but . . . a kind of long-distance touch' (Stewart 1997: 16). Similarly, in Wilde's 'Charmides', vision and touch coalesce. The sculptural bodies that we 'see' in the poem – Athena, the riders of the Parthenon frieze, and the pale, dead Charmides – function as conduits for Wilde's desire to 'touch' Keats from an unbridgeable distance. His focus on the sculptural monument to Keats in letters and in his essay, 'The Tomb of Keats', anticipates the statuephilic and necrophiliac longing expressed in 'Charmides'. Stating his preference for 'a coloured' and 'life-like' sculpture of Keats, Wilde reveals his desire to merge imaginatively and erotically with him, to do what Herder claims that the contemplation of sculpture allows: to touch him with the 'gentle fingers' of his 'inner sense' (2002: 80). The unsatisfying – and impossible – nature of such communion explains why, in 'Charmides', the relationship between the 'lovers', one besotted, the other dead, reaches fulfilment only in the afterlife. Unable to realise in life his enduring desire for Keats to whom he referred as 'the man I love', Wilde seems doomed, like his dryad, to wait for romantic reunion in the next world, a world of the poetic spirit but not of the flesh.

Following Wilde

Similar kinds of impossible love inform Olive Custance's statue poems, works that might be read as allusions to Wilde's 'Charmides'. Until the second half of the twentieth century, Custance's poetry received very little critical attention. Often confined to anthologies, if published at all, she was known, like so many women of her generation, more for her relationship with key male figures of the late nineteenth century than for her own literary output. Writing of Custance's relationship to late-Victorian Decadence in an introduction to an early bibliography of her work, Nancy J. Hawkey remarks:

> Although historically she is indeed in the Decadent period, her assignment to the Decadents seems to be based less on the characteristics of Olive Douglas['s] writing than on the association of her name with those of three of the period's most prominent men: her husband, Lord Alfred Douglas; a man she never met, Oscar Wilde; and her publisher, John Lane. (1972: 49)

Overshadowed by her notorious lover, a literary icon, and one of the *fin-de-siècle's* best-known publishers, it would be easy to agree with Hawkey and to dismiss Custance's importance. It is therefore vital to point to the fact that her work is significant in its own right, and that she anticipates other sapphic poets such as H.D. whose work engaged with Hellenism. She published regularly in periodicals during the 1890s, including the *Savoy*, and the *Living Age* (Thornton and Small 1996: ii); was 'a chief contributor to the *Yellow Book*' (Hawkey 1972: 49); and produced four volumes of poetry: *Opals* (1897), *Rainbows* (1902), *The Blue Bird* (1905) and *Inn of Dreams* (1911). More recently, Sarah Parker has identified work by Custance that extends well beyond the turn of the century and found that she continued to publish 'long after 1911, producing work throughout the 1920s, 30s, and 40s until her death in 1944' (2019: 57).

While Hawkey's introduction is often dismissive, it contributed to a revival of critical interest in Custance in the late twentieth century that has continued into the early decades of our own.[26] In his 2018 article, 'Olive Custance: A Poet Crossing Boundaries', Jad Adams, like Hawkey, highlights her relationships with prominent men of the late-Victorian period such as John Gray, Richard Le Gallienne, John Lane, Henry Harland and Alfred Douglas, but argues that her influences were 'the Romantic poets rather than any of the more modern writers of the fin de siècle' (Adams 2018: 61). However, as Caspar Wintermans remarks, Oscar Wilde and Walter Pater were among Custance's favourite authors (2004: 10). I would add Algernon Charles Swinburne as another significant influence; she owned an edition of *Poems and Ballads I* and notes in her diary that 'it certainly ought to be a "joy forever"' (Custance 2004: 45–6). But clearly Wilde is her most important touchstone: aside from their shared love for Lord Alfred Douglas, her diaries declare her admiration for Wilde's *Intentions* (1891) and contain quotes from *The Picture of Dorian Gray*.[27]

Continually overshadowed by the men she admired, in reclamations of lesbian writers' lives and works, she is likewise obscured by women she knew who had more sensational reputations such as Natalie Clifford Barney and Renée Vivien.[28] In his introduction to *The Selected Poems of Olive Custance*, published in 1995, Brocard Sewell attempts to distance her work from the more controversial aspects of the late-Victorian period. He concedes that a number of her poems 'have given her a place among the "Decadent" writers of the Eighteen-Nineties', but tempers this with the observation that 'with her, Decadence was more of a fleeting phase or mood than a deliberately cultivated attitude' (Sewell 1995: 13). This 'mood', according to Holbrook Jackson, is discernible in what he calls a 'minor note' and experienced collectively by those who epitomised the period, giving the poetry of the hour 'a hothouse fragrance; a perfume faint yet unmistakable and strange' (1913: 197). The use of the word 'strange' in this context is suggestive; as Ruth Vanita notes, it is a word that in the works of Walter Pater encodes homoeroticism and is often appropriated by his contemporaries and followers to complicate expressions of desire (1996: 66). Jackson's 'minor note' is therefore associated with complex negotiations of gender and sexuality, connotations that become increasingly clear in his extended discussion of the term:

> The eroticism which became so prevalent in the verse of the younger poets was minor because it was little more than a pose ... where the minor poets were both minor and poets was in that curious lisping note which many of them managed to introduce into their poems. This was

a new note in poetry, corresponding with the minor key in music . . . There was an unusual femininity about it; not the femininity of women, nor yet the feminine primness of men; it was more a mingling of what is effeminate in both sexes. This was the genuine minor note, and it was abnormal – a form of hermaphroditism. (1913: 96–7)

Jackson's book, published in 1913, demonstrates a retrospective consciousness of the clinical discourses that had begun, continued to define, and, in turn, to construct homosexuality. As Michel Foucault explains:

We must not forget that the psychological, psychiatric, medical category of homosexuality was constituted from the moment it was characterized . . . less by a type of sexual relations than by a certain quality of sexual sensibility, a certain way of inverting the masculine and the feminine in oneself. Homosexuality appeared as one of those forms of sexuality when it was transposed from the practice of sodomy onto a kind of interior androgyny, a hermaphroditism of the soul. (1981: 43)

Here Foucault refers more specifically to the attention paid by sexologists to male homosexuality, but lesbianism, while legally non-existent, had begun to come under scrutiny.[29] In 1886 Richard von Krafft-Ebing included lesbianism among the sexual perversions discussed in *Psychopathia Sexualis* and, according to his formulations, female homosexuality was to be suspected in women who wore their hair short, partook in male pastimes or sports, and enjoyed cross-dressing on or off stage (Showalter 1992: 23). In women, it appears, Foucault's 'hermaphroditism of the soul' swiftly becomes a 'hermaphroditism' of the body.

Beautiful Boys

Given the public denunciation of Lord Alfred Douglas's poetry published in the December 1894 edition of *The Chameleon*, which was cited by the prosecution at the first Wilde trial of 1895 as amplifying 'a defence of the vilest immorality' (Harris 1992: 159), it is unsurprising that Sewell tries to distance Custance from her more 'disreputable' contemporaries. This, despite the fact that she married Douglas, and that Natalie Clifford Barney – with whom she had a brief liaison – was known for her energetic sexual exploits with women, took Sappho as her model, and presided over a salon in Paris where one was certain to meet lesbians (Souhami 2004: 2). Custance's friendship with Barney developed following the latter's visit to the offices of The Bodley Head in search of a new translation of Sappho, during which John Lane encouraged her to purchase a copy of *Opals*.[30] Sewell relates that Barney, 'much pleased with these poems', wrote to Custance expressing her admiration and sent her a collection of her own work, *Quelques portraits: sonnets de femmes* (1900) (Sewell 1975: 11–12). Barney records in her memoir that Opal – as Custance liked to be called – responded warmly ('avec feu'), and quotes an extract from a poem that Custance addressed to her in her reply:

> For I would dance to make you smile, and sing
> Of those who with some sweet mad sin have played,
> And how Love walks with delicate feet afraid
> 'Twixt maid and maid. (1960: 51)[31]

Notwithstanding the homoerotic implications of Custance's romantic friendship with Barney, Sewell glosses over their relationship, claiming that by the spring of 1902, when she went to Venice with Barney, Custance carried with her a picture of a statue of Antinous (Figure 4.2) which she said reminded her of Lord Alfred Douglas

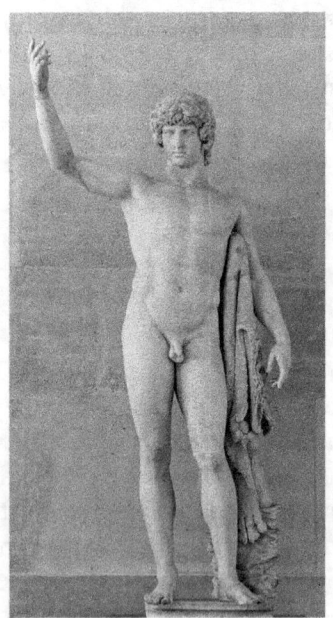

Figure 4.2   *Braschi Antinous*, second century CE, marble (Musée du Louvre, Paris). Jastrow / Wikipedia / CC BY-SA 4.0

'with whom she was ... in love', a problem that Barney hoped to resolve by suggesting that she herself should marry Douglas and that they should set up a *ménage-à-trois* (Sewell 1975: 13–17). Earlier in the biography Sewell also records how Custance, at the age of sixteen, developed a teenage passion for the poet John Gray, whom she met in 1890 and whom he describes as 'the most beautiful young man in London' at the time (1975: 7). Thought to be the model for Wilde's Dorian Gray, John Gray, like Douglas later, was reputedly Wilde's lover.[32]

Given the homosexual past of Custance's love-objects and female friends, Sewell's efforts to heterosexualise her are not entirely successful and it is evident from his biography that he is well aware of her penchant for women and feminine men. Alfred Douglas, in his autobiography, acknowledges this complication and its effect on their marriage:

> I fell desperately in love with Olive... In the end, after we were married, I was more in love with her than she was with me... But how could I know or guess that the very thing she loved in me was that which I was always trying to suppress and keep under: I mean the feminine part of me. As soon as I was married I deliberately tried to become more manly. The more manly I became, the less attractive I was to Olive. (qtd in Sewell 1975: 20)

Douglas's assessment of their marriage and of his own effeminacy accords not only with descriptions of his appearance, but also recalls the 'masculine' role adopted by Custance during the early stages of their courtship. Douglas is described as having been 'girlishly pretty' (Harris 1992: 87), while Olive is 'pretty in a boyish way, feminine but not girly' (Murray 2000: 124) and in her early correspondence with Douglas, Custance addresses him as her 'Prince' while she calls herself his 'page' (Murray 2000: 123). Indeed, the gender ambiguity that characterises their relationship is discussed by Douglas in a letter to Custance dated 13 November 1901 in which he writes: 'You are a darling Baby and you are exactly like a boy and you know perfectly well that I love you better than anyone else, boy or girl... I used to wish you were a boy, now I am glad you are not' (qtd in Murray 2000: 127). Later, Douglas, in attempting to explain his attraction to Custance, would declare: 'I believe that almost everyone is more or less bisexual' (qtd in Murray 2000: 124).

As Margaret Stetz and Mark Samuels Lasner have observed, this bisexuality is evident in both Custance's life and in her poetry. In their discussion of *Opals* and of Custance's relationship with Douglas they write:

> The androgynous and highly un-Victorian sexual yearning that fills all the poems in this, the author's first book, also shaped Olive Custance's own destiny. Although his practices and inclinations remained homosexual, Douglas was powerfully drawn to the beautiful young poet, who had herself photographed in knee-breeches much like those worn by Wilde in the 1880s and who referred to herself as Douglas's page ... Custance's poems from the Nineties suggest, however, that her strongest attachments were really to other women. (1990: 26–7)

Custance's adoption of the role of 'page', both in her letters and in the photograph mentioned by Stetz and Lasner, suggests a desire to present herself as an adolescent boy, a figure that has significant implications, the young, beautiful, beardless and effeminate boy often acting as the focus and/or mediator of homosexual desire in *fin-de-siècle* literature. Martha Vicinus argues that 'Even though many male homosexuals were not pederasts and most lesbians did not look like boys, the boy was the defining, free agent who best expressed who they were', and she suggests that we should always 'look – and then look again – to see the hidden meaning of the beautiful boy' (1994: 92). Among the 'beautiful boys' mentioned in this chapter so far are the cross-dressed figure of Olive Custance; John Gray and Lord Alfred Douglas; and the statue of Antinous, whose image reminded Custance so strongly of her husband-to-be. If we look again, as Vicinus suggests, at the 'hidden meaning' behind this particular boy, we find a homosexual coupling: that of Antinous and the Roman emperor Hadrian, who deified him after his premature death at the height of his beauty (Paglia 1991: 134).[33] However, in Custance's 'Antinous', this allusion to male homosexuality is problematised by the uncertain gender of the poem's speaker.

Loving Statues

'Antinous' appears in the collection *Rainbows*, dedicated to 'The Fairy Prince', thought to be Lord Alfred Douglas (Thornton and Small 1996: iv), and is one of her three statue poems, the others being 'The White Statue', published in *Opals*, and 'Statues', which appeared in her later collection *The Blue Bird*. According to Sewell, these poems are 'among her best', full of what he calls 'a strong "perversity"' that makes her a true poet of the *fin de siècle* (1975: 14). In order to explore the 'perversity' of Custance's treatment of sculpture, it is worth considering her statue poems alongside those works by Swinburne, Pater and Wilde that share her interest in the sculptural body. Swinburne's 'Hermaphroditus', inspired as noted in Chapter 2 by the antique statue of a sleeping hermaphrodite at the Louvre, centres on the 'curious beauty' (Pater 2010: 65) of its androgynous body in which 'Sex to sweet sex with lips and limbs is wed,/Turning the fruitful feud of hers and his/To the waste wedlock of a sterile kiss', and celebrates its ambiguity and its combination of the masculine and the feminine (Swinburne 1904: 79, ll. 17–19) . In contrast, Pater's essay, 'Winckelmann', in *The Renaissance*, is more preoccupied with forging a connection between the historian's 'romantic, fervid friendships with young men' and 'the Greek ideal [that] expressed itself pre-eminently in sculpture' (2010: 93–104). However, for Pater, the beauty of the Greek statues is a 'sexless beauty' that allows Winckelmann to finger the pagan marbles with 'unsinged hands, with no sense of shame or loss' (2010: 111–12). In both works, sculpture is seemingly desexualised while simultaneously permitting an erotic engagement that is ostensibly 'cleansed' by art: the white marble, emitting from its 'gleaming surfaces' a purifying 'white light purged from the angry, blood-like stains of action and passion' (Pater 2010: 106). In Wilde's *The Picture of Dorian Gray*, a similar form of sterilisation is at work. Dorian is described as 'a marvellous type', possessing grace and the kind of 'white purity of boyhood, and beauty' that is found in 'old Greek marbles' (1988: 33). Dorian's face is set to become to Basil Hallward what 'the face of Antinous was to late Greek sculpture' (1988: 14), and he shares with Charmides those 'finely curved scarlet lips', 'frank blue eyes' and 'crisp gold hair' that also recall the 'crisp curls, and flowerlike mouths' of the statues to which Symonds alludes in *Studies of the Greek Poets*, suggesting a coded homoeroticism ready to be deciphered by those in the know (Nelson 2004: 134). In 'Charmides', the speaker warns those 'who have never known a lover's sin' to read no more but urges those 'who have learned who Eros is' to 'listen yet awhile' (Wilde 1881a: 109). He then proceeds to detail Charmides' ardour, telling the reader how 'all night long he murmured honeyed word,/And saw her [Athena's] sweet unravished limbs, and kissed/Her pale and argent body undisturbed' (1881a: 110). Later, the speaker once again implies that those who have not known such love 'Will never know of what I try to sing' (1881a: 110) and after his sexual endeavours Charmides wears a 'strange and secret smile' (1881a: 112). The knowing reader is encouraged to see that those aware of 'strange' desires, those initiated into the secret codes of statue love, will understand the subtext of a poem that ostensibly presents two versions of heterosexual (albeit unnatural) love. Evidently, in calling to those who have known 'a lover's sin' and 'who have learned who Eros is', Wilde speaks to future readers like Custance, who have played with a 'sweet mad sin' and who like Douglas, recognise 'the love that dare not speak its name' (Murray 2000: 36). I would argue that Charmides' own sculptural beauty and the homoerotic implications of Wilde's poem are appropriated by Custance and developed into her own poetic and sculptural aesthetic through which she expresses the complexity of her own sexual proclivities.

Charmides, like the figure of Antinous, is an example of what Solomon-Godeau terms 'ephebic masculinity', denoting the 'feminized masculine' associated in antiquity with the hermaphrodite, the androgyne and the faun (1997: 202). Clearly, such feminised male bodies have a special significance in the works of Custance's antecedents and contemporaries, who 'summoned frequently' the 'nude male bodies of Greek statuary . . . as objects of the male homoerotic "gaze"' (Laity 1996: 45). However, as Cassandra Laity notes, this 'gaze' – and, by implication, visual 'touch' – can be appropriated by women, manifesting itself in a variety of 'trace images' that represent the object of desire: 'whiteness, crystal, marble statuary, the burning "hard gemlike flame," or the transparently veined white body' (1996: 65). I suggest that, in her statue poems, Custance plays with the 'trace images' of this gaze. In 'Statues' the speaker tells how he or she has worshipped 'the white form of stone' (Custance 1905: 12, l. 12); in 'Antinous' 'The faint light widens to fair day/round a white statue' (Custance 1902: 51); and the title 'The White Statue' speaks for itself (Custance 1897: 67). However, despite the impenetrable solidity of their marble whiteness, Custance's sculptural bodies seem to soften in the shifting lights of sunrises, twilights and moonlights. Coloured with 'The morning rainbows of an opal sky' (1897: 12), seen through the 'silver veils' of a 'Mysterious moon behind a mask of gold' (1897: 13), draped in 'veils of dusk diaphanous'; tinged by a sky 'stained with scarlet fire' (Custance 1902: 50–1), and tinted by a 'mauve-silver twilight' (Custance 1897: 67), Custance's statues either burn at sunrise with the 'hard gemlike flame' of Paterian aestheticism, or give the illusion of frail life, 'veined' by the delicate hues of twilight. What seems particularly significant is that these moments of colour occur in the liminal spaces of dawn and dusk, transitional temporal spaces that express and reflect the sexual duality of the statues and the ambiguity of the speakers' desires.[34]

Each of Custance's statue poems concerns itself with what Laity calls 'statue-love' (1996: 65), but fails to make the speaker's gender explicit. In 'Antinous', a poem that highlights the speaker's unrequited love for a male statue, this ambiguity is heightened by the first two lines: 'I spoke of you, Antinous, with her who is my heart's delight' (Custance 1902: 50). This endearment, which might suggest a male speaker, homoeroticises the poem, for, if this is the case, then the poem describes homosexual love, and if not, then bisexual desire is implied. This ambiguity is equally present in 'The White Statue', where neither the speaker's nor the sculpture's sex is defined. Moreover, the Greek term 'poikilos', a word belonging 'specifically to the homoerotic vocabulary of late-Victorian Aestheticism' captures the shimmering rays that illuminate Custance's statues (Dowling 1989: 1). Used to describe 'the play of light or texture' and having, as Robert Crawford observes, a range of meanings including 'pied', 'dappled', 'flashing', 'intricate' and 'ambiguous' (qtd in Dowling 1989: 1), the term is especially appropriate to denote the changing colours and surfaces that characterise Custance's sculptural bodies, the 'play of light and texture' she employs enabling a fantasmatic tactility that is experienced through the lover's gaze.

In adopting the homoerotic gaze and sculptural aesthetic of her male predecessors and contemporaries, Custance is a forerunner of H.D. who, according to Laity, is one of the group of women modernists, including Katherine Mansfield, Willa Cather and Renée Vivien, who identified with writers such as Swinburne, Pater and Wilde, rather than with their female antecedents (1996: x). She explains that:

> Unable or unwilling to recognize a tradition of women poets in the nineteenth century, H.D. and others used the Decadents to fashion a modernist poetic of female desire. In the next generation of male poets, theories of modern poetry authored by Eliot, Pound, Yeats, and others repeatedly raise the spectres of the femme fatale and the Aesthete to warn against the 'hedonism' they believed had plunged Romanticism into decadence and decay. Women modernists such as H.D., however, responded differently to the powerful feminine subjectivities of their early reading that were presently driving their male contemporaries toward a foreboding masculinization of poetry. The ready agents of a sexually transgressive poetic – the fatal woman and the Aesthete androgyne – therefore articulated a fluid range of forbidden sexualities, including androgyny, homoeroticism, and role reversal, not available in the modernist poetic of male desire, which . . . prompted the twentieth-century woman writer to evolve alternative modernisms. (Laity 1996: xi–xii)

While Custance is omitted from this list, like H.D. and the other women Laity mentions, she also identified with Swinburne, Pater and Wilde. Her sonnet, 'St. Sebastian', which appears in *The Blue Bird*, suggests a special identification with Wilde, and with Wilde's poem, 'The Grave of Keats' in which Keats is associated with the murdered saint (Skelton 1990: 6). In Custance's poem, the anguished speaker declares:

> Marvellous beauty . . . target of the world,
> How all Love's arrows seek thy joy, Oh, Sweet!
> And wound the white perfection of thy youth.
> How all the poisoned spears of hate are hurled
> Against thy sorrow when thou darest to meet
> With martyrdom men's mockery of the truth!
> (1905: 25, ll. 10–15)

Given that St Sebastian is often claimed as the patron saint of homosexuals; that Wilde expressed his fondness for Guido Reni's painting of St Sebastian (Ellmann 1988: 68); and that, after his release from Reading Gaol in 1897, Wilde used the name 'Sebastian Melmoth' as his alias in France (Ellmann 1988: 74), Custance's sonnet reads as a tribute to and comment on Wilde. The poem 'Hyacinthus' that also features in *The Blue Bird* might equally be read in this light. In Greek myth Hyacinthus is Apollo's young lover whom the god accidentally kills while playing a game of quoits.[35] Yet, Hyacinthus is also among the 'beautiful boys', including Hylas and Narcissus, mentioned in Wilde's 'Charmides'. The speaker in Custance's poem imagines a loving tryst between Hyacinthus and Apollo:

> Perchance I saw thee then, so glad and fleet,
> Hasten to greet Apollo, stoop to bind
> The gold and jewelled sandals on his feet,
> While he so radiant, so divinely kind,
> Lured thee with honeyed words to be his friend,
> All heedless of thy fate, for Love is blind.
> (1905: 15, ll. 7–12)

Custance's use of 'honeyed words' in this context couples her poem with Wilde's own, echoing the 'honeyed word' that Charmides murmurs all night long during his encounter with the statue of Athena (1881a: 110).[36] The speaker goes on to lament the sad nature of this meeting between god and mortal and blames its outcome on 'Some God' who, having witnessed Apollo kissing Hyacinthus, 'is jealous of the mute caress' (Custance 1905: 15, l. 18). However, Hyacinthus's death is not to be mourned, for, slain in his youth by 'the sweet hands of Love', he will remain 'for ever young and fair' (1905: 16, ll. 29–30).

The figures of Apollo and his young lover in 'Hyacinthus' cannot of course be mapped exactly on to Douglas and Wilde. The Greek model of male love between an older man and a young boy would suggest that, if this poem is an implicit comment on Wilde's decline and fall, Wilde, as the older partner, should be cast in the role of Apollo. Indeed, in a letter to Douglas sent in January 1893 Wilde writes: 'I know Hyacinthus, whom Apollo loved so madly, was you in Greek days' (qtd in Ellmann 1988: 367). Yet, it seems that, in Custance's poem, Wilde is associated not with Apollo, but with Hyacinthus the beautiful boy.[37] The coupling of Hyacinthus and Apollo also resonates with Keats, that other beautiful boy who, for Wilde 'was as lovely as Hyakinthos, or Apollo, to look at' (Wilde 1962: 41–2). While necessarily complicating any simple reading of Custance's poem as a mythical representation of the Douglas–Wilde relationship, the image of Wilde as beautiful boy has interesting implications: her desire for John Gray and for Lord Alfred Douglas serving as a covert form of identification with him, as well as an allusion to Wilde's own impossible love for Keats.[38] In loving the men that Wilde loved, and in marrying the love of Wilde's life, Custance, in a sense, usurps Wilde's position as lover, while marking the impossibility of her own boyish congress with Wilde.

Yet Custance problematises the Dorian aesthetic embraced by her male contemporaries as a cipher of male homosexuality and uses it to express a more inclusive bisexuality that is encoded in the colours that play over her sculptural bodies. As suggested earlier, for writers such as Pater the importance of the white statue seemingly lies in its ability to purify unruly desires. Greek sculpture represents a sexless pristine purity, a purity that is associated with 'white light', from which 'the angry, blood-like stains of action and passion' have been purged (Pater 2010: 106). However, in Custance's statue poems, the purity of this whiteness is compromised by the play of light that dapples the sculptural figure, the transient movement of shadow and light threatening to expose the 'lurid colour' of those desires. Eileen Gregory has pointed out that for H.D. who, like Custance, employs the Dorian tradition in her work, colour, with its homoerotic connotations, functions as an anxiety that must be resolved. Gregory argues that in her 1920 essay on Sappho H.D. felt compelled to 'apologize for her own poetic and erotic dispositions', treating Sappho 'as much as possible in the acceptable terms of a Dorian aesthetic' (1997: 105–6). In 'The Wise Sappho', H.D. comments on Sappho's fragments:

> 'Little, but all roses' is the dictate of the Alexandrine poet, yet I am inclined to disagree. I would not bring roses, nor yet the great shaft of scarlet lilies. I would bring orange blossoms . . . 'Little, but all roses' true there is a tint of rich colour . . . violets, purple woof of cloth, scarlet garments, dyed fastening of a sandal, the lurid, crushed and perished hyacinth, stains on cloth and flesh and parchment. There is gold too. Was it a gold rose the poet meant? . . . 'Little, but all roses.' I think, though the stains are deep on the red and scarlet cushions, on the flaming cloak of love, it is not warmth we look for in these poems . . . but another element containing all these, magnetic, vibrant; [a] white, unhuman element containing fire and light and warmth, yet in essence differing from all these . . . I think of the words of Sappho as these colours, or states rather, transcending colour yet containing . . . all colour. (1988: 57–8)

In her analysis of this passage Gregory observes:

> The operative rhetorical construction here – 'True . . . but' – is necessary because the *tinted*, *dyed*, *lurid*, and *stained* belong to a prurient iconography of Sappho, exemplified in Gautier's *Mademoiselle de Maupin*, in Baudelaire's and Swinburne's "lesbian," and in Pierre Louÿs's *Chansons de Bilitis*. (1997: 106; original emphasis)[39]

But, she argues, 'H.D. redeems Sappho's color-taint . . . by indicating that the words of Sappho are themselves "states" of colour, "transcending colour yet containing . . . all colour". This is . . . the traditional color iconography of white marble' (1997: 106). Gregory suggests that H.D.'s anxiety stems from the distinction made by Victorian critics, including Pater, between the Dorian and Ionian models of art. The Dorian, associated with Sparta and Apollo, is 'austere' and 'masculine', whereas the Ionian, associated with Athens and Aphrodite, is 'effeminate, luxurious and morally weak', indicating that the Ionian constantly needs to be 'corrected' by the Dorian (1997: 91–2). The Dorian is represented by whiteness, clarity and brilliance, whereas the Ionian manifests itself in colours: gold, ivory, yellow, purple, crimson and red (1997: 105). While H.D. feels compelled to 'redeem a too-Ionian, too-Aphroditic' Sappho (1997: 105), thus purifying Sappho's words in the prismatic 'white light' of Dorian aestheticism, Custance, inspired by the 'prurient' colour iconography that exemplifies the decadent lesbian, plays with colour in her poetry and appropriates it in order to express bisexual desire.

Her white statues are touched with rainbows, coloured by gold, scarlet, mauve and silver; her statue poems restore the colours of her Dorian statues, reimposing them artificially on sculptural bodies that function simultaneously as objects and expressions of love. Suffused with colour, these statues appear in collections whose titles are themselves stained, tinged and tinted with colour: *Opals*, *Rainbows* and *The Blue Bird*. Custance's 'strange passion' for opals, and her desire 'to be called, and to call herself, Opal' (Sewell 1975: 9) suggests that these stones share properties with the statues in her poems: white, or transparent, they often display or reflect the shifting colours that mirror the capricious nature of her own erotic desires.

Decadent Parnassianism

Yet, while the colours that play on the white surfaces of her statues locate her in a Sapphic tradition, her statue poems and her passion for opals also recall the Parnassian poets' investment in hard materials and sculpted forms. Like the Parnassians, in her work Custance privileges craftsmanship, beauty and permanence, subscribes to the tenet 'art for art's sake', and uses 'hard' materials such as gems and marble, as well as traditional poetic forms. Like the Parnassians, she engages in a 'cult of form' that, in Parnassian poetry, emerges in expressions of statuephilia (Johnson 2008: 117). Lothar Hönnighausen observes that this 'pronounced interest in the visual arts' is also recognisable in the 'Parnassian ideal of gem-carvers and engravers' which emerges in French collections such as Gautier's *Émaux et camées* (1852) and Banville's *Améthystes* (1862) (Hönnighausen 2010: 118). Like Gautier, Custance understands the correlation between poetry and gemstones; for her, as for Gautier, 'Verse, marble, onyx, and enamel' are the 'rebellious' forms from which the work of art emerges', and like that other minor poet, Arthur O'Shaughnessy, she sculpts in marble and seals her 'floating dream' forever in the 'resistant block' (qtd in Johnson 2008: 118). Writing of Gautier's *Émaux et camées*, Robert Denommé asserts that, as enamels are 'miniatures that require delicate manipulation' and cameos are 'precious stones whose beauty may be further enhanced by elegantly sculptured shapes and contours', the title of Gautier's collection conveys 'the poet's resolve to consider each of the poems as individually polished works of art' (1972: 52). Furthermore, he contends that 'the octosyllabic verse structure of the overwhelming majority of poems' contained in the collection, contributes to the idea of 'miniature jewels' suggested by the title *Émaux et camées*, and renovates the use of a 'familiar sixteenth-century form' (1972: 52). As discussed in Chapter 2, Gautier's influence is discernible in the work of those poets labelled the 'English Parnassians' (Gosse 1913: 362) such as Swinburne, Morris, Rossetti and O'Shaughnessy and in that of the generation that followed. For example, the correlation of poetry, form and sculpture informs Swinburne's 'Hermaphroditus' as well as Morris's 'Pygmalion and the Image' in *The Earthly Paradise*, and occurs most noticeably in Arthur O'Shaughnessy's collection, *Songs of a Worker* (1881). Similarly, the concern with statuary and precious stones is notable in the work of Pater, and in poems such as Swinburne's 'A Cameo' (1866) and Arthur Symons's later continuation of the tradition in 'Opals' (1896) which, as Hönnighausen observes, draws on 'the enumerative catalogue of precious stones' in Gautier's *Mademoiselle de Maupin* (2010: 120). Moreover, the return to traditional verse forms is noticeable, for example, in sonnet sequences such as those by Rossetti and Eugene Lee-Hamilton, and in Swinburne's roundels.[40]

Such concerns with poetic form, sculpture and precious stones also manifest themselves in the work of Olive Custance. Her collection, *Opals*, includes poems entitled 'Villanelle' and 'Virelay', while *Rainbows* and *The Inn of Dreams* feature madrigals.[41] Considered in this context, Custance's own Parnassian engagement with sculpture becomes clear in her statue poems: 'The White Statue', 'Antinous' and 'Statues'. According to Barbara Johnson:

> A characteristic associated with both statues and resistance in the minds of the Parnassian poets was whiteness. Gautier's 'Symphonie en blanc majeur' is a monochromatic tour de force in which a woman's pure, white body is compared to snow, satin, marble, frost, silver, opal, ivory, ermine, alabaster, dove, down, swans, hawthorn flowers, and other white substances. (2008: 119)

This concern with whiteness is also evident in Leconte de Lisle's 'Vénus de Milo' in which the statue's white body is equated with purity, 'alabaster' and 'doves' (Johnson 2008: 113). Custance's own statue poems, while they are touched with colours that express Sapphic desire, feature similar imagery: Antinous is a 'white statue', he is the 'flower of flowers' by whom the speaker watches 'pale and dumb' as the 'silver Dawn' rises (1902: 51). In 'The White Statue', the speaker presses her 'warm lips' against the sculpture's 'cold white mouth' (Custance 1897: 67); in 'Statues' the first line of each stanza begins with the expression: 'I have loved statues', and goes on to describe the speaker's erotic responses, how they have inspired her to chant 'curious madrigals/To charm their coldness' and how her body has 'worshipped the white form of stone' (Custance 1905: 12, ll. 5–6, 12). Above, I have suggested that the 'whiteness' of the sculptural body in Custance's work is complicated by her use of colour, as indeed it is, but I would argue that her focus on whiteness and coldness, and her investment in prosodic forms, situate her work in the Parnassian tradition. Her return to traditional forms both in sculpture and in poetry resonate with what Johnson has described as the Parnassian poets' 'impassioned apostrophes' to 'an unfeeling statue' (2008: 111). In addition, 'whiteness' pervades her poetry and is most apparent in 'opals' both in the title of her collection, and in the poem 'Opal Song' which appears in *The Inn of Dreams*.[42] Common opals, white, hard and beautiful, share properties with the statues in her poems. While the special place reserved for opals in Custance's imagination might appear an idiosyncratic affectation – she had 'a strange passion' for them and liked 'to be called, and to call herself, Opal' (Sewell 1975: 9) – her 'passion', I would argue, highlights the parallels between Custance's work and the theories of French Parnassianism, implying a greater complexity in her use of this precious stone.[43] Her work is evidently informed by that of British writers who influenced and enriched English decadence, but her engagement with traditional verse forms, marble statuary, and precious stones, shows that, for her, the nickname 'Opal' represented not only her alluring, mercurial character, but also marked her affinity with Parnassian poets, both British and French. However, her deployment of statue love, ready to be deciphered by those in the know, also suggests an acknowledgement of the complexities of her sexual desires and their entombment in the sepulchral materiality of her sculptural bodies.

Notes

1. Hamo Thornycroft (1850–1925) became an important purveyor of the New Sculpture, which rejected conventional neoclassical forms, and focused on naturalistic detail. As Getsy notes, 'the label "New Sculpture" must be used with caution' as it covers 'a wide range of experimentation in sculpture theory, subject matter, and representation that characterized the competitive and active climate of sculptural production in late-Victorian Britain' (2004: 3). See also Susan Beattie (1977).

2. In this series of articles, Gosse argued that English sculpture of the nineteenth century has been influenced by 'three dying rivulets' of sculptural tradition: that of Antonio Canova (1757–1822) and John Gibson (1790–1866); that of Francis Chantrey (1781–1841) and William Behnes (1795–1864); and, finally, that of John Flaxman (1755–1826), William F. Woodlington (1806–93) and Thomas Woolner (1825–92) (Gosse 1894: 138). In contrast, the New Sculpture movement in England was influenced by 'the French school of the last generation' including Paul Dubois (1829–1905), Henri Chapu (1833–91), Albert-Ernest Carrier-Belleuse (1824–87) and Jules Dalou (1838–1902); he also considered George Frederick Watts's *Clytie* (*c*.1865–9) a 'true forerunner of the New Sculpture', and identified Frederic Leighton's *Athlete Wrestling a Python* (1877) as the starting point for the new movement (Gosse 1894: 139–40).
3. Building on Getsy's research, Jason Edwards observes that works by Thornycroft and Leighton were of particular interest to those invested in 'homoerotic Aestheticism', such as Wilde, Symonds and Henry James (2006: 12). His own book focuses on the homoerotic resonances of works by Alfred Gilbert who is best known for his sculpture of Anteros as 'The Angel of Christian Charity', that graces the Shaftesbury Memorial in Piccadilly Circus, London, and is commonly known as *Eros*. In Greek myth, Anteros is the god of requited love who avenges the unrequited.
4. This statue is referred to in Gosse's 'New Sculpture' articles in *The Art Journal* as 'Putting the Stone'.
5. Frederick Walker (1840–75) was a social realist painter and illustrator; Jules-Félix Coutan (1848–39) was a French sculptor whose best-known work is the sculpture that sits above New York City's entrance to the Grand Central Terminal; Louis-Albert Lefeuvre (1845–1924) was a French sculptor known for allegorical works such as *Pour la patrie* (1890).
6. In this essay, Tyrwhitt reviews Symonds's *Studies of the Greek Poets* (1873, 1876) alongside Matthew Arnold's *Poems* (1853), *Essays in Criticism* (1865) and *Culture and Anarchy* (1869).
7. The *Dionysiaca* is an epic poem from the late fourth or early fifth cenury BCE. Nonnus's myth presents the story of Kalamos and Karpos. The two youths are competing in a swimming contest in the Meander River when Karpos drowns. Distraught with grief, Kalamos drowns himself and is transformed into a water reed.
8. The word 'desiderium' signifies 'an ardent desire or wish; a longing, properly for a thing once possessed and now missed', capturing 'a sense of loss' (*Oxford English Dictionary* n.d.).
9. *Artemis* is the sculpture that catapulted Thornycroft to fame and established him as 'the leading innovator in British sculpture in the early 1880s' (Getsy 2004: 65).

10. The poet Olive Custance (1874–1944), who later married Lord Alfred Douglas, was a contributor to *The Yellow Book* in the 1890s and is associated primarily with the Decadent movement of the late nineteenth century.
11. Adonis is the mortal lover of the goddess Aphrodite.
12. Richard Ellmann argues that 'the novel's theme, and the relation of passion to art' can be traced back to 'Charmides' (1988: 313).
13. Wilde's reference to 'the love of things impossible' suggests an allusion to Pater's essay, 'Leonardo da Vinci', in which he writes that Leonardo was 'smitten with a love of the impossible' (2010: 59). While Pater equates this with Leonardo's desire to perforate mountains, change the course of rivers and raise great buildings, the 'love of things impossible' might also be considered 'against nature', and thus function as a covert reference to Leonardo's sexuality.
14. This potentially alludes to the myth of Endymion.
15. Interestingly, Sam Singleton's response to Hudson's beauty – he looks at Roderick as if he were 'a statue on a pedestal' (James 1986: 119) – resonates with the male reaction to Charmides in Socrates' palaestra, and therefore reinforces Singleton's homoerotic attraction to the sculptor.
16. Published posthumously in 1898, the poem is often read as Keats's chilling address to his lover Fanny Brawne. For an extended discussion of Keats's poem, see Najarian (2002) and Hopkins (1984).
17. See also Iain Ross (2013).
18. In the *Letters of Oscar Wilde*, edited by Rupert Hart-Davis, this letter is listed as written sometime in June 1877 (Wilde 1962: 41), whereas the more recent *Complete Letters of Oscar Wilde*, edited by Merlin Holland and Rupert Hart-Davis, dates the letter as written in May the same year (Wilde 2000: 50).
19. Wilde's desire for a coloured bust of Keats suggests his knowledge that Greek statues were originally polychromous. On marble statues, colours were applied discreetly; only the hair, lips, eyes and possibly part of the drapery would have been tinted (see Beazley and Ashmole 1966: 15).
20. The bust to which Wilde refers is that of Rajaram Chuttraputti (1849–70) of Kohlapur who died in Florence. An elaborate gilded and tinted monument in the Cascine in Florence marks the site of his funeral pyre.
21. Charles Armitage Brown (1787–1842) was a close friend of both Keats and the artist Joseph Severn (1793–1879); John Hamilton Reynolds (1774–1852) was one of Keats's key correspondents.
22. Shelley's *Adonais*, written seven weeks after Keats's death, is a pastoral elegy modelled on classical elegies. In it Shelley suggests that the harsh criticism of Keats's work had contributed to his untimely death.
23. Medusa's dismembered head also recalls Keats's death mask. For a detailed discussion of Keats's death masks, see Malone (2012).

24. Charmides' 'crisp brown curls', lips 'made to kiss' and liminal existence between sleep and death recall Wilde's Endymion – his tribute to Keats's own – whose hair is similarly 'brown and curly' and has 'lips that should be kissed' (Wilde 1881b).
25. See Lene Østermark-Johansen (2011) for a discussion of the riders on the Parthenon frieze as they appear in Théophile Gautier's *Mademoiselle de Maupin* (1835) and their homoerotic significance for Pater and Wilde.
26. Karl Beckson includes poems by her in his 1982 anthology: *Aesthetes and Decadents of the 1890s*; Margaret D. Stetz and Mark Samuels Lasner, discuss Custance in *England in the 1890s* (1990); a selection of Custance's poetry is published with an introduction by Brocard Sewell in 1995; and a facsimile collection of *Opals* and *Rainbows*, introduced by R. K. R. Thornton appears in 1996. Eight years later, in 2004, edited selections from Custance's 1905–10 diary entries are published under the title: *I desire the moon: The diary of Lady Alfred Douglas*, with an introduction by Caspar Wintermans; and in that same year Custance makes a cameo appearance in Diana Souhami's 2004 book, *Wild Girls: Paris, Sappho and Art*, and Linda Hughes analyses Custance's poetry in 'Women Poets and Contested Spaces in *The Yellow Book*'. In 2007, in an article published in *Studies in English Literature*, Sally Ledger lists Custance among the women who contributed to *The Yellow Book* and my own essay on her work, 'Tinted and Tainted Love: The Sculptural Body in Olive Custance's Poetry' appears in *The Yearbook of English Studies*. More recently, Custance's work has been treated in depth in a monograph by Sarah Parker, *The Lesbian Muse and Poetic Identity* (2013), and in her more recent article, 'Olive Custance, Nostalgia, and Decadent Conservatism' (2019) and Jad Adams's 'Olive Custance: A Poet Crossing Boundaries' (2018) reads Custance's diaries alongside material that has been recently been made available as part of the Eccles Bequest to the British Library.
27. Custance uses an epigraph from Swinburne's 'A Song in Season' (*Poems and Ballads II*, 1878) in her poem 'God Took Great Roses Rare and Pale', which appears in *The Blue Bird*, and the Swinburnean language that informs 'Doubts', published in *Opals*, is clearly informed by Swinburne's 'Anactoria' (1866), published in *Poems and Ballads I*.
28. Natalie Clifford Barney (1876–1972) was an American poet, novelist and playwright who lived in Paris and whose salon attracted prominent artists and writers; Renée Vivien (Pauline Mary Tarn, 1877–1909) was a British poet who wrote in French and was influenced by French Symbolist and Parnassian poets. Barney and Vivien were lovers.
29. Terry Castle notes that 'The law has traditionally ignored female homosexuality', and that when, in 1921, members of the House of Lords had the opportunity to amend the Criminal Law Amendment Act of 1885 to include 'acts of gross indecency' between women, they decided not to for fear it would encourage their frequency (1993: 6).

30. Sewell suggests that this visit took place either in late 1900 or early in 1901 (1975: 11).
31. Douglas Murray reads this poem as a pastiche of Lord Alfred Douglas's early homosexual poetry. In 'Two Loves' Lord Alfred Douglas had written 'I am the love that dare not speak its name' (qtd in Murray 2000: 36); and in 'In Praise of Shame' he declared that 'Of all sweet passions Shame is the loveliest' (qtd in Murray 2000: 55). Murray notes that 'shame' was homosexual slang for homosexual love' (2000: 36). Later, Barney relates Custance's eagerness to join her commune of women poets in Paris (based on that of Sappho at Mytilene), and records Opal's excitement at the prospect of meeting her, prompted by the sight of Carolus Duran's portrait of her dressed as a page, which appeared as the frontispiece of Barney's *Quelques portraits*' (1960: 51).
32. Neil McKenna writes that there 'could be no doubt in the minds of Oscar's friends and contemporaries that John Gray was the model for Dorian Gray' from whose 'exquisite reality' Wilde 'had fashioned his exquisite amoral hero'; moreover, in the only letter from John Gray to Oscar Wilde that survives, Gray signs himself 'Dorian', and McKenna records that Wilde 'was in the habit of referring to him as "Dorian" in conversations with Ada Leverson and others' (2004: 164). Custance dedicated two poems to Gray: 'Ideal' and 'Reminiscences', published in *Opals* and *Rainbows*, respectively.
33. See also Lambert (1997).
34. According to John Dixon, 'poets of the nineties' often used Dante Gabriel Rossetti's device of comparing the 'images of his soul with some momentous hour of the day', and he notes that twilight was 'especially popular as the appropriate landscape for an uneasy soul' (1968: 114). Lillian Faderman has pointed out the more explicitly homoerotic significance of this word, claiming that 'twilight love' has long been identified with 'the love that dares not speak its name' (1981: 6). Faderman notes that the word 'twilight' was appropriated by American pulp fiction titles of the 1950s and 1960s that depicted lesbian desire (1981: 6). A Custance poem 'Twilight' appears in *Opals* (1897: 5–6), and twilight features in a number of other poems in her *oeuvre*.
35. Eileen Gregory has observed that he is a figure to whom Pater repeatedly returns in his work. In addition to appearing in 'Apollo in Picardy' in *Miscellaneous Studies* (1895), Hyacinthus is also mentioned in *The Renaissance* (1873), *Greek Studies* (1895) and *Plato and Platonism* (1895), (Gregory 1997: 270, n. 37). Laity notes that H.D. appropriates the Hyacinth myth in her own work (1996: 54–60).
36. H.D. also alludes to 'Charmides' in *Paint It Today* (1921) (Laity 1996: 69).
37. Interestingly, Douglas also wrote a poem entitled 'Hyacinthus', which was accepted for publication in the *Artist* in April 1892 (Murray 2000: 50). Although it is not certain that this poem was addressed to Wilde,

it is clear that 'Hyacinthus' is a homosexual pseudonym, and one that suggests a slippage between Wilde as lover and Douglas as beloved.
38. Wickes suggests that Barney's engagement to Douglas functions in this way (1977: 11).
39. Théophile Gautier's *Mademoiselle de Maupin* (1835) features complex negotiations of desire, and questions of sexual ambiguity; Gregory's references to 'Baudelaire's and Swinburne's "lesbian"' allude to works such as Baudelaire's 'Femmes damnées' and 'Lesbos' that appeared in *Les Fleurs du Mal* (1857), and Swinburne's 'Anactoria' which was published in *Poems and Ballads I* (1866). All represent same-sex desire. Pierre Louys's *Chansons de Bilitis* (1894) is a collection of erotic lesbian poetry.
40. See Rossetti's *House of Life* (1881) which contains 100 sonnets; Eugene Lee-Hamilton's *Imaginary Sonnets* (1888) and *Sonnets of the Wingless Hours* (1894); Swinburne invented the 'roundel' as a counterpart to the French 'rondeau'. Both use stylised patterns and refrains.
41. As is commonly known, the villanelle, modelled on the French revival of the form, entered English poetry in the nineteenth century, while the virelay is a medieval French form, one of the traditional 'fixed forms', advocated by Théodore de Banville in *Le Petit Traité de poésie Française* (1870), alongside other medieval and Renaissance forms such as the rondel, ballade, envoi, sonnet, rondeau, rondeau redouble, triolet and lai, which Banville admired.
42. Whiteness is a repeated motif in Custance's poetry; see Pulham (2007).
43. Renée Vivien was also considered to have been influenced by the Parnassians (see Goujon 1985).

Chapter 5

Between Death and Sleep: Libidinal Entombments

The ambiguities that characterise Olive Custance's life and work are equally evident in the letters and poetic production of her antecedents, Katherine Bradley (1846–1914) and Edith Cooper (1862–1913), who wrote under the name 'Michael Field'. Like Custance, this 'lesbian aunt-and-niece couple' (Vicinus 2009: 753) use sculptural bodies to play with gender and mediate their sexual proclivities. Moreover, in Michael Field's work, as in Custance's, sculpture functions 'as a complex metaphor' for a 'modern, dissident poetics, a metaphor for the sexual and sensual body, for the intellect and ideal, [and] for their decadence' (Vadillo 2019: 68). For Michael Field and Olive Custance, sculpture, poetic craft and sexual expression are intricately intertwined. As Ana Vadillo demonstrates in *Michael Field: Decadent Moderns*, 'the imprint of sculpture on Michael Field was profound and significant' and especially visible in their writings from what she calls their 'marble period' (*c.*1878–90); during those years, it featured prominently in their poems and correspondence, and Cooper's '"white sculptural thought" contributed to a number of "marble books"' (2019: 68).[1] According to Vadillo, in the late 1870s sculpture emerges as 'a collaborative mode of thinking for Bradley and Cooper' and continued to inform their writings in the decade that followed (2019: 71). 'To Apollo—The Conqueror', inspired by the *Apollo Belvedere*, is one of Edith Cooper's early poems written in 1878; statues of Antinous, the *Laocoön*, the *Capitoline Venus*, the *Venus de Milo* and the tomb of Ilaria del Carretto by Jacopo della Quercia are mentioned in their letters to each other during this period; and their first joint publication, the poetic drama, *Bellerophôn*, published in 1881, was prompted in part by their study of sculpture at the British Museum.[2]

In Michael Field's writings, statues are used both to express alternative gender identities and facilitate sexual expression: after cutting her hair like a boy, Cooper compares herself to Antinous, Hadrian's beloved, and in her poem 'To Apollo—The Conqueror', dedicated to Bradley, Cooper describes an eroticised union between a statue of Apollo and the speaker, a priestess. For Vadillo, this poem 'is about poetry and sex: indeed, poetry is sex' (2019: 73). 'Dower me with thine own lips' the priestess begs Apollo as she channels the language taken from his 'fair Greek mouth', and later refers to his 'thrilling touch', taking inspiration from him to become, through poetry, 'mother to all beauteous things' (qtd in Vadillo 2019: 73). In this poem, poetic inspiration doubles as sexual congress and functions as a thinly veiled allusion to Cooper's dual initiation into poetic production and lesbian love:[3]

> The priestess sees Apollo's poetic inspiration as a sexual encounter ... In this transgressive poem, Apollo is a statue and the beloved, the embodiment of Bradley, a heterosexual intercourse encoding an incestuous lesbian relationship. Bradley is indeed represented, metaphorically speaking, as the sculptor who, 'with thrilling touch' sculpts the priestess, the young initiate, into a poet. (Vadillo 2019: 73)

Apollo, here, is a figure of both sexual allure and poetic fame; he inspires Michael Field's decadent poetics, and his sculptural counterpart encrypts the doubly transgressive desire between Bradley and Cooper. The *Apollo Belvedere* was clearly an important touchstone in their relationship: when Bradley visited Rome in 1880, she 'run madly' to see the statue and it has been suggested that a cast of Apollo may have played a part in a 'marriage ceremony' between the two women (Vadillo 2019: 74). Yet, as Vadillo notes, female statues were of equal importance in expressions of love between Bradley and Cooper and were often utilised to 'negotiate their personal incestuous relationship' (2019: 80). Among these is the *Venus de Milo*; in a letter to Cooper, Bradley describes the statue as 'the perfect woman' who has 'no thought of man, no entreaty for his love; yet breasts so sweet one longs to drink from them' (qtd in Vadillo 2019: 80). Similarly, when Bradley sees the *Capitoline Venus* (Figure 5.1) she confesses to Cooper her delight in finding that 'her garments are beside her, not on her', and takes pleasure in the 'circling beauty' of her loins, though she finds 'the bosom heave' of the *Venus de Milo* 'unrivalled' by her counterpart in Rome (qtd in Vadillo 2019: 83–4). However, Bradley and Cooper's interest in statues was also intrinsically related to their poetic craft. 'To Apollo—The Conqueror' binds libidinal desire with poetic prowess and, similarly, prompted by her encounter with the *Venus de Milo*, Bradley writes to Cooper of her

Figure 5.1 *The Capitoline Venus*, Roman copy of a Greek original by Praxiteles, fourth century BCE, marble (Capitoline Museums, Rome). G. Dagli Orti / De Agostini Picture Library / Bridgeman Images

intention to compose '3 sonnets one to each Venus', the others being the 'Venuses of the Pitti and the Capitol' (qtd in Vadillo 2019: 82). Writing about sculpture becomes simultaneously part of their aesthetic pleasure and their professional process; it becomes 'a metaphor for composition, decomposition, and recomposition' that conceives of poetry as sculpture (Vadillo 2019: 84). According to Vadillo, this investment in sculpture culminates in their 'marble books', which were 'bound in white', mainly in vellum, and constructed the book itself as an 'art object, a sculptural icon . . . a 3-D block on which the writing appeared as if it were bas-relief' (2019: 89).

In their appropriation of sculptural figures such as the *Apollo Belvedere* and the statue of Antinous, Michael Field, like Custance, engage with the 'nude male bodies of Greek statuary posited by male contemporaries as objects of the 'homoerotic "gaze"'' (Laity 1996: 45). It is clear that Bradley and Cooper would have been aware of Winckelmann's significance in this context as their early work was 'influenced by Winckelmann's vision of Romanticism in Greek sculpture, both directly and indirectly, by way of Pater' and, by 1880, it is certain that they would have read Pater's essay on 'Winckelmann', collected in *Studies in the History of the Renaissance* (Vadillo 2019: 75). The sexual ambiguities implicit in the slippages between heterosexual and homoerotic responses to statuary in Michael Field's writings also chime with Custance's statue poems in which the gender of speakers and statues remains unarticulated or, as in 'Antinous', complicates the speaker's sexuality. Anticipating Custance's engagement with statuary, Michael Field's writings both blur gender identity and suggest bisexuality, a libidinal response that becomes more visible and problematic for their relationship following their introduction to the art critic Bernard Berenson in the summer of 1890. As Martha Vicinus observes, soon 'both women were deeply in love with his androgynous physical beauty and charismatic intellectual drive' and gave him nicknames that highlighted his own ephebic masculinity:

> His dark, curly hair, close-trimmed beard and beautiful hands and feet gave him a youthful, otherworldly appearance, so Bradley and Cooper soon added 'Faun' and 'Dionysus' to their pet names. They had long played with contrary genders in their poetry and lives, so it is no surprise that they reversed a literary cliché of the aesthetic movement by transforming a beautiful man, rather than a woman, into an erotic object. (2009: 753-4)

This 'reversal' depends, of course, on whether one conceives of their love as prompted by heterosexual desire or gender identification. As Vicinus notes, Bradley and Cooper 'reveled in gender play': they 'called each other a variety of male nicknames' and their use of the professional name 'Michael Field' might be read as an 'adoption of male cultural authority', 'self-conscious sexual play', 'a symbol of their personal and literary collaboration', or 'an evasion of any simple sexual, literary and gender identity' (2009: 754). Cooper, especially, identified increasingly with Berenson, falling in love 'with a masculine version of herself'; having 'assumed the part of an adolescent boy' in her relationship with her aunt, she now 'reworked her boy-role, not only to differentiate herself from her aunt, but also to confirm her androgynous faun-like resemblance to Berenson' (Vicinus 2009: 754). Although both women were bitterly disappointed by Berenson's relationship with Mary Costelloe, with whom he began an affair in 1891 and eventually married in 1900, they visited the couple in Florence in 1895 and once again 'found themselves in thrall to Berenson's androgynous beauty' and to his 'theory of empathic pleasure in art, based upon what he called "giving tactile values to retinal sensations"' (Vicinus 2009: 758).[4] While by the end of 1895 Cooper writes, 'a spiritual obscession [*sic*] has lifted' to mark the formal end of her infatuation with Berenson, Vicinus argues that she continued to think of Berenson as 'her own soul', that 'her heterosexual love for him actually confirmed her homosexual identity', the renounced Berenson, living 'on inside her, as part of the Bradley-Cooper dyad' (2009: 760).

Cooper's identification as a 'boy' recalls Custance's own – she is a 'page' to Alfred Douglas's 'Prince', and has a boyish beauty (Murray 2000: 123) – but the 'queer triangle' formed by Cooper, Bradley and Berenson (Vicinus 2009: 754) also resonates with the triangular desire between Miriam and Hilda, mediated by another Dionysian faun, Donatello, in Hawthorne's *The Marble Faun*. Like Michael Field, whose poetic collaboration Bradley thought of as a form of marriage, for Hilda, friendship with Miriam is a union of hearts 'call them marriage, or whatever else' where each is taken 'for better, for worse' (Hawthorne 1990a: 85). Moreover, like Michael Field who were 'mother and daughter, sisters, lovers', as well as aunt and niece (Thain and Vadillo 2009: 25, n. 4), the close relationship between the women in Hawthorne's novel crosses boundaries between sisterly, maternal and erotic love. The 'incestuous' nature of such desires is symbolised in Hawthorne's text by the images of Beatrice Cenci, in whom Hilda's and Miriam's reflections combine, and by Harriet Hosmer's sculpture of Beatrice which, though unmentioned, haunts the novel evoking 'entombment'; that 'strange sisterhood' of women artists to whom Hosmer belonged; and the 'ghost' of Hosmer's lesbian identity (Fryd 2006: 300–6).

Girls in Marble

For Michael Field, however, it is an earlier renaissance woman, Ilaria del Carretto (1379–1405), whose marble effigy mediates lesbian desire. In response to Bradley's assertion that she plans to write three sonnets each dedicated to one of the famous statues of Venus she has seen on her travels through Europe, Cooper writes:

> The thought of consecrating a sonnet to each fair manifestation of Venus delights me. If you have bent before the 'Eternal Womanhood' at the Louvre, this morning you will Kiss the perfect woman at Lucca, and thank God for having sent her on Earth and Jacopo della Quercia for having kept her there. I have sent a pilgrim-Kiss; may it reach you in time to be pressed by your lips on her shrine! (qtd in Vadillo 2019: 82)

Figure 5.2 Funerary monument to Ilaria del Carretto by Jacopo della Quercia, fifteenth century, marble and stone (Cathedral of San Martino, Lucca). De Agostini Picture Library / G. Nimatallah / Bridgeman Images

As Vadillo notes, 'Bradley accepted the role play and in her next letter to Cooper from Florence' describes her encounter with Ilaria (Figure 5.2):

> I bear on my lips the marble of Ilaria's brow! I walked straight to the left transept, and saw her, and by the bye they *all* left me, and I kissed her on the calm forehead, the tremulously sweet lips, the sweet round chin. And I saw the breast 'heaving like a low wave of the sea,' the softly-folded hands. (qtd in Vadillo 2009: 82–3; original emphasis)

The quotation 'heaving like a low wave of the sea' comes from John Ruskin's 'Three Colours of Pre-Raphaelitism' (1878) in which he writes of Ilaria's tomb and observes how 'As a soft, low wave of summer sea, her breast rises; no more' (1878: 1080). For Vadillo, Bradley and Cooper's response to Ilaria is 'more erotic and closer to Winckelmann's (and Pater's) sensual reading of the art of sculpture' (2019: 83). She argues that 'they saw the beauty of Ilaria as a sexual beauty', that Bradley's 'reaction was sexual', and that 'Bradley acts here as receiver, transmitter, and agent of homoerotic agalmatophilia' (2019: 83). While Ruskin's language is certainly less suggestive, I would argue that a powerful eroticism is implicit in his long-standing love for Caretto's marble double, which he describes in detail in Volume 2 of *Modern Painters* (1846). Here it is posited as 'an instance of the exact and right mean between the rigidity and rudeness of the earlier monumental effigies, and the morbid imitation of life, sleep, or death, of which the fashion has taken place in modern times' (Ruskin 1906: 76). In his note on this 'fashion', Ruskin asserts that, in monumental work, the sculptor should aim for a careful balance between realism and art:

> The statue should be felt to be a statue, not look like a dead or sleeping body; it should not convey the impression of a corpse, nor of sick and outwearied flesh, but it should be the marble *image* of death or weariness. (1906: 76, n. 1; original emphasis)

In Ruskin's view, Ilaria's effigy epitomises this equilibrium, and his interest may be read as part of a wider concern with early Renaissance tomb sculpture that manifests itself in the works of contemporaries and successors who revisit its importance. In Volume 3 of *Renaissance in Italy* (1877), John Addington Symonds mentions della Quercia's Ilaria as one who had 'long been dear to English students of Italian art', before remarking of Antonio Rossellino's tomb of the Cardinal of Portugal at S. Miniato a Monte in Florence that 'The sublimity of the slumber that is death has never been more nobly and feelingly portrayed than in the supine figure and sleeping features of this most beautiful young man, who lies watched by angels beneath a heavy-curtained canopy' (1877: 153).[5] Similarly, Vernon Lee notes the 'modesty, the simplicity, the awful and beautiful repose of the dead' to be found in both these tomb sculptures; for her, Ilaria represents 'the most beautiful lady ... that the art of the fifteenth century has recorded', while the Cardinal's effigy is so delicately executed that the young priest 'in his virginal dignity is almost a noble woman' (1883: 572). Later, following in Ruskin's footsteps, in *Earthwork Out of Tuscany* (1895) Maurice Hewlett pays his own visit to Lucca and depicts Ilaria as a form of sleeping beauty; in words that resonate with Ruskin's in *Modern Painters*, he claims that as he gazed at her, it seemed 'as if her bosom rose and fell', despite the inevitable fact that 'Death had his way with her' (1901: 39–40).

Ruskin's own concern with the tombs of Italy re-emerges in *The Stones of Venice* (1851–3) in the final volume of which he traces the increasing degradation of Venice via an engagement with funerary art, but it is the beautiful Ilaria who inhabits a special place in Ruskin's heart. He first encounters her at Lucca in 1845, and revisits her in 1874, before making his final pilgrimage to her tomb in 1882. Perhaps the death of a young woman always elicits a special sympathy as it carries the dual poignancy of arrested beauty and stilled life; confronted with the effigy of Beatrice d'Este (1475–97) at the Certosa in Pavia, the poet Mary Robinson exclaimed, 'To think that she is dead, and to think she was a woman! Impossible. She is a lively child, fallen asleep in playtime: motionless, but full of a contained vivacity' (1889: 312).[6] In contrast to this image of spontaneous life momentarily suspended, Ruskin's initial description of Ilaria centres on her stillness:

> The hair is bound in a flat braid over the fair brow, the sweet and arched eyes are closed, the tenderness of the loving lips is set and quiet; there is that about them which forbids breath; something which is not death nor sleep, but the pure image of both. The hands are not lifted in prayer, neither folded, but the arms are laid at length upon the body, and the hands cross as they fall. The feet are hidden by the drapery, and the form of the limbs concealed, but not their tenderness. (1906: 77)

The gentleness and sensitivity of Ruskin's literary gaze foreshadows Ilaria's future significance as the artistic embodiment – or, more accurately, encorpsement – of those dead young girls that later come to inhabit his imagination. As Lindsay Smith notes, *Praeterita* (1885–9) 'is full of the [figurative or literal] loss of young girls' and she demonstrates how, following the death of Ruskin's beloved Rose La Touche in 1875, he 'reads back his past relationships with little girls as a consequence of this later tragedy' (2002: 53–6).[7] In other words, in these lost friendships he retrospectively 'finds the death of Rose already writ large' (Smith 2002: 56). Catherine Robson traces a similar pattern in *Praeterita*. In response to Kenneth Clark's rhetorical question: 'Was there ever an autobiography in which girls are more vividly remembered' (2001: 96), Robson writes:

> What Clark does not comment upon . . . is the fact that very nearly all of these girls have their lives cut short by early death . . . Sometimes the deaths are imagined, rather than literal: the lives of formerly beloved girls who are lost to Ruskin in one way or another are effectively truncated by *Praeterita*'s refusal to grant their adulthood any representation

> ... On occasion, even when the beloved female does indeed die at a relatively early age, she is remembered and depicted primarily as a much younger being. Here the most important figure is the love of Ruskin's middle age and early old age, Rose La Touche, through the lens of which all the girl-deaths of *Praeterita* are filtered. Although Rose died at the age of twenty-seven of brain fever, she lives in the autobiography primarily as a high-spirited nine-year-old. (2001: 103)

Although the deaths (real or imagined) of these young girls are all filtered through La Touche, the lasting impact of Ilaria's effigy on Ruskin doubtless informs his subsequent investment in the dead Rose's image. John Rosenberg argues that, even before Ruskin met Rose as a young child, 'their meeting had been prefigured thirteen years earlier, in 1845, in the Church of San Martino in Lucca':

> There he saw, and never forgot, Jacopo della Quercia's exquisitely sculptured effigy of the young bride Ilaria di Caretto. In his close-up study of her head, drawn in the same year as his profile of the dying Rose, he renders della Quercia's delicate chiselling of a lock of her hair as if it were still moist from the fever flush of death. And he transposes the fillet that rings Ilaria's forehead into the lace-like coronet that encircles Rose's hair. (2005: 85–6)

Twinned in death and united in Ruskin's art, Rose and Ilaria become almost interchangeable. Yet the cold, sculpted marble body of Ilaria is also clearly inscribed in the metaphorical language Ruskin uses to express his love for and questionable interest in other young girls including his erstwhile wife, Effie Gray.[8]

As Robson observes, in *Praeterita* Effie is mentioned 'only parenthetically as the "little girl" for whose amusement *The King of the Golden River* was written' (2001: 103). Given their disastrous marriage, it is understandable that Ruskin might want to recall the happy young girl rather than the unhappy wife, yet it seems that Effie's girlishness was always an important part of her charm. In his analysis of their relationship, Barry Bullen points to the 'series of passionate letters' Ruskin wrote to Effie 'between November 1847 and February 1848 during the six-month period of their engagement' (2002: 71). He notes that in these letters, 'two contradictory images' of Effie emerge; the first is of a 'child bride, "*girlish*" and "youthful"', while the second is of a cold, hard and dangerous woman (2002: 71–3; original emphasis). In a letter to Effie dated 15 December 1847, Ruskin's imagery expresses this duality:

> You are like a sweet forest of pleasant glades and whispering branches – where people wander on and on in its playing shadows they know not how far – and when they come near the centre of it, it is all cold and impenetrable . . . You are like the bright soft – swelling – lovely fields of a high glacier covered with fresh morning snow – which is heavenly to the eye – and soft and winning on the foot – but beneath, there are winding clefts and dark places in its cold – cold ice – where men fall, and rise not again. (qtd in Bullen 2002: 73)

These images of coldness, imperviousness and innocence resurface in *The Ethics of Dust* (1865). Robson argues that the 'central conceit' of this text is simply: 'girls are crystals and crystals are girls' (2001: 115).[9] In her astute analysis of this work, Robson highlights how images of girlish softness and 'flexible moistness' are juxtaposed with and outnumbered by 'evocations of [the girls'] rocklike impenetrability and adamantine brilliance' (2001: 123). She suggests that Ruskin's 'besetting habit of viewing the beloved as both a hard and an aesthetic object is not a defense against the erotic, but a component of it. Reversing the Pygmalion myth, Ruskin transforms the mutable girl into stone' (2001: 123). To support her thesis, Robson provides a series of examples: in *Praeterita*, Ruskin expresses his penchant for 'crystalline blonde[s]'; Emily La Touche (Rose's sister) is described as 'a perfectly sweet, serene, delicately chiselled marble nymph of fourteen'; in *The Cestus of Aglaia* (1864), the breasts of a ten-year-old Turinese girl are defined as 'white – marble-like – but, as wasted marble, thin with scorching rains of Time' (qtd in Robson 2001: 123–4). Elsewhere, Phyllis Rose writes that Ruskin's perfect woman would probably be 'highly idealized, like classical statues' and cites Rose La Touche as a key example of this type (1984: 56). Brian Gregory dismisses this claim on the grounds that if Ruskin 'desired the physical form of a classical Greek statue', he would hardly 'seek the love of a ten-year-old girl' (1999: 80).[10] However, if in Ruskin's imagination, 'girls are crystals and crystals are girls' as Robson suggests, they naturally embody the crystalline quality of marble statuary.[11] As a result, they also function as repetitions of that crystalline beauty, the marble effigy of Ilaria.

In *Men in Wonderland*, Robson asserts that it is 'an open secret that Ruskin the famous Victorian sage is also Ruskin the infamous Victorian pedophile' although there is 'no evidence that Ruskin sexually abused little girls' (2001: 122). In view of Ruskin's interest in sculptural bodies we might also suggest that Ruskin – like Hardy's sculptor Jocelyn Pierston, whose Well-Beloved had a similar tendency to migrate from one woman's body to another – is a closet necrophiliac aroused by dead girls or, indeed, agalmatophiliac, one who 'establishes a personal relationship with a complete statue as a statue' (Scobie and Taylor 1975: 49). While it is, of course, easy and perhaps unreasonable to impose such labels on a dead author who cannot challenge or dispute such accusations, Ruskin's investment in the marble body of Ilaria del Carretto and the young girls in *Praeterita* whose arrested lives she embodies nevertheless provoke such readings. Ruskin's passion for the cold, impenetrable body of Effie Gray is clear from his letter to her, and the recurrent references to dead girls and, indeed, to dead civilisations in his work suggest 'a passionate attraction to all that is dead' (Downing 2003: 4). In addition, in reversing the Pygmalion myth and metaphorically converting 'mutable girl[s] into stone' (Robson 2001: 123), Ruskin demonstrates a desire 'to transform that which is alive into something which is unalive' (Downing 2003: 4).

In her discussion of necrophilia in Vladimir Nabokov's notorious novel *Lolita* (1955), Lucy Maddox forges an interesting connection between nympholepsy, necrophilia and aestheticism:

> The nympholepsy which is the bane and blessing of his [the protagonist Humbert's] life is symptomatic of a more general, essentially aesthetic impulse to possess and preserve the beautiful, while his abhorrence of the mature woman, the 'coffin of coarse female flesh within which my nymphets are buried alive' . . . is a specific instance of a general horror of physical decay. He is attracted to the idea of death, therefore, as a saving stasis, a way of preventing the loss of the beautiful. (1982: 368)

The language of sex, death and aestheticism Maddox identifies in *Lolita* resonates with Ruskin's privileging of dead girls – real, imagined or preserved in marble stasis – in his writings. His ekphrasis of Ilaria's tomb effigy maintains a balance between the living and dead beloved; in it he finds 'something which is not death nor sleep' and, though her body is imaged in marble, he imagines the 'tenderness' of her 'loving lips', and the equal 'tenderness' of her concealed limbs (1906: 77). While the repetition of 'tenderness' may allude to her young age at the time of death, Ruskin's coupling of the word with 'loving lips' and 'limbs concealed' implies a tactile response; an imagined kiss and the fondling of Ilaria's limbs beneath the sculpted drapery. In effect, this focus on the marble body functions as a lover's 'tender' touch, enabling a phantasmatic tactility that simultaneously channels and yet buries Ruskin's nympholepsy in Ilaria's tomb. In Ruskin's case, the aesthetic beauty and stillness of Ilaria's marble body facilitates a tactile encounter that releases and yet conceals a paedophilic impulse, an erotic compulsion that remains taboo, unmentionable and forbidden.

Cultural Sepulchres

Tombs, entombment and the dead have been recurring motifs in the preceding chapters, reaffirming my contention that the sculptural body in Victorian literature is not simply about Pygmalionesque animation, but also about the figurative 'burial' and containment of an active and transgressive eroticism that is retrieved from the sculptural body through touch and metaphors of tactility. The dangers of touch are tacitly acknowledged in Chapter 1, where those Victorian Ovids, Morris and Woolner – like MacDonald's Anodos – use sound, in the form of poetic song, rather than touch to bring their Galateas to life. In the works discussed, touch is prohibited and in Morris's 'Pygmalion and the Image' and Woolner's *Pygmalion*, the caresses that bring Pygmalion's statue to life in *Metamorphoses* are mediated by the goddess, Venus Aphrodite, and thus elevated, leaving their sculptors' purity intact. Judging from his preface to *Songs of a Worker*, O'Shaughnessy was similarly keen to counter any accusation of immorality, to ensure that his 'thoughts in marble' were of 'the purest Parian' (qtd in Deacon 1881: viii). Yet, as becomes clear in my analysis of those 'thoughts' in his poetry, the line between living and sculptural women is incredibly fine; watching his wayward Venus's post-coital sleep in 'Living Marble', the speaker-sculptor wishes 'That [her] sleep indeed were endless, even as death' (O'Shaughnessy 1881: 103, l. 26), and expresses a desire to embed her in marble. Similarly, it is no accident that in 'Dialogue between Two Venuses', it is the *Cnidian Venus*, modelled on Praxiteles' courtesan lover, Phryne, who has taken 'marble for a grave' (1881: 113, l. 15). Moreover, in O'Shaughnessy's poetry, as in Hardy's *The Well-Beloved* and Wilde's 'Charmides', death and loss underscore a libidinal investment in sculptural form, while in Custance's poetry as in Wilde's and Michael Field's, forbidden desire is concealed in a tactile communion with statues.

In Hawthorne's novel, the expression and burial of transgressive desire figures more prominently in *The Marble Faun*'s allusions to excavation and interment, and in the repeated motif of bacchanals and sarcophagi that litter the text. The image first appears early in the narrative when, walking through the Borghese gardens, Miriam and Donatello meet a carnival crowd and join in their festivities. These are described in sculptural terms: their dance in 'a wild ring of mirth' is like 'the realization of one of those bas-reliefs where a dance of nymphs, satyrs, or bacchanals is twined around the circle of an antique vase', or 'like the sculptured scene on the front and sides of a sarcophagus, where, as often as any other device, a festive procession mocks the ashes and white bones that are treasured up within' (Hawthorne 1990a: 88). This image is later repeated in the frescoes of the antique saloon in Donatello's ancestral home, which depict a faded 'wreath of dancing figures' that seem 'like the ghosts of dead and buried joys' (1990a: 226). It finally re-emerges in the carnival described toward the end of *The Marble Faun* where, according to Sheldon Liebman, it represents a 'final sarcophagus scene' that functions as 'a marriage pageant for Kenyon and Hilda, and a funeral march for Donatello and Miriam' (1967: 76). However, I suggest that it also acts as a closing comment on those carnivalesque reversals of gender and sexuality that inform the text. Here, the volatile, metamorphic figures of Miriam and Donatello are replaced by Kenyon, the 'man of marble' (Hawthorne 1990a: 103) and his 'marble' bride-to-be, simultaneously ridding Hawthorne of his unruly characters and ossifying the union between Kenyon and Hilda, thus burying their own sexual ambiguities and, symbolically, those of Miriam and Donatello.

Sculpture and death also coalesce in Wilde's 'Charmides', to express 'a sensuality which feeds on statues and dead bodies' (qtd in Beckson 1974: 32), and the same might be said of James's *Roderick Hudson*, in which the male corpse is aestheticised and acquires a sculptural form. In Chapter 3, I argued that Hudson's beautiful cadaver, 'a vague white mass' whose 'clothes and hair were as wet as if the billows of the ocean had flung him upon the strand' (James 1986: 386) anticipates the reclining figure in Onslow Ford's *Shelley Memorial*, unveiled in 1893 and housed at University College, Oxford (Plate 4). According to Hilary Fraser, Ford's sculpture 'attracted considerable critical attention in the art press of the day' (2018: 44). She notes that the language of tactility often surfaced in responses to it, and shows how, writing of Ford, Marion Hepworth Dixon commends 'the hand which portrayed the impassioned poet', a hand which 'could caress even marble' (qtd in Fraser 2018: 47). But Dixon is also aware of the 'daring' nature of the statue; Ford's statue of Shelley confronts the viewer with a body that is 'lifeless, nude, cold, but still beautiful, inexpressibly beautiful' (qtd in Fraser 2018: 45).[12] As Fraser observes, effigies 'conventionally play with such ambiguities – the funeral shroud that is like a blanket, the sarcophagus that is like a bed, the death that is like sleep', but Ford's presents 'a body that is unmistakeably a corpse' (2018: 45). While Ruskin's Ilaria seemingly exists in a liminal space between death and sleep, Shelley's effigy highlights the fact that 'the sculptural figure as a form shares some disquietingly common characteristics with the corpse' (Fraser 2018: 45). Unlike Ruskin, who argues that, in memorial sculpture, the statue 'should be felt to be a statue', should not look like a dead body, and 'should not convey the impression of a corpse' (1906: 76, n. 1), Ford set out to 'capture the symbiosis of materiality and representation' in the form of a 'sensuous sculptural realism' (Getsy 2004: 128). Here, Shelley is not symbolised but presented as 'a lifeless corpse'; as Getsy asserts, 'This is not a portrait with its implications of intellectual life, but a rendering of a dead body. The white marble of the effigy approximates colorless, dead flesh . . . It is cold, pale, and motionless' (2004: 133). In contrast to the effigy 'in sepulchral sculpture in which the body is presented asleep or peacefully at rest', Ford's sculpture breaks with these conventions to offer the viewer 'a toppled, lifeless body in disarray' (2004: 133).

While this is indeed the case, there is no doubt that this 'lifeless body in disarray' is nevertheless sexually alluring and poetic; like Roderick Hudson's corpse, the recumbent statue of Shelley is, in Dixon's words, 'still beautiful, inexpressibly beautiful' (qtd in Fraser 2018: 45). Moreover, Luisa Calè and Stefano Evangelista note that the marble is sculpted to make it appear 'soft and tactile' (2018: 19) and that, in 'turning the grotesque body into a classical body, Onslow Ford draws attention to Shelley's own classicism or what one could call Shelley's Greekness', thus invoking the homoerotic code of Victorian Hellenism (2018: 21). As Calè and Evangelista argue, Ford restores 'to the body of the male poet the classical beauty that Wilde had missed in the medallion portrait of Keats', turning 'the male body into an object of desire' (2018: 26). Ford's *Shelley Memorial* was created 'in a culture that was discovering new and sometimes transgressive meanings in the poetic and sculptural male body'; the statue reopened debates surrounding Shelley's effeminacy and sexuality, and Symonds, in particular, was eager 'to discover a queer Shelley', to read 'Shelley's "flight towards the region of impossible ideals"' as 'a gloss on . . . "l'amour de l'impossible" – an expression he uses to spiritualize homoerotic desire' (Calè and Evangelista 2018: 26).

Like Roderick Hudson's aestheticised corpse, Ford's statue of Shelley elicits homoerotic interest, but it also recalls the figure of the *Sleeping Hermaphrodite* in the Louvre, celebrated in Swinburne's poem, 'Hermaphroditus'. Calling attention to its androgyny, it embodies, like Hudson's corpse, a sterile beauty that elicits an impossible love in both men and women.[13]

In his discussion of Quatremère de Quincy's views on the removal of works of art from their original contexts, quoted in my introduction, Bruce Haley explains that Quatremère's model 'for the artifactual corpse' was 'an emblematic tomb figure, lifeless as the body it is supposed to honor, an allegory arousing no "emotion" for the viewer' (2003: 16). However, as my study shows, the transference of sculptural bodies from the museum space to Victorian literature appears to have had a very different effect, even when the statues or sculptural artefacts in question literalise death. In this context, the libidinal economy that circulates between artworks, social transgression and sexual repression in the Victorian sculpture gallery remains entombed but is revealed through metaphors of tactility that also inspire creative endeavours. Responding to the democratisation of museum culture, the rise of the Victorian art gallery, and popular access to classical, renaissance and New Sculpture through exhibitions, engravings and photography, the poetry, novels and prose writings considered in *The Sculptural Body in Victorian Literature* utilise the three-dimensionality of sculptural form, and the intersections between touch and vision in the experience of statuary, to explore its transgressive potential. In these literary works, thoughts in marble create sculptures that double as sepulchres of forbidden desire.

Notes

1. Vadillo notes that Bradley and Cooper always lived surrounded by sculptures; they owned sculptures by artist contemporaries; collected casts of ancient Greek and Roman statues; and bought photographs of sculptures to hang in their writing room (2019: 70).
2. *Bellerophôn* was published under the names 'Arran and Isla Leigh', names that, as Yopie Prins has suggested, blur gender boundaries, and suggest 'various possible [familial] relationships' (1999: 55). As Thain and Vadillo note, this is 'an ambiguity utterly appropriate for an aunt and niece who were also mother and daughter, sisters, lovers' (2009: 25, n. 4).
3. The deployment of gallery artworks as a means of mediating lesbian desire has been discussed by Diana Maltz (2000), in an essay which

charts the role of psychological aesthetics in the relationship between the writer and aesthete Vernon Lee (Violet Paget, 1856–1935) and her long-term lover and companion, Clementina Anstruther-Thomson (1857–1921). For a discussion of sculpture and gender identification in Lee's work, see Pulham (2008a).

4. As Hilary Fraser notes, while Cooper 'was an experienced art critic' in her own right, and had published with Bradley a series of ekphrastic poems, *Sight and Song* 'based on their collaborative response to a series of paintings in British and Continental galleries', Berenson valued her as 'a "mirror" that enables the connoisseur to see more, and more profoundly, what is present in the picture' (2014: 2). Berenson's dismissal of women's art criticism and experimentation reaches a particularly unpleasant height in his accusation of plagiarism against Vernon Lee and Clementina Anstruther-Thomson whose work on psychological aesthetics he believed to be informed by his own theories. For an interesting discussion of this accusation and its dismissal see Jo Briggs (2006).

5. Antonio Gamberelli (1427–79), named 'Rossellino' due to his hair colour, was a Renaissance sculptor thought to have studied under Donatello, now best known for his bronze sculpture, *David* (c.1440s), which can be seen at the Bargello in Florence.

6. Agnes Mary Frances Robinson (1857–1944) was a poet, critic, writer and translator who was Vernon Lee's companion and lover prior to Robinson's marriage. Robinson was also a close friend and favourite of John Addington Symonds.

7. Ruskin's *Praeterita* is an autobiography. Rose La Touche (1848–75) became Ruskin's pupil. He met her in 1858 when she was nine years old and Ruskin continued to tutor her until she was eighteen. Ruskin, almost thirty years older than La Touche, fell in love with Rose and asked for her hand in marriage following the annulment of his unconsummated marriage to Effie Gray. Rose's parents refused. La Touche died at the age of twenty-seven; the reasons for her tragic death are unclear, though 'brain fever' and anorexia are suggested causes.

8. Euphemia (Effie) Gray (1828–97) married Ruskin in 1848 at the age of twenty. He knew her as a child and, when she was twelve, wrote the *King of the Golden River* (1851) for her. The marriage was unconsummated at Ruskin's request, and later annulled. Gray went on to marry the artist John Everett Millais in 1855.

9. As Robson notes, *The Ethics of Dust* is a 'curious work' (2001: 115). According to Robson, subtitled 'Ten Lectures to Little Housewives on the Elements of Crystallisation', *The Ethics of Dust* 'was intended, Ruskin maintained, to function as a gloss on the chapter entitled "Compact Crystallines" in the fourth volume of *Modern Painters*' (2001: 115). The 'Little Housewives' mentioned in the title were the pupils of Winnington Hall in Cheshire, a school for wealthy girls, and the book is written 'as

a series of quasi-Socratic dialogues between a "Lecturer" (a figure who is never named "Ruskin" in the text but who is self-evidently the author of *Modern Painters* and his other books) and twelve "girls" between the ages of nine and twenty' (Robson 2001: 115).
10. La Touche's age on first meeting Ruskin is not consistent in critical works and varies between nine and ten.
11. I refer in Chapter 2 to the fact that marble is a crystalline material that comes from limestone. It is formed of calcite which is a crystalline form of calcium carbonate.
12. Marion Hepworth Dixon (1856–1936) was the sister of New Woman writer, Ella Hepworth Dixon (1857–1931).
13. It was rumoured that Ford had used a female model for the Shelley statue, though his son later revealed that he had posed for it (Calè and Evangelista 2018: 26).

Bibliography

Abraham Nicolas, and Maria Torok (1986), *The Wolf-Man's Magic Word: A Cryptonomy*, trans. Nicholas Rand, Minneapolis: University of Minnesota Press.

Adams, Jad (2018), 'Olive Custance: A Poet Crossing Boundaries', *ELT, 1880–1920*, 61:1, 35–65.

Altick, Richard D. (1978), *The Shows of London*, Cambridge, MA: Belknap Press of Harvard University Press.

Alworth, David J. (2015), 'Henry James, Fredric Jameson, and the Social Art of Sculpture', *Henry James Review*, 36: 3, 212–25.

American Heritage Dictionary (2001), 4th edn, Boston: Houghton Mifflin.

Amtower, Laurel, and Jacqueline Vanhoutte (2009), *A Companion to Chaucer and his Contemporaries: Texts and Contexts*, Peterborough, ON: Broadview Press.

Angel, Sara (2011), 'The Mnemosyne Atlas and the Meaning of Panel 79 in Aby Warburg's Oeuvre as a Distributed Object', *Leonardo*, 44: 3, 266–7.

Anon. (1854), 'Popular Art', *The Era*, 28 May.

Anon. (1882a), 'Mr. Woolner's "Pygmalion"', *The Spectator*, 7 January, pp. 25–7, <http://archive.spectator.co.uk/page/7th-january-1882/27> (last accessed 22 August 2019).

Anon. (1882b), 'Mr Woolner's "Pygmalion"', *St James's Gazette*, 7 February, pp. 6–7.

Arscott, Caroline (2000), 'Venus as Dominatrix: Nineteenth-Century Artists and Their Creations', in Caroline Arscott and Katie Scott (eds), *Manifestations of Venus in Art and Sexuality*, Manchester: Manchester University Press, pp. 109–25.

Arscott, Caroline (2008), 'Introduction', *William Morris and Edward Burne-Jones: Interlacings*, New Haven and London: Yale University Press, pp. 9–27.

Arscott, Caroline, and Katie Scott (eds) (2000), 'Introducing Venus', *Manifestations of Venus in Art and Sexuality*, Manchester: Manchester University Press, pp. 1–23.

Aske, M. (1985), *Keats and Hellenism*, Cambridge: Cambridge University Press.

Aspley, Keith, Elizabeth Cowling and Peter Sharratt (eds) (1999), *From Rodin to Giacometti: Sculpture and Literature in France, 1880–1950*, Amsterdam: Rodopi.

Auerbach, Jonathan (1980), 'Executing the Model: Painting, Sculpture, and Romance-Writing in Hawthorne's *The Marble Faun*', *ELH*, 47: 1, 103–20.

Balzer, David (2015), *Curationism: How Curating Took over the Art World and Everything Else*, London: Pluto Press.

Barnard, John (1999), 'Hazlitt's *Liber Amoris, or the New Pygmalion* (1823): Conversations with the Statue', in Shirley Chew and Alistair Stead (eds), *Translating Life: Studies in Transpositional Aesthetics*, Liverpool: Liverpool University Press, pp. 181–98.

Barney, Natalie (1960), *Souvenir Indiscrets*, Paris: Flammarion.

Barrett Browning, Elizabeth (1995), 'Hiram Powers' Greek Slave', in Robert Glorney Bolton and Julia Bolton Holloway (eds), *Aurora Leigh and Other Poems*, London: Penguin, p. 375.

Baym, Nina (1971), '*The Marble Faun*: Hawthorne's Elegy for Art', *The New England Quarterly*, 44: 3, 355–76.

Beattie, Susan (1977), *The New Sculpture*, New Haven: Yale University Press.

Beazley, J. D. and B. Ashmole (1966), *Greek Sculpture and Painting to the End of the Hellenistic Period*, Cambridge: Cambridge University Press.

Beckson, K. (1974), *Oscar Wilde: The Critical Heritage*, London: Routledge & Kegan Paul.

Bell, Millicent (2004), 'Introduction', Henry James, *Beloved Boy: Letters to Hendrik C. Andersen, 1899-1915*, Charlottesville and London: University of Virginia Press, pp. ix–xxxv.

Blanchard, Marc (2000), 'The Dandy and the Commissar: Notes on the History of Culture', *MLN*, 115: 4, 662–89.

Booth, Michael (1981), *Victorian Spectacular Theatre 1850-1910*, London and New York: Routledge.

Boyiopoulos, Kostas (2015), *The Decadent Image: The Poetry of Wilde, Symons, and Dowson*, Edinburgh: Edinburgh University Press.

Breitenberger, Barbara (2007), *Aphrodite and Eros: The Development of Greek Erotic Mythology*, New York: Routledge.

Briggs, Jo (2006), 'Plural Anomalies: Gender and Sexuality in Bio-Critical Readings of Vernon Lee', in Catherine Maxwell and Patricia Pulham (eds), *Vernon Lee: Decadence, Ethics, Aesthetics*, Basingstoke: Palgrave Macmillan, pp. 160–73.

Brodhead, Richard H. (1990), 'Introduction', *The Marble Faun: Or, The Romance of Monte Beni*, London: Penguin, pp. ix–xxix.

Bronfen, Elisabeth (1992), *Over Her Dead Body: Death, Femininity and the Aesthetic*, Manchester: Manchester University Press.

Browning, Robert (1855), *Men and Women*, 2 vols, London: Chapman and Hall.

Buchanan, Robert (1871), 'The Fleshly School of Poetry: D.G. Rossetti', *Contemporary Review*, 18, 334–50.

Bullen, J. B. (1986), *The Expressive Eye: Fiction and Perception in the Work of Thomas Hardy*, Oxford: Clarendon Press.

Bullen, J. B. (2002), 'Ruskin, Gautier, and the Feminization of Venice', in Dinah Birch and Francis O'Gorman (eds), *Ruskin and Gender*, Basingstoke: Palgrave Macmillan, pp. 64–85.

Butler, Marilyn (1984), 'Satire and the Images of the Self in the Romantic Period: The Long Tradition of Hazlitt's Liber Amoris', in Claude Rawson (ed.), *English Satire and the Satiric Tradition*, New York: Blackwell, pp. 209–25.

Calè, Luisa, and Stefano Evangelista (2018), '"A bright erroneous dream": The Shelley Memorial and the Body of the Poet', *Word & Image*, 34: 1, 16–30.

Candlin, Fiona (2010), *Art, Museums and Touch*, Manchester: Manchester University Press.

Carroll, Noël (2006), 'Aesthetic Experience: A Question of Content', in Matthew Kieran (ed.), *Contemporary Debates in Aesthetics and the Philosophy of Art*, Oxford: Blackwell, pp. 69–97.

Casillo, Robert (1997), 'Twilight of the Sacred: René Girard Reappraised', *Annals of Scholarship: An International Quarterly in the Humanities and Social Sciences*, 11: 4, 405–31.

Castle, Terry (1993), *The Apparitional Lesbian: Female Homosexuality and Modern Culture*, New York: Columbia University Press.

Challis, Debbie (2008), 'Modern to Ancient: Greece at the Great Exhibition and the Crystal Palace', in Jeffrey A. Auerbach and Peter H. Hoffenberg (eds), *Britain, the Empire, and the World at the Great Exhibition of 1851*, Burlington: Ashgate Press, pp. 173–90.

Chandler Moulton, Louise (1894), *Arthur O'Shaughnessy: His Life and Work with Selections from his Poems*, Cambridge and Chicago: Stone & Kimball.

Classen, Constance (2012), *The Deepest Sense: A Cultural History of Touch*, Champaign: Illinois University Press, pp. i–xvii.

Coltman, Viccy (2006), *Fabricating the Antique: Neoclassicism in Britain, 1760-1800*, Chicago: The University of Chicago Press.

Coltman, Viccy (2009), *Classical Sculpture and the Culture of Collecting in Britain since 1760*, Oxford: Oxford University Press.

Connell, Brian (1957), *Portrait of a Whig Peer: Compiled from the Papers of the Second Viscount Palmerston*, London: Andre Deutsch.

Cook, Brian F. (1985), *The Townley Marbles*, London: British Museum Press.

Curtis, Gregory (2003), *Disarmed: The Story of the Venus de Milo*, Stroud: Sutton Publishing Ltd.

Custance, Olive (1897), *Opals*, London and New York: John Lane.

Custance, Olive (1902), *Rainbows*, London and New York: John Lane.

Custance, Olive (1905), *The Blue Bird*, London: Marlborough Press.

Custance, Olive (1911), *The Inn of Dreams*, London and New York: John Lane.

Custance, Olive (2004), *I desire the Moon: The Diary of Lady Alfred Douglas (Olive Custance), 1905-1910*, ed. Caspar Wintermans, New York: Avalon Press.

Cutting, Andrew (2005), *Death in Henry James*, Basingstoke: Palgrave Macmillan.

Dabakis, Melissa (2014), *A Sisterhood of Sculptors: American Artists in Nineteenth-Century Rome*, Philadelphia: Pennsylvania State University Press

Davis, Whitney (2010), *Queer Beauty: Sexuality and Aesthetics from Winckelmann to Freud and Beyond*, New York: Columbia University Press.

De Biasio, Anna, Anna Despotopoulou and Donatella Izzo (eds) (2013), 'Introduction', *Transforming Henry James*, Newcastle upon Tyne: Cambridge Scholars Publishing, pp. 1–8.

Deacon, A. W. Newport (1881), 'Preface', *Arthur O'Shaughnessy, Songs of a Worker*, London: Chatto & Windus, pp. v–viii.

Denommé, Robert T. (1972), *The French Parnassian Poets*, London and Amsterdam: Feffer & Simms Inc.; Carbondale and Edwardsville: Southern Illinois University Press.

Dent, P. (ed.) (2014), 'Introduction', *Sculpture and Touch*, Aldershot: Ashgate, pp. 1–24.

Derrida, Jacques (1986), '*Fors*: The Anglish Words of Nicolas Abraham and Maria Torok', trans. Barbara Johnson, in Nicolas Abraham and Maria Torok, *The Wolf Man's Magic Word: A Cryptonomy*, Minneapolis: University of Minnesota Press, pp. xi–xlviii.

Di Bello, Patrizia (2010), 'Photography and Sculpture: A Light Touch', in Patrizia di Bello and Gabriel Koureas (eds), *Art History and the Senses: 1830 to the Present*, Burlington: Ashgate Press, pp. 19–34.

Dixon, John (1968), *The Pre-Raphaelite Imagination, 1848–1900*, London: Routledge & Kegan Paul.

Docherty, John (1990), 'The Sources of *Phantastes*', *North Wind: Journal of George MacDonald Studies*, 9, 38–53.

Donnellan, Victoria (2019), 'Ethics and Erotics: Receptions of an Ancient Statue', in Jana Funke and Jen Grove (eds), *Sculpture, Sexuality and History: Encounters in Literature, Culture and the Arts from the Eighteenth Century to the Present*, London: Palgrave Macmillan, pp. 145–67.

Dowling, Linda (1989), 'Ruskin's Pied Beauty and the Constitution of a "Homosexual Code"', *Victorian Newsletter*, 1–8.

Dowling, Linda (1994), *Hellenism and Homosexuality in Victorian Oxford*, Ithaca: Cornell University Press.

Downing, Lisa (2003), *Desiring the Dead: Necrophilia and Nineteenth-Century French Literature*, Oxford: Legenda.

Eck, Stefanie (2014), *Galatea's Emancipation: The Transformation of the Pygmalion Myth in Anglo-Saxon Literature since the 20th Century*, Hamburg: Anchor Academic Publishing.

Edwards, Jason (2006), *Alfred Gilbert's Aestheticism: Gilbert amongst Whistler, Wilde, Leighton, Pater and Burne-Jones*, Burlington: Ashgate Press.

Eliade, Mircea (1982), *History of Religious Ideas, Volume 2: From Gautama Buddha to the Triumph of Christianity*, trans. Willard. R. Trask, Chicago and London: Chicago University Press.

Eliot, George [1871–2] (2003), *Middlemarch*, ed. Rosemary Ashton, London: Penguin.

Ellis, Havelock [1905] (1936), *Studies in the Psychology of Sex*, 8 vols, New York: Random House, vol. 4.

Ellmann, Richard (1984), 'Henry James among the Aesthetes', *Proceedings of the British Academy*, vol. 69, London: The British Academy, pp. 209–28.

Ellmann, Richard (1988), *Oscar Wilde*, London: Vintage Books.

Evangelista, Stefano (2009), *British Aestheticism and Ancient Greece: Hellenism, Reception, Gods in Exile*, Basingstoke: Palgrave Macmillan.

Faderman, Lillian (1981), *Surpassing the Love of Men: Romantic Friendship and Love between Women from the Renaissance to the Present*, London: Junction Books.

Faulkner, Peter (2012), 'Morris and Pre-Raphaelitism', *Journal of William Morris Studies*, 19: 4, 40–62.

Fernie, Deanna (2011), *Hawthorne, Sculpture and the Question of American Art*, Burlington: Ashgate Press.

Foucault, Michel (1981), *An Introduction*, vol. 1 in *The History of Sexuality*, trans. Robert Hurley, Harmondsworth: Penguin.

Fraser, Hilary (2014), *Women Writing Art History in the Nineteenth Century*. Cambridge: Cambridge University Press.

Fraser, Hilary (2018), 'Grief Encounter: The Language of Mourning in Fin-de-siècle Sculpture', *Word & Image*, 34: 1, 40–54.

Freedberg, David (1989), *The Power of Images: Studies in the History and Theory of Response*, Chicago and London: The University of Chicago Press.

Freud, Sigmund (1955), 'Delusions and Dreams in Jensen's *Gradiva*', in *The Standard Edition of the Complete Psychological Works of Sigmund Freud*, ed. and trans. James Strachey, Anna Freud, Alix Strachey and Alan Tyson, 24 vols, London: The Hogarth Press and the Institute of Psychoanalysis, vol. 9, pp. 7–93.

Freud, Sigmund (1977), 'Dora', in *The Pelican Freud Library*, ed. and trans. Angela Richards, 24 vols, London: Penguin, vol. 8, pp. 31–164.

Fryd, Vivien Green (2006), 'The "Ghosting" of Incest and Female Relations in Harriet Hosmer's *Beatrice Cenci*', *Art Bulletin*, 88: 2, 292–309.

Funke, Jana, and Jen Grove (eds) (2019), 'Introduction', *Sculpture, Sexuality and History: Encounters in Literature, Culture and the Arts from the Eighteenth Century to the Present*, London: Palgrave Macmillan.

Gaarden, Bonnie (2005), 'Cosmic and Psychological Redemption in George MacDonald's *Lilith*', *Studies in the Novel*, 37: 1, 20–36.

Gaiger, J. (2002), 'Introduction', *Sculpture: Some Observations on Shape and Form from Pygmalion's Creative Dream*, Chicago: Chicago University Press, pp. 1–29.

Gaimster, David (2001), 'Under Lock and Key: Censorship and the Secret Museum', in Stephen Bailey (ed.), *Sex: The Erotic Review*, London: Cassell & Co., pp. 126–39.

Getsy, David (2004), *Body Doubles: Sculpture in Britain, 1877–1905*, New Haven and London: Yale University Press.

Getsy, David (2014), 'Acts of Stillness: Statues, Performativity, and Passive Resistance', *Criticism*, 56: 1, 1–20.

Girard, René (1965), *Deceit, Desire, and the Novel: Self and Other in Literary Structure*, Baltimore: Johns Hopkins University Press.

Goethe, Johann Wolfgang von [1816–17] (1970), *Italian Journey*, trans. W. H. Auden and Elizabeth Mayer, London: Penguin.

Goethe, Johann Wolfgang von (1996), *Roman Elegies and Other Poems and Epigrams*, ed. and trans. Michael Hamburger, London: Anvil Press Poetry.

Gollin, Rita K., and John L. Idol, Jr. (1991), *Prophetic Pictures: Nathaniel Hawthorne's Knowledge and Uses of the Visual Arts*, New York: Greenwood Press.

Goodman, Martin (2014), 'Nature Vs Naturalist: Paths Diverging and Converging in Edmund Gosse's Father and Son', *Life Writing*, 11: 1, 85–101.

Gosse, Edmund (1879), 'Desiderium', *New Poems*, London: C. Kegan Paul & Co, pp. 70–2.

Gosse, Edmund (1894), 'The New Sculpture: 1879-1894', *The Art Journal* (New Series), London: J. S. Virtue & Co. Ltd. pp. 138–42, 199–203, 277–82, 306–11.

Gosse, Edmund (1913), *French Profiles*, London: Heinemann.

Gosse, Edmund (1925), *Silhouettes*, London: W. Heinemann Ltd.

Gosse, Edmund [1907] (2004), *Father and Son*, ed. Michael Newton. Oxford: Oxford University Press.

Goujon, Jean-Paul (1985), 'Renée Vivien et le Parnasse', *Bulletin des Etudes Parnassiennes*, 741–56.

Graham, Wendy (1999), *Henry James' Thwarted Love*, Stanford: Stanford University Press.

Gray, William (1996), 'George MacDonald, Julia Kristeva and the Black Sun', *Studies in English Literature, 1500-1900*, 36: 4, 877–93.

Gray, William (ed.) (2011), *Fantasy, Art and Life: Essays on George MacDonald, Robert Louis Stevenson and other Fantasy Writers*, Newcastle upon Tyne: Cambridge Scholars Publishing.

Gregory, Brian (1999), 'Sexual Serpents: Ruskin's The Queen of the Air', *Nineteenth-Century Prose*, 26: 2, 73–85.

Gregory, Eileen (1997), *H.D. and Hellenism: Classic Lines*, Cambridge: Cambridge University Press.

Gross, Kenneth (2006), *The Dream of the Moving Statue*, University Park: Pennsylvania State University Press.

Haley, Bruce (2003), *Living Forms: Romantics and the Monumental Figure*, New York: State University of New York Press.

Hall, Spencer (1970), 'Beatrice Cenci: Symbol and Vision in The Marble Faun', *Nineteenth-Century Fiction*, 25: 1, 85–95.

Hardy, Thomas (1902), 'Rome: The Vatican: Sala delle Muse', *Poems of the Past and Present*, New York and London: Harper & Brothers, pp. 50–2.

Hardy, Thomas (1978a), *Collected Letters of Thomas Hardy*, ed. R. L. Purdy and M. Millgate, 7 vols, Oxford: Clarendon Press, Volume 1: 1840–92.

Hardy, Thomas (1978b), *Selected Poetry*, ed. David Wright, London: Penguin.

Hardy, Thomas [1892; 1897] (1997), *The Pursuit of the Well-Beloved and The Well-Beloved*, ed. Patricia Ingham, London: Penguin.

Harris, Frank (1992), *Oscar Wilde*, New York: Carroll & Graf.

Haskell, Francis J., and Nicholas Penny (1981), *Taste and the Antique: Lure of Classical Sculpture, 1500–1900*, New Haven and London: Yale University Press.

Hatt, Michael (2001), 'Thoughts and Things: Sculpture and the Victorian Nude', in Alison Smith (ed.), *Exposed: The Victorian Nude*, London: Tate Trustees, pp. 37–49.

Hawkey, Nancy J. (1972), 'Olive Custance Douglas: Introduction to a Bibliography', *ELT, 1880–1890*, 15: 1, 49–51.

Hawthorne, Nathaniel, (1980), *The French and Italian Notebooks*, ed. Thomas Woodson, Columbus: Ohio State University Press.

Hawthorne, Nathaniel [1860] (1990a), *The Marble Faun: Or, The Romance of Monte Beni*, ed. Richard Brodhead, London: Penguin.

Hawthorne, Nathaniel (1990b), 'Preface', *The Marble Faun: Or, The Romance of Monte Beni*, ed. Richard Brodhead, London: Penguin, pp. 1–4.

Hazlitt, William (1818), 'On Poetry', *Lectures on the English Poets*, London: Taylor and Hessey, pp. 1–38.

Hazlitt, William [1823] (1998a), *Liber Amoris. The Selected Writings of William Hazlitt*, ed. Duncan Wu, 9 vols, London: Pickering & Chatto, vol. 7, pp. 2–73.

Hazlitt, William [1822] (1998b), 'On the Elgin Marbles', in *The Selected Writings of William Hazlitt*, ed. Duncan Wu, 9 vols, London: Pickering & Chatto, vol. 9, pp. 75–94.

H.D. (1988), *Notes on Thought and Vision; and The Wise Sappho*, London: Owen.

Heffernan, James (1993), *Museum of Words: The Poetics of Ekphrasis from Homer to Ashbery*, Chicago: Chicago University Press.

Hein, Ronald (1993), *George MacDonald: Victorian Mythmaker*, Nashville: Star Song.

Herder, Johann Gottfried [1778] (2002), *Sculpture: Some Observations on Shape and Form from Pygmalion's Creative Dream*, ed. and trans. J. Gaiger, Chicago: Chicago University Press.

Hersey, George L. (2009), *Falling in Love with Statues: Artificial Humans from Pygmalion to the Present*, Chicago and London: The University of Chicago Press.

Hewlett, Maurice [1895] (1901), *Earthwork Out of Tuscany*, London and New York: Macmillan & Co. Ltd.

Hillis Miller, J. (1982), *Fiction and Repetition: Seven English Novels*. Cambridge, MA: Harvard University Press.

Hogarth, William [1753] (1772), *The Analysis of Beauty: Written with a View to Fixing the Fluctuating Ideas of Taste*, London: W. Strahan.

Holmes, John (2004), 'Pursuing the Well-Beloved: Thomas Hardy, Jocelyn Pearston and the School of Rossetti', in David Clifford and Laurence Rousillon (eds), *Outsiders Looking in: The Rossettis Then and Now*, London: Anthem Press, pp. 237–51.

Hönnighausen, Lothar (2010), *The Symbolist Tradition in English Literature: A Study of Pre-Raphaelitism and Fin de Siècle*, trans. Gisela Hönnighausen, Cambridge: Cambridge University Press.

Hopkins, B. (1984), 'Keats and the Uncanny: "This Living Hand"', *Kenyon Review*, 11, 28–38.

Howes, David, and Constance Classen (2014), *Ways of Sensing: Understanding the Senses in Society*, New York: Routledge.

Hughes, Linda K (2004), 'Women Poets and Contested Spaces in *The Yellow Book*', *Studies in English Literature, 1500–1900*, 44: 4, 849–72.

Jackson, Holbrook (1913), *The Eighteen Nineties: A Review of Art and Ideas at the Close of the Nineteenth Century*, London: Grant Richards.

James, Henry (1883), *Hawthorne*, London: MacMillan and Co.

James, Henry [1875] (1907), *Roderick Hudson, New York Edition*, 24 vols, New York: Charles Scribner's Sons, vol. 1.

James, Henry (1974), *Letters*, ed. Leon Edel, 4 vols, Cambridge, MA: Harvard University Press, vol. 1: 1843–75.

James, Henry (1986), *Roderick Hudson*, London: Penguin.

James, Henry (2004), *Beloved Boy: Letters to Hendrik C. Andersen, 1899–1915*, ed. Rosella Mamoli Zorzi, Charlottesville and London: University of Virginia Press.

Jameson, Anna (1854), *A Handbook to the Courts of Modern Sculpture*, London: Bradbury and Evans.

Jeffreys, Sheila (1985), *The Spinster and Her Enemies: Feminism and Sexuality 1880–1930*, London: Pandora Press.

Jenkins, Ian (1992), *Archaeologists and Aesthetes in the Sculpture Galleries of the British Museum 1800-1939*, London: British Museum Press.

Jenkyns, Richard (1996), *The Victorians and Ancient Greece*, Oxford: Blackwell.

Johnson, Barbara (2008), *Persons and Things*, Cambridge, MA: Harvard University Press.

Johnson, Christopher D. (2012), *Memory, Metaphor, and Aby Warburg's Atlas of Images*, Ithaca: Cornell University Press.

Joshua, Essaka (2001), *Pygmalion and Galatea: The History of a Narrative in English Literature*, Aldershot: Ashgate.

Kaplan, Fred (1999), *Henry James, the Imagination of Genius: A Biography*, Baltimore: Johns Hopkins University Press.

Kasson, Joy S. (1992), 'Narratives of the Female Body: *The Greek Slave*', in Shirley Samuels (ed.), *The Culture of Sentiment: Race, Gender, and Sentimentality in 19th-Century America*, New York and Oxford: Oxford University Press, pp. 172–90.

Kaye, Richard (1999), '"Determined Raptures": St. Sebastian and the Victorian Discourse of Decadence', *Victorian Literature and Culture*, 27: 1, 269–303.

Keats, John (1988), *The Complete Poems*, ed. John Barnard, London: Penguin Classics.

Kenaan, Hagi (2014), 'Touching Sculpture', in Peter Dent (ed.), *Sculpture and Touch*, Burlington: Ashgate, pp. 45–60.

Kendrick, Walter (1987), *The Secret Museum: Pornography in Modern Culture*, New York: Viking.

Kern, Stephen (1996), *Eyes of Love: The Gaze in English and French Culture, 1840–1900*, London: Reaktion Books.

Kistler, Jordan (2012), '"I carve the marble of pure thought": Work and Production in the Poetry of Arthur O'Shaughnessy', *Victorian Network*, 4: 1, 73–90.

Kistler, Jordan (2016), *Arthur O'Shaughnessy, A Pre-Raphaelite Poet in the British Museum*, London and New York: Routledge.

Laity, Cassandra (1996), *H.D. and the Victorian Fin de Siècle: Gender, Modernism, Decadence*, Oxford: Oxford University Press.

Lambert, Royston (1997), *Beloved and God: The Story of Hadrian and Antinous*, London: Phoenix.

Larrabee, Stephen (1941), 'Hazlitt's Criticism and Greek Sculpture', *Journal of the History of Ideas*, 2: 1, 77–94.

Lear, Andrew, and Eva Cantarella (2008), *Images of Ancient Greek Pederasty*, London and New York: Routledge.

Ledger, Sally (2007), 'Wilde Women and *The Yellow Book*: The Sexual Politics of Aestheticism and Decadence', *ELT, 1880-1920*, 50: 1, 5–26.

Lee, Vernon (1883), 'The Portrait Art of the Renaissance', *Cornhill Magazine*, 47, 564–81.

Lee, Vernon (1884), *Miss Brown: A Novel in Three Volumes*, Edinburgh and London: William Blackwood and Sons.

Lee, Vernon (2006), 'Dionea', in *Hauntings and Other Fantastic Tales*, ed. Catherine Maxwell and Patricia Pulham, Peterborough, ON: Broadview Press, pp. 77–104.

Leland, Henry P. (1863), *Americans in Rome*, New York: Charles T. Evans.

Lester, C. Edwards (1845), *The Artist, the Merchant, and the Statesman in the Age of the Medici*, New York: Paine & Burgess.

Lewis, D. M., John Boardman, J. K. Davies and M. Ostwald (eds) (1992), *The Cambridge Ancient History*, Cambridge: Cambridge University Press, vol. 5, The Fifth Century BC.

Liebman, Sheldon W. (1967), 'The Design of the Marble Faun', *New England Quarterly*, 40, 61–78.

Livingston, Paisley (1992), *Models of Desire: René Girard and the Psychology of Mimesis*, Baltimore and London: Johns Hopkins University Press.

Long, Robert Emmet (1976), 'James's *Roderick Hudson*: The End of the Apprenticeship – Hawthorne and Turgenev', *American Literature*, 48: 3, 312–26.

McClellan, Andrew (1994), *Inventing the Louvre: Art, Politics, and the Origins of the Modern Museum in Eighteenth-Century Paris*, Cambridge: Cambridge University Press.

Macdermott, Edward (1854), *Routledge's Guide to the Crystal Palace and Park at Sydenham*, London: George Routledge & Co.

MacDonald, George [1858] (2008), *Phantastes: A Faerie Romance for Men and Women*, ed. Nick Page, London: Paternoster.

McGillis, Roderick (ed.) (2008), *George MacDonald: Literary Heritage and Heirs*, Cheshire: Winged Lion Press.

MacKay, Carol Hanbury (1984), 'Hawthorne, Sophia, and Hilda as Copyists: Duplication and Transformation in *The Marble Faun*', *Browning Institute Studies: An Annual of Victorian Literary and Cultural History*, 12, 93–120.

McKenna, Neil (2004), *The Secret Life of Oscar Wilde*, London: Arrow Books.

MacLachlan, Christopher, John Patrick Pazdziora and Ginger Stelle (eds) (2013), *Rethinking George MacDonald: Contexts and Contemporaries*, Glasgow: Scottish Literature International.

MacLeod, Catriona (2014), *Fugitive Objects: Sculpture and Literature in the German Nineteenth Century*, Evanston: Northwestern University Press.

Maddox, Lucy B. (1982), 'Necrophilia in *Lolita*', *Centennial Review*, 26: 4, 361–74.

Mallgrave, Harry F. (2006), 'Foreword. Johann Joachim Winckelmann', in *History of the Art of Antiquity*, trans. Harry F. Mallgrave, ed. Alex Potts, Los Angeles: Getty Publications, p. ix.

Malone, P. (2012), 'Keats's "Posthumous Existence" in Plaster', *The Keats-Shelley Review*, 26: 2, 125–35.

Malraux, André [1947] (1967), *Museum without Walls*, trans. Stuart Gilbert and Francis Price, London: Secker & Warburg.

Maltz, Diana (2000), 'Engaging "Delicate Brains": From Working-Class Enculturation to Upper-Class Lesbian Liberation in Vernon Lee and Kit Anstruther-Thomson's Psychological Aesthetics', in Talia Schaffer and Kathy Alexis Psomiades, *Women and British Aestheticism*, Charlottesville: University of Virginia Press, pp. 211–29.

Manlove, Colin (2005), 'Did William Morris Start MacDonald Writing Fantasy?' *North Wind: A Journal of George MacDonald Studies*, 24: 6, <http://digitalcommons.snc.edu/northwind/vol24/iss1/6> (last accessed 30 July 2018).

Marsh, Amy (2010), '"Love among the Objectum Sexuals', *Electronic Journal of Human Sexuality*, 13.

Marshall, Gail (1998), *Actresses on the Victorian Stage: Feminine Performance and the Galatea Myth*, Cambridge: Cambridge University Press.

Martin, Robert K. (1978), 'The "High Felicity" of Comradeship: A New Reading of *Roderick Hudson*', *American Literary Realism*, 11, 100–8.

Martin, Robert K. (2002), '"An Awful Freedom": Hawthorne and the Anxieties of the Carnival', in Robert K. Martin and Leland S. Person (eds), *Roman Holidays: American Writers and Artists in Nineteenth-Century Italy*, Iowa City: University of Iowa Press, pp. 28–40.

Martin, Robert K., and Leland S. Person (eds) (2002), *Roman Holidays: American Writers and Artists in Nineteenth-Century Italy*, Iowa City: University of Iowa Press, pp. 1–8.

Matthews, Thomas (1911), *The Biography of John Gibson, R. A., Sculptor, Rome*, London: William Heinemann.

Mendelssohn, Michèle (2003), 'Homosociality and the Aesthetic in Henry James's *Roderick Hudson*', *Nineteenth-Century Literature*, 57: 4, 512–41.

Mendelssohn, Michèle (2018), *Making Oscar Wilde*, Oxford: Oxford University Press.

Miller, Jane M. (1988), 'Some Versions of Pygmalion', in Charles Martindale (ed.), *Ovid Renewed. Ovidian Influences on Literature and Art from the Middle Ages to the Twentieth Century*, Cambridge: Cambridge University Press, pp. 205–14.

Miller, Mark J. (2016), *Cast Down: Abjection in America, 1700–1850*, Philadelphia: University of Pennsylvania Press.

Moores, John (2018), 'George Cruickshank and the British Satirical Response', in Katherine Astbury and Mark Philip (eds), *Napoleon's Hundred Days and the Politics of Legitimacy*, London: Palgrave Macmillan, pp. 255–74.

Morris, William (1882), 'The Lesser Arts', *Hopes and Fears for Art*, London: Ellis & White, pp. 1–37.

Morris, William [1868] (1888), 'Pygmalion and the Image', *The Earthly Paradise: A Poem*, London: F. S Ellis, vol. 2, pp. 588–613.

Murray, Douglas (2000), *Bosie: A Biography of Lord Alfred Douglas*, London: Hodder & Stoughton.

Murtaugh, Daniel J. (1996), 'An Emotional Reflection: Sexual Realization in Henry James's Revisions to *Roderick Hudson*', *The Henry James Review*, 17: 2, 182–203.

Najarian, James (2002), *Victorian Keats: Manliness, Sexuality and Desire*, Basingstoke: Palgrave Macmillan.

Natarajan, Uttara (2002), 'Hazlitt, Ruskin, and Ideal Form', *Philological Quarterly*, 81: 4, 493–503.

Nelson, James G. (2004), '"The Honey of Romance": Oscar Wilde as Poet and Novelist', in William Baker and Ira B. Nadel (eds), *Redefining the Modern: Essays on Literature and Society in Honor of Joseph Wiesenfarth*, Madison: Fairleigh Dickinson University Press, pp. 130–57.

Nichols, Kate (2013), 'Art and Commodity: Sculpture under Glass at the Crystal Palace', in John C. Welchman (ed.), *Sculpture and the Vitrine*, Burlington: Ashgate, pp. 23–46.

Nichols, Kate (2015), *Greece and Rome at the Crystal Palace: Classical Sculpture and Modern Britain, 1854–1936*, Oxford: Oxford University Press.

Nietzsche, Friedrich (2003), *The Birth of Tragedy*, ed. Michael Tanner, trans. Shaun Whiteside, London: Penguin.

Ormond, Leonee (1970), 'Vernon Lee as Critic of Aestheticism in *Miss Brown*', *Colby Library Quarterly*, 9: 3, 131–54.

O'Shaughnessy, Arthur (1874), *Music and Moonlight: Poems and Songs*, London: Chatto & Windus.

O'Shaughnessy, Arthur (1881), *Songs of a Worker*, London: Chatto and Windus.

O'Shaughnessy, Arthur (n.d.a), 'Pagan', Special Collections, McClay Library, Queen's University, Belfast, MS 8/3, pp. 95–110

O'Shaughnessy, Arthur (n.d.b), 'Notes on Books', Special Collections, McClay Library, Queen's University, Belfast, MS 8/4.

Østermark-Johansen, Lene (2011), *Walter Pater and the Language of Sculpture*, Burlington: Ashgate Press.

Ovid (2008), *Metamorphoses*, trans. A. D. Melville, ed. E. J. Kennedy, Oxford: Oxford University Press.

Oxford English Dictionary (n.d.), <https://www.oed.com> (last accessed 10 November 2019).

Page, Nick (ed.) (2008), 'Introduction', in *Phantastes: A Faerie Romance for Men and Women*, Milton Keynes: Paternoster, pp. 7–30.

Page, Norman (1999), 'Art and Aesthetics', in Dale Kramer (ed.), *The Cambridge Companion to Thomas Hardy*, Cambridge: Cambridge University Press, pp. 38–53.

Paglia, Camille (1991), *Sexual Personae: Art and Decadence from Nefertiti to Emily Dickinson*, New York: Vintage.

Parker, Sarah (2013), *The Lesbian Muse and Poetic Identity, 1889–1930*, London and New York: Routledge.

Parker, Sarah (2019), 'Olive Custance, Nostalgia, and Decadent Conservatism', *Volupté: Interdisciplinary Journal of Decadence Studies*, 2: 1, 57–81.

Parkins, Wendy (2013), *Jane Morris: The Burden of History*, Edinburgh: Edinburgh University Press.

Pater, Walter [1894] (1910), *Greek Studies*. London: Macmillan.

Pater, Walter [1873] (2010), *Studies in the History of the Renaissance*, ed. Matthew Beaumont, Oxford: Oxford University Press.

Paterson, Mark (2007), *The Senses of Touch: Haptics, Affects and Technologies*, New York: Berg.

Paulin, Tom (2008), 'Foreword', *William Hazlitt, On the Elgin Marbles*, London: Hesperus Press, pp. vii–ix.

Person, Leland S. (2002), 'Falling into Heterosexuality: Sculpting Male Bodies in *The Marble Faun* and *Roderick Hudson*', in Robert K. Martin and Leland S. Person (eds), *Roman Holidays: American Writers and Artists in Nineteenth-Century Italy*, Iowa City: Iowa University Press, pp. 107–39.

Person, Leland S. (2013), 'Manic James: The Early Letters and *Roderick Hudson*', in Anna De Biasio, Anna Despotopoulou and Donatella Izzo (eds), *Transforming Henry James*, Newcastle upon Tyne: Cambridge Scholars Publishing, pp. 40–53.

Pilgrim, Anne C. (1991), 'Hardy's Retroactive Self-Censorship: The Case of *The Well-Beloved*', in Judith Kennedy and John R. Reed (eds), *Victorian Authors and Their Works: Revision, Motivations and Modes*. Athens: Ohio University Press, pp. 125–39.

Pionke, Albert D. (2011), 'The Art of Manliness: Ekphrasis and/as Masculinity in George MacDonald's *Phantastes*', *Studies in the Novel*, 43: 1, 21–37.

Plato (2019), *Charmides*, trans. with Introduction, Notes and Analysis by Christopher Moore and Christopher C. Raymond, Cambridge and Indianapolis: Hackett Publishing Company, Inc.

Preston, Carrie J. (2011), *Modernism's Mythic Pose: Gender, Genre, Solo Performance*, Oxford: Oxford University Press.

Prickett, Stephen (1990), 'Fictions and Metafictions: *Phantastes, Wilhelm Meister*, and the Idea of the Bildungsroman' in William Reaper (ed.), *The Gold Thread: Essays on George MacDonald*, Edinburgh: Edinburgh University Press.

Prins, Yopie (1999), 'Greek Maenads, Victorian Spinsters', in Richard Dellamora (ed.), *Victorian Sexual Dissidence*, Chicago and London: The University of Chicago Press, pp. 43–81.

Pollock, Griselda (ed.) (1996), *Generations and Geographies in the Visual Arts: Feminist Readings*, London and New York: Routledge.

Pollock, Griselda (2007), *Encounters in the Virtual Feminist Museum: Time, Space, and the Archive*, London and New York: Routledge.

Potts, Alex (2000), *Flesh and the Ideal: Winckelmann and the Origins of Art History*, New Haven and London: Yale University Press.

Potts, Alex (2006), 'Introduction', *Johann Joachim Winckelmann, History of the Art of Antiquity*, Los Angeles: Getty Publications, pp. 1–53.

Poulot, Dominique (2012), 'Introduction', in Quatremère de Quincy, *Letters to Miranda and Canova on the Abduction of Antiquities from Rome and Athens*, trans. Chris Mille and David Gilks, Los Angeles: The Getty Research Institute.

Proctor, Nancy (2002), 'The Purloined Studio: The Woman Sculptor as Phallic Ghost in Hawthorne's *The Marble Faun*', in Robert K. Martin and Leland S. Person (eds), *Roman Holidays: American Writers and Artists in Nineteenth-Century Italy*, Iowa City: Iowa University Press, pp. 60–72.

Pulham, Patricia (2007), 'Tinted and Tainted Love: The Sculptural Body in Olive Custance's Poetry', *The Yearbook of English Studies*, 37: 1, 161–76.

Pulham, Patricia (2008a), *Art and the Transitional Object in Vernon Lee's Supernatural Tales*, Aldershot: Ashgate Press.

Pulham, Patricia (2008b), 'From Pygmalion to Persephone: Love, Art, and Myth in Thomas Hardy's *The Well-Beloved*', *Victorian Review*, 34: 2, 219–39.

Pulham, Patricia (2010), '"Of marble men and maidens": Sin, Sculpture, and Perversion in Nathaniel Hawthorne's *The Marble Faun*', *The Yearbook of English Studies*, 40: 1–2, 83–102.

Pulham, Patricia (2012), 'The New Pygmalions: Idealism and Disillusionment in Hazlitt's *Liber Amoris* and Vernon Lee's *Miss Brown*', in Carmen Casaliggi and Paul March-Russell (eds), *Legacies of Romanticism: Literature, Culture, Aesthetics*, New York and London: Routledge, pp. 101–16.

Pulham, Patricia (2016a), 'Eyes That Trace Like Fingers: Keats, Wilde, and Victorian Statue Love', *La Questione Romantica*, 5: 1–2, 129–49.

Pulham, Patricia (2016b), 'Marmoreal Sisterhoods: Classical Statuary in Nineteenth-Century Women's Writing', *19: Interdisciplinary Studies in the Long Nineteenth Century*, 22, <http://doi.org/10.16995/ntn.763> (last accessed 27 March 2020).

Raeper, William (1987), *George MacDonald: Novelist and Victorian Visionary*, Tring: Lion Publishing.

Ramazani, Jahan (1991), 'Hardy and the Poetics of Melancholia: Poems of 1912–13 and Other Elegies for Emma', *English Literary History*, 58: 4, 957–77.

Read, Herbert (1956), *The Art of Sculpture*, London: Faber & Faber.

Reis, Richard (1962), 'George MacDonald's Fiction: A Study in the Nature of Realism and Symbolism', dissertation, Brown's University, Providence, RI.

Reynolds, Joshua (1891), 'Discourse III', in *Sir Joshua Reynolds's Discourses*, ed. Edward Gilpin-Johnson, Chicago: A. C. McClurg & Company.

Robinson, Agnes Mary Frances (1889), *The End of the Middle Ages: Essays and Questions in History*, London: T. Fisher Unwin.

Robson, Catherine (2001), *Men in Wonderland: The Lost Girlhood of the Victorian Gentleman*, Princeton and Oxford: Princeton University Press.

Rose, Phyllis (1984), *Parallel Lives*, New York: Random House.

Rosenberg, John (2005), *Elegy for an Age: The Presence of the Past in Victorian Literature*, London: Anthem Press.

Ross, Iain (2008), '*Charmides* and *The Sphinx*: Wilde's Engagement with Keats', *Victorian Poetry*, 46: 4, 451–65.

Ross, Iain (2013), *Oscar Wilde and Ancient Greece*, Cambridge: Cambridge University Press.

Rossetti, Christina (1994), 'In an Artist's Studio', in *Poems and Prose*, ed. Jan Marsh, London: Everyman, p. 52.

Rossetti, Dante Gabriel (1881), *Ballads and Sonnets*, London: F. S. Ellis.

Rowe, John Carlos (2002), 'Hawthorne's Ghost in James's Italy: Sculptural Form, Romantic Narrative, and the Function of Sexuality in *The Marble Faun*, 'Adina' and *William Wetmore Story and His Friends*', in Robert K. Martin and Leland S. Person (eds), *Roman Holidays: American Writers and Artists in Nineteenth-Century Italy*, Iowa City: University of Iowa Press, pp. 73–106.

Ruskin, John (1851), *King of the Golden River, or The Black Brothers: A Legend of Stiria*, London: Smith, Elder & Co.

Ruskin, John (1853), *The Stones of Venice. Volume the Third. The Fall*, London: Smith, Elder & Co.

Ruskin, John (1855), 'Pre-Raphaelitism', *Lectures in Architecture and Painting*, London: Smith, Elder and Co., Lecture IV, pp. 189–232.

Ruskin, John (1878), 'The Three Colours of Pre-Raphaelitism', *Nineteenth Century*, 4, November–December, 925–32; 1072–82.

Ruskin, John [1846] (1906), 'Of the Imaginative and Theoretic Faculties', *Modern Painters*, 5 vols, London: George Allen, vol. 2.

Ruskin, John [1885] (2012), *Praeterita*, ed. Francis O'Gorman, Oxford: World's Classics.

Ryan, Michael (1979), 'One Name of Many Shapes: *The Well-Beloved*', in Dale Kramer (ed.), *Critical Approaches to the Fiction of Thomas Hardy*, Basingstoke: The Macmillan Press Ltd.

Salomon, Nanette (1996), 'The Venus Pudica: Uncovering Art History's "Hidden Agendas" and Pernicious Pedigrees', in Griselda Pollock (ed.), *Generations and Geographies in the Visual Arts: Feminist Readings*, London and New York: Routledge, pp. 69–87.

Salzman-Mitchell, Patricia (2008), 'A Whole out of Pieces: Pygmalion's Ivory Statue in Ovid's *Metamorphoses*', *Arethusa*, 41: 2, 291–311.

Scobie, A., and A. J. W. Taylor (1975), 'Perversions Ancient and Modern: 1. Agalmatophilia, The Statue Syndrome', *Journal of the History of the Behavioral Sciences*, 11, 49–54.

Scott, David (2006), 'Tensions dynamiques: le rapport sculpture/poétique en France, 1829–1859', *Nineteenth-Century French Studies*, 35: 1, 132–50.

Scott, Grant F. (1994), *The Sculpted Word: Keats, Ekphrasis, and the Visual Arts*, Lebanon and New York: University Press of New England.

Sedgwick, Eve Kosofsky (1993), *Tendencies*, Durham, NC: Duke University Press.

Sedgwick, Eve Kosofsky (2016), *Between Men: English Literature and Male Homosocial Desire*, New York: Columbia University Press.

Sewell, Brocard (1975), *Olive Custance: Her Life and Work*, London: Eighteen Nineties Society.

Sewell, Brocard (1995), 'Introduction', *The Selected Poems of Olive Custance*, London: Cecil Woolf.

Shelley, Percy Bysshe (1977), 'On Love', in Donald H. Reiman and Sharon B. Powers (eds), *Shelley's Poetry and Prose*, New York: Norton, pp. 473–4.

Showalter, Elaine (1992), *Sexual Anarchy: Gender and Culture at the Fin de siècle*, London: Virago.

Skelton, Robin (1990), *Celtic Contraries*, Syracuse: Syracuse University Press.

Smith, Alison (1996), *The Victorian Nude: Sexuality, Morality and Art*, Manchester: Manchester University Press.

Smith, Lesley Willis (2015), 'MacDonald's Crystal Palace: Diamonds and Rubies, Coal and Salt in *At the Back of the North Wind*', *North Wind: Journal of George MacDonald Studies* 34, 13–57.

Smith, Lindsay (2002), 'The Foxglove and the Rose: Ruskin's Involute of Childhood', in Dinah Birch and Francis O'Gorman (eds), *Ruskin and Gender*, Basingstoke: Palgrave Macmillan, pp. 47–63.

Sofer, Naomi Z. (1999), 'Why "different vibrations walk hand in hand": Homosocial Bonds in *Roderick Hudson*', *The Henry James Review*, 20: 2, 185–205.

Solomon-Godeau, Abigail (1997), *Male Trouble: A Crisis in Representation*, New York: Thames & Hudson.

Souhami, Diana (2004), *Wild Girls: Paris, Sappho and Art: The Life and Loves of Natalie Barney and Romaine Brooks*, London: Weidenfeld & Nicolson.

Staël, Madame de [1807] (2008), *Corinne, or Italy*, ed. and trans. Sylvia Raphael, Oxford: World's Classics.

Steele, Jeremy V. (2006), 'Plato and the Love Goddess: Paganism in Two Versions of *The Well-Beloved*', in Keith Wilson (ed.), *Thomas Hardy Reappraised: Essays in Honour of Michael Millgate*, Toronto: University of Toronto Press, pp. 199–218.

Stetz, Margaret D., and Mark Samuels Lasner (1990), *England in the 1890s: Literary Publishing at The Bodley Head*, Washington, DC: Georgetown University Press.

Stewart, A. (1997), *Art, Desire and the Body in Ancient Greece*, Cambridge: Cambridge University Press.

Stoichita, Victor I. (2008), *The Pygmalion Effect: From Ovid to Hitchcock*, trans. Alison Anderson, Chicago: The University of Chicago Press.

Stokes, J. (1997), 'Wilde the Journalist', in P. Raby (ed.), *The Cambridge Companion to Oscar Wilde*, Cambridge: Cambridge University Press, pp. 69–79.

Sutherland, Helen (2013), 'Pictures on a Page: George MacDonald and the Visual Arts', in Christopher MacLachlan (ed.), *Rethinking George MacDonald: Contexts and Contemporaries*, Glasgow: Scottish Literature International, pp. 216–34.

Swinburne, Algernon Charles [1866] (1904), *Poems and Ballads, First Series*, London: Chatto & Windus.

Symonds, John Addington (1877), *Renaissance in Italy*, 7 vols, London: Smith, Elder & Co., vol. 3, The Fine Arts.

Symonds, John Addington (1901), *A Problem in Greek Ethics: Being an Inquiry into the Phenomenon of Sexual Inversion*, London: Privately Printed.

Symonds, John Addington (1969), 'Letter to Edmund Gosse, 9 November 1890', *The Letters of John Addington Symonds*, ed. Herbert M. Schueller and Robert L. Peters, 3 vols, Detroit: Wayne State University Press, vol. 3 1885–93.

Talbot, William Henry Fox (1844), *The Pencil of Nature*, London: Longman, Brown, Green, and Longmans.

Tarnowsky, Benjamin [1886] (1898), *The Sexual Instinct and Its Morbid Manifestations*, trans. W. C. Costello and Alfred Allinson, Paris: Charles Carrington.

Thain, Marion, and Ana Parejo Vadillo (2009), 'Introduction', *Michael Field, The Poet: Published and Unpublished Materials*, Peterborough, ON: Broadview Press, pp. 23–52.

Thomas, Jane (2018), 'The Mower, The Sower, and The Mayor: Thomas Hardy and Hamo Thornycroft, Encounters and Affinities', *Word & Image*, 34: 1, 7–15.

Thornton, R. K. R., and Ian Small (1996), 'Introduction to Olive Custance', in *Opals, with Rainbows*, Poole: Woodstock, pp. i–vii.

Thwaite, Ann (2007), *Edmund Gosse: A Literary Landscape*, Stroud: Tempus.

Turner, Frank M. (1981), *The Greek Heritage in Victorian Britain*, New Haven: Yale University Press.

Tyrwhitt, John (1877), 'The Greek Spirit in Modern Literature', *Contemporary Review* 29, 522–66.

Vadillo, Ana (2019), 'Sculpture, Poetics, Marble Books: Casting Michael Field', in Sarah Parker and Ana Parejo Vadillo (eds), *Michael Field: Decadent Moderns*, Athens: Ohio University Press, pp. 67–99.

Vanita, Ruth (1996), *Sappho and the Virgin Mary: Same-Sex Love and the English Literary Imagination*, New York: Columbia University Press.

Vicinus, Martha (1994), 'The Adolescent Boy: Fin-de-siècle Femme Fatale?' *Journal of the History of Sexuality*, 5, 90–114.

Vicinus, Martha (2004), *Intimate Friends: Women Who Loved Women, 1778–1928*, Chicago and London: The University of Chicago Press.

Vicinus, Martha (2009), 'Faun Love: Michael Field and Bernard Berenson', *Women's History Review*, 18: 5, 753–64.

Waterfield, Giles (2015), *The People's Galleries: Art, Museums, and Exhibitions in Britain, 1800-1914*, London: Yale University Press.

Whitman, Walt (2004), *The Complete Poems*, ed. Francis Murphy, London: Penguin.

Wickes, George (1977), *The Amazon of Letters: The Life and Loves of Natalie Barney*, London: Allen.

Wilde, Oscar (1881a), 'Charmides', *Poems*, Boston: Roberts Brothers, pp. 101–42.

Wilde, Oscar (1881b), 'Endymion', *Poems*, Boston: Roberts Brothers, pp. 95–7.

Wilde, Oscar (1913), 'Art and the Handicraftsman', *Essays and Lectures by Oscar Wilde*, London: Methuen & Co., pp. 175–96.

Wilde, Oscar (1919), *A Critic in Pall Mall: Being Extracts from Reviews and Miscellanies*, London: Methuen & Co. Ltd.

Wilde, Oscar (1962), *Letters of Oscar Wilde*, ed. R. Hart-Davis, London: Rupert Hart-Davis.

Wilde, Oscar (1970), 'The Tomb of Keats', R. Hart-Davis (ed.), *The Artist as Critic: Critical Writings of Oscar Wilde*, London: W. H. Allen, pp. 3–5.

Wilde, Oscar [1890–1] (1988), *The Picture of Dorian Gray*, ed. Donald L. Lawler, New York and London: Norton.

Wilde, Oscar (1997), *Complete Poetry*, ed. Isobel Murray, Oxford: World's Classics.

Wilde, Oscar (2000), *Complete Letters of Oscar Wilde*, ed. Merlin Holland and Rupert Hart-Davis, New York: Henry Holt & Company.

Winckelmann, Johann Joachim [1764] (2006), *History of the Art of Antiquity*, trans. Harry Francis Mallgrave, Los Angeles: Getty Publications.

Wintermans, Caspar (2004), 'Introduction', *I Desire the Moon: The Diary of Lady Alfred Douglas (Olive Custance), 1905–1910*, New York: Avalon Press.

Wolff, Robert Lee (1961), *Golden Key: A Study in the Fiction of George MacDonald*, New Haven: Yale University Press.

Woods, Gregory (1999), 'The Art of Friendship in Roderick Hudson', in John R. Bradley (ed.), *Henry James and Homo-Erotic Desire*, Basingstoke: Macmillan Press, pp. 69–77.

Woolner, Thomas (1881), *Pygmalion*, London: Macmillan and Co.

Wright, Nathalia, (1965), *American Novelists in Italy: The Discoverers*, Philadelphia: University of Pennsylvania Press.

Wright, William C. (1974), 'Hazlitt, Ruskin, and Nineteenth-Century Art Criticism', *The Journal of Aesthetics and Art Criticism*, 32: 4, 509–23.

Yeates, Amelia (2018), 'Poetic Narrative in William Morris's and Edward Burne-Jones's Pygmalion Project', in Sophia Andres and Brian Donnelly (eds), *Poetry in Pre-Raphaelite Paintings*, New York: Peter Lang, pp. 107–20.

Zinkiewicz, Grzegorz (2017), *William Morris' Position between Art and Politics*, Newcastle upon Tyne: Cambridge Scholars Publishing.

Ziolkowski, Theodore (1977), *Disenchanted Images: A Literary Iconology*, Princeton: Princeton University Press.

Zuchert, R. (2009), 'Sculpture and Touch: Herder's Aesthetics of Sculpture', *The Journal of Aesthetics and Art Criticism*, 67: 3, 285–99.

Index

Abraham, Nicolas, 3, 27n
Adonis, 16, 154, 157, 160, 161, 162, 179n
aesthete, 102n, 134, 171, 180n, 198n
aestheticism, 19, 21, 36, 52, 60, 77, 88, 89, 142, 170, 171, 174, 178n, 193
agalmatophilia, 32–3, 40, 61n, 91–2, 103n, 127, 189, 193; see also pygmalionism; statue love; statuephilia
Andersen, Hendrik, 136–9, 146n
androgyne, 170, 171
androgyny, 118, 158, 162, 165, 168, 169, 171, 186, 197
animation, 13, 25, 43, 44, 53, 59, 91, 104, 109, 116–18, 127, 194; see also reanimation
Antinous, 16, 109, 110, 118, 144n, 166, 168, 169, 170, 171, 176, 183, 185, 186
Aphrodite, 29, 31, 42–5, 47–9, 63n, 72, 74, 81, 86, 89, 91, 92, 98, 101n, 103n, 155, 158, 174, 179n
Apollo, 19, 25, 105, 110, 116–17, 118, 132, 139, 159, 162, 172–3, 174, 183–4
Apollo Belvedere, 5, 7, 9, 10, 15, 36, 104, 116–17, 132, 183–5
Arnobius, 29, 32, 61n
Arscott, Caroline, 50, 72, 77, 79, 80, 81

Athena, 155, 158, 159, 161, 162, 169, 172

Bacchus, 105, 118, 135, 146n
Barnard, John, 35, 36, 38
Barney, Natalie Clifford, 164, 165–7, 180n, 181n, 182n
Baudelaire, Charles, 67, 69, 100n, 101n, 174, 182n
Baym, Nina, 110, 126, 144n, 145n
Beatrice Cenci, 113, 114; see also Cenci, Beatrice
Boston marriage, 114, 144n
Bradley, Katherine see Field, Michael
British Museum, 2, 4, 6, 7, 14, 27n, 28n, 57, 66, 70, 71, 102n, 104, 183
Browning, Elizabeth Barrett, 12, 17
Browning, Robert, 51, 64n, 66
Bullen, Barry, 84, 89, 90, 99, 191, 192
Burne-Jones, Edward Coley, 21, 49, 50, 51, 63n, 88, 89

Capitoline Museums, 9, 84, 108, 109, 110, 115, 119, 131, 144n
Capitoline Venus, 9, 183, 184, 185
Castle, Terry, 114, 144n, 180n
Cenci, Beatrice, 108, 112, 113, 114, 119, 121, 123, 143n, 144n, 187

Chandler Moulton, Louise, 66, 76, 77, 94
Christianity, 19, 83, 145n
Classen, Constance, 21, 22, 24, 60, 153
classical sculpture, 2, 8, 14, 16, 20, 70, 71, 84
Clement of Alexandria, 29, 30, 32, 59, 61n
Cnidian Aphrodite, 17
Cnidian Venus, 72, 74, 78–9, 81, 92, 158, 194
collecting, 3–9
Cooper, Edith *see* Field, Michael
corpses, 12, 13, 91, 92, 97, 99, 140, 141, 189, 190, 195, 196, 197
crypt *see* tomb
Crystal Palace, 4, 5, 18, 19; *see also* Great Exhibition
Custance, Olive, 26, 153, 154, 163–4, 165–77, 179n, 180n, 181n, 182n, 183, 185, 186, 187, 194
  I desire the Moon, 180n
  Opals, 163, 166, 168, 175, 176, 180n, 181n
  Rainbows, 163, 168, 175, 176, 180n, 181n
  The Blue Bird, 163, 168, 172, 175, 180n
  The Inn of Dreams, 163, 176, 177

Deacon, Alfred Newport, 67, 69, 70, 194
death, 3, 12, 13, 26, 51, 54, 56, 66, 67, 75, 76, 77, 78, 81, 83, 87, 92–7, 99, 106, 109, 118, 129, 137, 140, 141, 143n, 154, 157, 160, 161, 162, 163, 168, 173, 179n, 180, 183, 189–91, 193–7, 198n
  death-in-life, 91, 92, 93
Decadence, 163, 164, 171, 177, 183
del Carretto, Ilaria, 26, 28n, 183, 187–91, 192, 193–4, 196

della Quercia, Jacopo, 26, 183, 187, 188, 189, 191
desire
  bisexual, 171, 174
  encrypted, 3, 24
  heterosexual, 25, 121, 123, 130, 186
  homosexual, 168
  mimetic, 119, 121, 130; *see also* Girard, René
  object of, 7, 91, 119, 126, 156, 162, 170, 196
  sensory, 59
  sexual, 13, 17, 21, 58, 74, 92, 107, 117, 121, 177
  transgressive, 1, 2, 100, 184, 194
Dionysus, 47, 118, 144n, 162, 186, 187
Discobolus, 5, 6, 73
Douglas, Lord Alfred, 146n, 153, 154, 163, 164, 165, 166, 167, 168, 170, 173, 179n, 181n, 182n, 187
Dowling, Linda, 133, 150, 171
Downing, Lisa, 96, 97, 140, 193
Dying Gladiator, 5, 7, 9, 109–10, 131

effigy, 25, 75, 76, 155, 187, 189, 190, 191, 192, 193, 196; *see also* tomb
ekphrasis, 13, 42, 56, 116, 117, 193
Elgin Marbles, 8, 14, 28n, 34, 36–7, 39, 46, 70–1, 101n, 104, 147, 162
Eliot, George, 12, 104, 171
Ellis, Havelock, 32, 91, 92
Ellmann, Richard, 134, 142, 145n, 158, 172, 173, 179n
Endymion, 131, 159, 179n
entombment, 25–6, 114, 177, 187, 194; *see also* tomb

eroticism, 2, 19, 20, 25, 49, 81, 84, 128, 158, 189, 194
Evangelista, Stefano, 117, 156, 196, 199n

Faderman, Lillian, 114, 144n, 181n
Faun or *Faun of Praxiteles*, 108, 109, 111, 114, 115, 117, 119, 131, 143n
Fernie, Deanna, 8, 20, 108
Field, Michael, 26, 183–8, 194
Fraser, Hilary, 195, 196, 198n
Freud, Sigmund, 27n, 52, 64n, 96, 124

Ganymede, 131, 145n
Gautier, Théophile, 60, 67, 68, 69, 100n, 101n, 174, 175, 176, 180n, 182n
gems *see* jewels
gender, 26, 164, 167, 168, 171, 183, 186, 195
Getsy, David, 20, 60, 147, 148, 149, 152, 177n, 178n, 196
Gibson, John, 17, 18, 57, 79, 80–1, 106, 107, 143n, 178n
Girard, René, 119, 121, 122, 130, 144n
Goethe, Johann Wolfgang von, 14, 15, 24
Gosse, Edmund, 12, 18, 19, 26, 28n, 66, 67, 87, 102n, 147, 148, 149, 150, 151, 152, 153, 176, 178n
  'Desiderium', 151–3
  Father and Son, 18
  'The New Sculpture: 1879–1894' *see* New Sculpture
Gray, Effie, 191, 193, 198n
Gray, John, 153, 164, 167, 168, 173, 181n
Great Exhibition, 4, 16, 57, 80
Gross, Kenneth, 20, 91–2

Haley, Bruce, 10, 13, 197
Hamilton, Emma, 14–15; *see also* poses plastiques
Hamilton, William, 14–15
Hardy, Emma, 93, 99
Hardy, Thomas, 12, 25, 60, 84–100, 102n, 104, 193, 194
  'Rome: The Vatican: Sala delle Muse', 12, 84, 91, 99
  The Well-Beloved, 12, 25, 60, 84–93, 95–9, 102n, 193, 194
Hatt, Michael, 14, 16, 17, 80, 102n
Hawthorne, Nathaniel, 12, 26, 100, 104–9, 111–19, 121–7, 129, 131, 143n, 144n, 145n, 187, 194–5
  The French and Italian Notebooks, 104, 105, 143n
  The Marble Faun, 12, 26, 100, 104, 107–14, 118–29, 130, 143n, 144n, 187, 194–5
Hazlitt, William, 30, 33–9, 46, 62n, 63n, 88, 147
  Liber Amoris, or The New Pygmalion, 30, 34–40, 88
  'On the Elgin Marbles', 36, 37, 39
H.D., 163, 171, 172, 173, 174, 181n
Hebe, 47, 48, 59, 63n
Hellenism, 133, 163, 196
Herder, Johann Gottfried, 22, 84, 162
hermaphrodite, 21, 25, 69, 101n, 153, 165, 169, 170, 176, 197
Hersey, George, 20, 42, 61n, 79
Hillis Miller, J., 87, 96, 97, 98
homoerotic(ism), 118, 120, 124, 130, 133, 136, 139, 151, 154, 155, 164, 169, 171
homosexuality, 1, 21, 124, 129, 133, 142, 165, 168, 173, 180n

homosocial(ity), 121, 122, 129–30, 133, 141
Hosmer, Harriet, 106, 108, 113, 114, 122–3, 127, 129, 143n, 144, 187
Hyacinthus, 110, 143n, 162, 172–3, 181–2n

imaginary museum, 9, 11, 13, 26, 56

James, Henry, 12, 26, 107, 113, 114, 122, 129, 130–42, 143n, 145n, 146n, 151, 178n, 179n, 195
  Roderick Hudson, 12, 26, 100, 107, 129–32, 134–42, 143n, 146n, 147, 149, 151, 153, 195, 196, 197
jewels, 16, 42, 43, 57, 68, 81, 91, 101, 172, 175, 176
Johnson, Barbara, 69, 70, 175, 176, 177
Joshua, Essaka, 20, 29, 30, 34
Juno, 41, 84, 86, 88, 109, 110, 111, 118, 125, 144n

Keats, John, 10, 13, 26, 28n, 70, 153–5, 157–63, 172, 173, 179n, 180n, 196; *see also* Shelley, Percy Bysshe; Wilde, Oscar
Kenaan, Hagi, 21, 23, 24, 130
Kistler, Jordan, 66, 67, 68, 70, 74, 76, 83, 93, 94, 100n

La Touche, Rose, 190–2, 198n
Laity, Cassandra, 170, 171, 172, 181n, 185
Laocoön, 5, 7, 9, 10, 143n, 183
Lasner, Mark Samuels, 167, 168, 180n
Leconte de Lisle, Charles Marie René, 67, 69, 70, 77, 100n, 101n, 176

Lee, Vernon, 12, 62n, 100, 189, 198n
literary gallery, 25–6
Louvre, 9, 10, 69, 70, 72, 166, 169, 187, 197
Lycian Apollo, 109, 110, 118

MacDonald, George, 12, 25, 30, 51–3, 55–60, 63n, 64n, 65, 78, 81, 98, 194
  Phantastes, 12, 25, 30, 51–60, 64n, 65, 81
Malraux, André, 10–11, 13
Marshall, Gail, 8, 15, 20, 30, 33–4, 88
Martin, Robert K., 108, 114, 115, 134
Medici Venus, 7, 9, 10, 16, 72, 105, 145n
Mendelssohn, Michèle, 130, 141, 142, 158
Merleau-Ponty, Maurice, 23–4, 130
Michelangelo, 73, 75, 104, 134, 135, 145n, 146n
Miller, Jane, 31, 32, 35, 40, 45
monument, 3, 26, 69, 79, 98, 100, 135, 158, 159, 162, 179, 188, 189; *see also* effigy; tomb
Morris, Jane, 40, 62n, 63n
Morris, William, 25, 30, 36, 40–6, 50, 59, 60, 62n, 64, 66, 69, 78, 98, 148, 176, 194
  'Pygmalion and the Image', 25, 30, 36, 41–3, 49, 51, 55, 58, 69, 89, 103n, 194
Murtaugh, Daniel J., 136, 138, 139, 142
museum culture, 1, 4, 197

Najarian, James, 153, 154, 160, 161, 179n
Napoleon, 8, 9, 12, 28n, 34, 38, 62n

necrophilia, 1, 91, 92, 95, 96, 97, 103n, 127, 140, 141, 155, 157, 161, 162, 193
neoclassical sculpture, 19, 28n, 57, 89, 102n, 107, 143n, 147, 177n
New Sculpture, 146n, 147, 148, 152–3, 177n, 178n, 197; see also Gosse, Edmund; Thornycroft, Hamo

Onslow Ford, Edward, 140, 146n, 195, 196
O'Shaughnessy, Arthur, 12, 25, 60, 65–78, 81–4, 88, 91, 92, 93, 94, 95, 98, 99–100, 107, 149, 175, 176, 194
  Music and Moonlight: Poems and Songs, 66, 68, 100n
  'Pagan', 65
  Songs of a Worker, 12, 25, 60, 67, 68, 69, 93, 94, 176, 194
  'Thoughts in Marble', 12, 25, 60, 66, 67, 68, 69, 70, 72, 73, 74, 76, 77, 83–4, 93, 98, 99, 100, 194
O'Shaughnessy, Eleanor, 93–4, 98, 103n
ossification, 97, 109, 195; see also stasis
Ovid, 25, 29, 30–2, 33, 35, 36, 41, 42, 43, 45, 49, 50, 51, 59, 60, 61n, 74, 91, 98, 106, 194
  Metamorphoses, 29, 30, 35, 194; see also Pygmalion

paganism, 2, 19, 29, 65, 74, 76, 81, 82, 83, 86, 107, 108, 109, 118, 125, 126, 135, 145n, 169
Pater, Walter, 21, 88–9, 90, 92, 116, 117–18, 133–4, 135, 139, 145n, 146n, 149, 155, 157, 158, 164, 169, 170, 171, 172, 173, 174, 176, 179n, 180n, 181n, 185, 188

Person, Leland, 108, 121, 122, 129, 131, 135, 138
Philostephanus of Cyrene, 29, 31, 32, 61n, 74
photography, 10, 13, 197
Phryne, 79, 81, 194
Pionke, Albert, 52, 55, 56
Plato, 61n, 87, 88–9, 92, 102n, 133, 156, 181n
polychromy, 16, 17, 80, 179n
poses plastiques, 14, 16
Powers, Hiram, 16–17, 57, 58, 106, 107
Praxiteles, 78, 79, 81, 82, 92, 103n, 104, 105, 107, 108, 109, 111, 114, 115, 117, 119, 131, 185, 194
Pre-Raphaelites, 16, 39, 40, 51, 62n, 66, 87, 89, 155, 188
Propoetides, 30, 31, 36, 41, 45
Pulham, Patricia, 28n, 62n, 124, 143n, 182n, 198n
Pygmalion, 1, 12, 15, 20, 21, 22, 25, 28n, 29–36, 40–51, 53, 55–6, 58–60, 61n, 62n, 63n, 69, 74, 78, 81, 86, 88, 89, 91, 92, 96, 98, 103n, 104, 106, 117, 127, 128, 141, 142, 153, 176, 192, 193, 194
pygmalionism, 1, 32–3, 74, 91, 98; see also 'agalmatophilia'; statue love; statuephilia

Quatremère de Quincy, Antoine, 12–13, 28n, 197

reanimation, 93, 95
Reynolds, Joshua, 37, 40, 46
Robinson, Agnes Mary Frances, 190, 198n
Robson, Catherine, 190, 191, 192, 193, 198n, 199n

Romanticism, 25, 33, 52, 56, 70, 87, 88, 100n, 153, 154, 164, 171, 185
Ross, Iain, 157, 158–9, 161, 179n
Rossetti, Christina, 51, 52, 63n, 66, 89
Rossetti, Dante Gabriel, 51, 40, 60, 63n, 66, 67, 69, 89, 90, 101n, 176, 181n, 182n
Rousseau, Jean-Jacques, 34, 62n
Rowe, John Carlos, 113, 120, 143n
Ruskin, John, 26, 39, 40, 51, 52, 64n, 67, 148, 188–94, 196, 198n, 199n
The Stones of Venice, 189–80
Praeterita, 190–3, 198n
Ryan, Michael, 88, 89, 92

Sappho, 154, 155, 165, 166, 173–4, 180n, 181n
Scobie, A., 33, 91, 103, 193
sculptural nude, 2, 16, 18, 19, 57, 58, 79, 80, 107, 115, 170, 185
Sedgwick, Eve Kosofsky, 130, 134, 145n
senses, the, 12, 22, 23, 24, 44, 59, 63n, 65, 76, 130, 157; *see also* sight; touch; vision
Sewell, Brocard, 164, 165, 166, 167, 168, 175, 177, 180, 181
sexuality, 1, 20, 26, 30, 33, 38, 98, 108, 114, 136, 142, 143n, 144n, 164, 186, 195, 196; *see also* gender
Shaw, George Bernard, 35–6, 62n
Shelley Memorial, 140, 195–6
Shelley, Percy Bysshe, 10, 87, 88, 90, 161, 179n, 195–7; *see also* Onslow Ford, Edward; *Shelley Memorial*

sight, 22, 23, 63n, 73, 76, 77, 83, 134, 142, 159, 161, 181n; *see also* vision
Sofer, Naomi, 129, 131, 132, 151
stasis, 13, 25, 34, 44, 109, 193
statue love, 1, 29, 30, 33, 42, 43, 84, 158, 170, 177; *see also* statuephilia
statuephilia, 26, 153, 155, 147, 153, 155, 175
Stetz, Margaret, 167, 168, 180n
Swinburne, Algernon Charles, 60, 66, 67, 69, 89, 100n, 101n, 164, 169, 171, 172, 174, 176, 180n, 182n, 197
Symonds, John Addington, 89, 149, 150, 151, 155, 156, 169, 178n, 189, 196, 198n

tableaux vivants, 14
tactility *see* touch
Tarnowsky, Benjamin, 32, 61n, 62n
Taylor, A. J. W., 33, 91, 103n, 193
The Greek Slave, 16, 57
The Tinted Venus, 17, 18, 79, 81, 106
Thornycroft, Hamo, 19, 26, 89, 102n, 147, 148, 149, 150, 151, 152, 153, 177n, 178n
tomb, 2–3, 13, 25–6, 77, 157, 160, 183, 188–90, 193–4, 197; *see also* entombment
Torok, Maria, 3, 27n
touch, 2, 3, 21–5, 26, 29, 31, 37, 42, 43, 44, 46, 47, 48, 49, 51, 53, 56, 58, 59–60, 74, 76, 78, 83–4, 90, 98, 106, 108, 109, 116, 120, 127, 128, 130, 134, 135, 136–9, 142, 148, 152, 153, 157–8, 159, 161–2, 170, 171, 175, 176, 184, 186, 193, 194, 195, 196, 197

Townley, Charles, 2, 27n
Townley Marbles, 7, 71–2
Townley Venus, 5, 6
Tyrwhitt, John, 150, 156, 178n

Vadillo, Ana, 183–6, 187–8, 197n
Venus, 1, 15, 16, 17, 19, 25, 29, 30, 31, 32, 40, 43, 51, 56, 59, 64n, 70, 73, 74, 77–83, 86, 98, 99, 105, 106–7, 125, 126, 145n, 162, 185, 187, 194
Venus Aphrodite, 25, 29, 31, 32, 41, 42, 43, 44, 59, 76, 125, 194
Venus de' Medici, 5, 105, 106, 107, 126, 145n
Venus de Milo, 62n, 69, 70, 72, 84, 101n, 147, 183, 184
Vicinus, Martha, 114, 168, 183, 186, 187
Virgin Mary, 108, 123, 124, 125, 126, 145n
vision, 21, 22, 23, 24, 32, 47, 58, 89, 91, 92, 99, 130, 135, 142, 157, 161, 162, 185, 197; *see also* sight

Wetmore Story, William, 108, 111, 129, 138, 143n, 145n
Whitman, Walt, 150–1
Wilde, Oscar, 21, 26, 145n, 146n, 149, 153–70, 171–3, 178n, 179n, 180n, 181n, 182n, 194, 195, 196
  'Charmides', 26, 153, 154, 155–7, 158–9, 161–3, 169–70, 172, 179n, 180n, 181n, 194, 195
  'The Tomb of Keats', 154, 160, 162
Winckelmann, Johann Joachim, 7, 8, 12, 37, 79, 116–17, 118, 132, 133–5, 139, 143n, 145n, 169, 185, 188
Woolner, Thomas, 12, 25, 30, 45–6, 48, 49, 51, 58–9, 60, 63n, 89, 98, 102n, 178n, 194
  Pygmalion, 12, 25, 30, 36, 45–6, 58–9, 63n, 89, 194

Yeates, Amelia, 49, 50, 51, 63n

Zeus, 47, 131, 145n

EU representative:
Easy Access System Europe
Mustamäe tee 50, 10621 Tallinn, Estonia
Gpsr.requests@easproject.com

www.ingramcontent.com/pod-product-compliance
Lightning Source LLC
Chambersburg PA
CBHW070346240426
43671CB00013BA/2421